4-.5-2014

MW00975876

To Kiddie
Many Blessings!

DANCING MY WAY
THROUGH HELL!

AN AUTOBIOGRAPHY

Gene Shirley Richey

GENE SHIRLEY RICHEY

Copyright © 2014 by Gene Shirley Richey
First Edition – February 2014

ISBN
978-1-4602-3679-6 (Hardcover)
978-1-4602-3680-2 (Paperback)
978-1-4602-3681-9 (eBook)

GREG RONATO: Photographer
Appears On: Back Cover

ROSALIND BORDERS: Foreword
Appears On: Page xi

GREG RONATO - chief photographer, Norwegian Sun, Dec. 2012.
Grateful for patience and expertise. Permission for photo use on file

ROSALIND BORDERS - deep appreciation for excellent contribution to the book

JKIM WINN - younger daughter of the author, gratitude for her
poems, "Light in the Darkness" and "Granddaddy's Hands"

MARY ANN OGLESBY NEELEY - appreciation for picture in
"Montgomery in the 20th Century" - HPN Books, 2012, page 30.

RON LAMMERT - Pres., HPN, permission to use preceding picture, as follows: "From
Carolyn Voshell Collections, as published in 'Montgomery in the 20th Century' by HPN
Books"

All rights reserved.

No part of this publication may be reproduced in any form, or by any means, electronic or
mechanical, including photocopying, recording, or any information browsing, storage, or
retrieval system, without permission in writing from the publisher.

Produced by:

FriesenPress
Suite 300 – 852 Fort Street
Victoria, BC, Canada V8W 1H8

www.friesenpress.com

Distributed to the trade by The Ingram Book Company

Table of Contents

ACKNOWLEDGMENTS

HEARTFELT thanks go to many people who, during the eight years of the writing of this true life story, have given their forbearance and patience, their constant support, and their faith and friendship.

My Nurse Aide professor and registered nurse, Lelia Poteet, heads my list, for it was she who first suggested, then encouraged me publicly (in class) to write my story, finally placing a note on my final grade sheet saying, "Gene, I'm looking forward to your book!" I truly believe that, if it had not been for Lelia, this book would not have been written.

A special word of gratitude is very appropriate to the Reverend Bob Konrad, who told me fifteen years ago, when I was in South Florida, that I would be moving to the mountains and would be writing a book; he later made the suggested name change for the book; he has continued his faithful words of encouragement.

I give special appreciation to the following for their quick eyes and thoughts related to their contributions to correct typos and to proffer changes of words and expressions:

- My daughter, Carol, with her college background
- Carol's husband, Ray, with his background as college English professor
- My daughter, Kim, and my son, Steve, with almost daily calls of support
- Patricia Inman, who never stopped reading, always with an open eye

My wonderful friend in West Palm Beach, Rosalind Borders, was always available for food, fun and fellowship and, now, she has lent regular encouragement in my writing. I give you a very special word of appreciation, Roz, for the *Foreword*.

Finally and emphatically, many thanks to the one who expects it the least and deserves it the most, my loyal and understanding fact checker, researcher bloodhound and computer key punch operator. You're the best, Richard!!

DEDICATION

THIS true story of my life is warmly dedicated to every reader, especially to those who have been rejected and wounded in one way or another by a parent or a husband or wife on whom everything depended. In the great storehouse of our memories, where our hurts and pains lie buried too deep for ordinary prayer, certainly too deep for any audible prayer—this is where emotional healing takes place through God's touch in our lives. I pray that these words will begin the healing process for those in need and provide a basis for genuine forgiveness to thrive. Only in forgiveness can peace be found.

ADVANCE PRAISES FOR STRUGGLE AND VICTORY OVER REAL LIFE SITUATIONS

Everyone likes a love story, and this is a special one. Gene Shirley Richey entered this life already an "old soul," one with resilience and the gift of forgiveness. Even as a young girl, she was a seeker of truth and the deeper meanings of the events in her life. Readers will be uplifted by her spirit for, despite many hardships, she always lands on her feet, not just standing, but dancing on a higher plane.

– Lelia T. Poteet, RN, BSN; Nurse Aide Instructor/Program Director (retired) Rappahannock Community College, Warsaw, Virginia

You will take away so much more than Gene's amazing life story. You will be rewarded with her invaluable spiritual insights and penetrating wisdom and, through her diversity of experiences, she will unveil the healing power of love and forgiveness. Her quest for the answers to life's most esoteric questions and her courage and stamina through her many challenges, will uplift and inspire you to better face those in your own life.

– Rosalind Borders, Broker-Property Manager Borders Realty, West Palm Beach, Florida

"Dancing My Way Through Hell" is a beautiful story of one woman's spiritual journey. This inspiring story will offer hope for those currently dancing their way through their own hell. What guided this writer through her difficult and painful childhood, adolescence and early adulthood turmoil was an infinite, invisible, indwelling spirit that lifted her out of her darkness into the light. Just as the author discovered that infinite, invisible Shepherd guiding her through her life, the reader will discover, or reconfirm, that same Spirit which dwells in every one of us.

– The Reverend Bob Konrad, Pastor, Tequesta, Florida

FOREWORD

GENE Shirley Winn had no idea who I was when I boldly showed up on her doorstep, only that I desperately wanted something she had. It was 1991, and a dear friend had mentioned meeting a woman named Gene who shared my passion for the work of spiritual mystic, Joel Goldsmith. This friend told me that Gene also had several tape recordings of some of the actual talks Joel had given worldwide, and I was absolutely intent on finding this woman and listening to those tapes.

I feel certain that it was preordained that we would be friends in this lifetime, as Gene felt like a familiar soul from the moment we met. What bonded us together in the beginning was our deep connection to *The Infinite Way* teachings of Joel Goldsmith. What has kept us friends for all these years was not only a deep spiritual bond, but our connection as women who have known the intense joys and heartaches of being mothers, wives, daughters of challenging mothers, lovers of cats, our shared pet peeve of irritating noises, and so much more.

Gene is not a movie star. She didn't invent something life-altering, nor is she a famous artist. Picking up this book, one might ask, "Why would I want to read her autobiography?" I'll tell you why! Some of the most memorable biographies I have ever read have been about ordinary people who have lived extraordinary lives, and Gene has most definitely lived an extraordinary life. From the very first chapter you will delight in the unique way in which she tells her story. She will take you on a journey from her strict church upbringing in Alabama to the opulent and excessive lifestyles of the rich and famous in Palm Beach. You will get to know this remarkable woman as a runaway fourteen-year-old bride, as the wife of an abusive but brilliant artist, as a business woman, psychic intuitive, talented violinist, tap dancer, teacher, single mother of three and as the personal assistant and nurse of the owner of famous art galleries in Palm Beach, Chicago, New York and Paris. And you will read the heart-warming story of the synchronistic meeting of her beloved husband, Richard, not seen by each other since the tenth grade, now a missionary and preacher with whom she fell in love at the age of 78 while researching this book.

In the end, you will take away so much more than Gene's amazing life story. You will be rewarded with her invaluable spiritual insights and penetrating wisdom, and through her diversity of experiences, she will unveil the healing power of love and forgiveness. Her quest for the answers to life's most esoteric questions and her courage and stamina through her many challenges, will uplift and inspire you to better face those in your own life. So, take a deep breath, strap on your dancing shoes, and be prepared for the many twists and exhilarating turns as you experience the extraordinary life story of Gene Shirley Richey "dancing her way through hell."

The illumined walk without fear – by Grace. (Joel Goldsmith)

Rosalind Borders
Broker - Property Manager
Borders Realty - **West Palm Beach, Florida**

DANCING MY WAY
THROUGH HELL

PREFACE

FROM the very young age of five I vividly recall my love and curiosity about God and the questions which ran through my mind. Questions ... mostly because of my mother's belief in God's harsh judgment. You see, as far back as my memory goes, I had music and rhythm in my bones, and I wanted to dance! However, **my mother warned me that I would dance my way to hell!!**

I somehow knew at that early age that God loved His creation and was a forgiving God. I had many questions to which I wanted answers. How could God answer so many prayers all at the same time? Why were some destined to live in sick and crippled bodies? Some rich and some poor? And why did so many think that they were better than the rest? I suppose that at that age I didn't know that the word for that was "prejudice."

My early marriage relationships and physical abuses were quite traumatic. My questions concerning God seemed to fade in the midst of so many problems. I eventually came to realize that some of our most horrific experiences sometimes become our most rewarding joys of life (children, grandchildren, great grandchildren).

In my early 40s, I became very depressed, although I had three beautiful children and a good job. In searching for a way out of my deep depression, I knew that I just had to find the answers to my lifelong questions about God. As the Greek philosopher, Socrates, once said, *"Know thyself,"* words took on a new meaning for me, and I realized that my early paranormal experiences were a great tool to help me understand myself and my relationship to God. Several career fields in five states kept me continuously employed until my 78th year. At that time my true soul mate came into the picture. I returned to my "first love" (the violin) and to the writing of my life's true story.

CHAPTER 1

EARLY

CHILDHOOD

MOTHER went to St. Margaret's Hospital in Montgomery, Alabama to deliver her baby. Both she and Daddy were hoping for a boy. They were planning to name the baby Gene, after Mother's brother Eugene. The problem with that – the baby turned out to be me. However, they went ahead and named me Clara Gene Shirley. I would never use my first name Clara. To this day, 85 years later, the spelling of G-e-n-e has caused problems with my mail addressed as Mr. Gene Shirley, Mr. Gene Parker, Mr. Gene Albertsson, Mr. Gene Winn or Mr. Gene Richey. I'm sure my Mother with her rigid, hard-shelled Baptist religion, didn't intend for me to have so many marriages. I know she's happy now that I'm married to a preacher. She thought that this final relationship was my sole purpose in life. I will write more about this chapter later.

My birth didn't happen in the hospital as the physician, Dr. Dawson, sent her home, believing she wasn't ready to deliver. Very soon after arriving home, her water broke, so Dr. Dawson came to the house on Hull Street, where I was born on February 18, 1928. My sister, Helen, who was five years old at the time, greeted the doctor and wanted to know if he had a baby in his black bag.

My first memory is that I caught my leg in a swing on the front porch of the house on East Jeff Davis. I must have been about two and a half years old, as you see me on the book cover. My next memory is that we had moved to a different address on Hull Street. About that time, I must have been curious about what I looked like naked. I remember looking into a full-length mirror with no clothes on!

Our next move was to Sayre Street. I can only recall three or four incidents at that location. One was learning to skate, which I'm sure produced lots of bruises. All these years later, I can still see the boundaries on the sidewalk that Mother had insisted we stay in. Helen and I were skating one day when she fell and cut her chin open, requiring a trip to the hospital. It was at this very young age that I discovered the great myth of Santa Claus. Helen and I were "home alone." I suppose Mother felt that Helen was old enough to babysit me. Helen found our Christmas presents in a cedar chest in Mother and Daddy's room. Somehow, Mother found out, and no doubt we got a whipping, but later, she told us there was no Santa Claus! One day, Helen had her friend, Doris, visiting. I thought Doris was the most beautiful girl I had ever seen, mostly because she had a big dimple in her chin. Throughout my younger years (maybe all my life?), I have wanted a dimple in my chin. When I was growing up, I would often squeeze my chin trying to make a dimple.

Chapter 2

My Mother

6 Hannon Street, Montgomery

My family sure moved a lot. Our next move was to 6 Hannon Street, where I was to have memories, some of which were profound and some which have guided me over the years. Things that would puzzle me for years and, later, have some understanding and meaning to them, would take place in my fourth, fifth, sixth and seventh years. I would often hear my name called, and thinking Mother had called me, find out that she had not called. One morning, I was on my back porch, and I saw several very small people milling around on our neighbor's back porch. I realize today that they resembled the Lilliputians of Swift's Gulliver's Travels. The neighbors were not supposed to be home. I vividly remember hearing the sounds of footsteps running inside our house. I remember the times lying in my bed and feeling so very lonesome, almost like I was homesick! But I was at home with my family. Country music, or hillbilly music, as we called it then, which was so often heard by radio in those days, always left me depressed.

Uncle Eugene and Papa Arnold

Mother, who probably missed her calling (for becoming a preacher) would take Helen and me to church twice on Sunday, every Wednesday night and sometimes seven nights a week if there was a revival meeting at the church. My grandfather, who we called Papa, lived with us. He and I were very close. Mother told me years later that Papa, who at the time lived in Georgia with Aunt Detty, his oldest daughter, returned to Montgomery when I was born and told my Mother that I was "his baby." He and I were buddies over the years. On his daily trips downtown, he most often would bring me candy or some little gift. He was a tall, handsome man, but never remarried after Grandmother Lucy passed away.

We did not have a car – very few people had cars in those days. So we walked, but I didn't have to walk so much, because Papa would carry me. He never refused me when I would say "Papa tote me." Papa and I often got a scolding from Mother, and he and I would make plans to run away.

Mother had a very narrow vision for what God's plan was for using my musical talent. She believed it should be used only for her church (or any church that had her beliefs). I was given expression lessons which led to my performance at the Annual Church Christmas Pageant. At five years of age, I started reciting 'Twas the Night before Christmas and continued to do so at ages six and seven. In my seventh year, I decided to shorten my recitation by saying "Xmas" instead of "Christmas." To my great humiliation the congregation laughed! I have several memories engraved in my mind from my early childhood: the Xmas humiliation and a more positive one of my anticipation of receiving brown bags filled with candy, fruits and nuts.

One of my very first memories was playing, or banging, on the piano at age three. My parents said I could pick out a tune at that age. I was playing hymns with two hands by ear when I was five years old. Mother sent my sister and me to Mrs. Stella Mable Morrison to take piano lessons. Mrs. Morrison and her children attended our church, The Gospel Tabernacle. She lived two miles from us, so my sister and I would walk to her home once a week to take music lessons. I would play all the lessons for my mother with no problems, until she started quizzing me about the names of the notes. I didn't know the first note. I didn't need to, because I could play by ear, but that ended my piano lessons. I don't recall why mother decided to have me take violin lessons, but I started taking lessons at age eight. More will come later about my first love, the violin.

My education began when I was six years of age, at which time I was enrolled at Goode Street Grammar School. Mother had given me one of Helen's old spelling books, which I treasured. Someone wanted to buy it for their child. Mother gave it to them, and I've wondered all these years if that didn't adversely affect my spelling skills! I can remember being so proud of the words I was learning. One day I told Daddy, "I know how to spell God." He said, "Spell it for me." My reply was, "D. O. G." Of course, he laughed. Nell Wilson started attending Goode Street School that same year, and while we didn't visit each other often, we became close friends after our marriages failed. We continued to be friends through the years. Nell was a very pretty girl and her brother, Ray, was a good-looking boy the girls all liked. .

In my later years, I would believe and repeat many times that I was not a product of my environment. This was very true on my soul level; however, on a conscious level I was somewhat influenced by my mother. A good example occurred at six years of age. I felt a need to call on my neighbors to urge them to go to church in order to be Christians. My next-door neighbor, Mrs. Ellis, told me, "You don't have to go to church to be a Christian." This was filed away in my mind as something I needed to investigate.

Mother's brother, Uncle Eugene, Aunt Dorothy and their two children, Dorothy Ann and Eugene Jr., came to visit us all the way from California. We believed they were very rich, being able to travel in their car all the way to Alabama. Why, Uncle Eugene even had a movie camera! And 80 years later, I have a video made from that visit! That was the year I started school. In second grade, I had my next humiliation. My teacher, Mrs. Bennett, asked the class if there was anyone who had *never* been to a movie (We called them "picture shows."). I slumped down in my seat as I didn't want anyone to know I had never been to a movie. If my mother had her way I never would, because she believed that was a sinful place to go. However, one of my classmates spoke up and said "Gene Shirley has never been to a picture show." Of course, the whole class turned and looked at me!

Other Hannon Street memories were of the black ladies selling fresh vegetables on our street. They would start early in the morning walking with baskets on their heads and calling out loudly, "Get your fresh vegetables. I have corn, string beans, peas, okra and black-eyed peas." I often wondered how they could walk balancing a basket of vegetables on their heads. Mother would frequently buy from them. Quite often, a black male or female would come by the house asking for food. Mother would give them something to eat, as I'm sure she thought this was the Christian thing to do, but not in *her* dishes. She would put the food in something she didn't intend to keep, and they would have to come to the back door to receive it. At a soul and conscious level, I knew this was wrong. At that young age, I didn't know and probably didn't hear the word "prejudice," but I realized more and more as the years passed that my parents and most of the people I knew were wrong to treat blacks as they did.

Mother and the preacher at the Tabernacle were very good friends. His name was John Scalf. Their children were John Jr., Bobby and Doris. The pastor had a car, so it was a big deal to go shopping with all of us riding along. The grown-ups would leave John Jr., Bobby and me in the car while they shopped, which was something I looked forward to until John Jr. kept trying to kiss me, causing me to move back and forth from one side of the car to the other. I don't remember any consequence from this, and I suppose at that young age I knew better than to tell Mother.

One day, we discovered we had a mouse. Since Daddy was working downtown, and the preacher didn't live far away, Mother asked him to come over and catch the mouse. I don't remember much more about it, except he was chasing the mouse with a broom, and it ran up his pant leg. I put that in the category as being one of the worst things that could happen to a person.

Our next street address was to be two locations on Jones Street. We moved to the first house in my seventh year and moved across the street for my eighth to tenth years. Mother's second home was our church – The Gospel Tabernacle, which was located on Sayre Street between Hannon and Jones Street.

Children in my growing-up years were a world apart in their behavior from the children of the last few decades. If I ever dared to step out of line, my mother was quick to tell me I was getting a whipping when I got home, which was really two punishments – the dreaded waiting to get home and the whipping itself. Papa disapproved of Mother whipping me and would occasionally speak to her about it. She would just tell him he could move out if he didn't like it.

Mother, Helen and I made a weekly trip every Saturday evening downtown to meet Daddy in front of the J. C. Penney Store. The sole purpose of going to meet him was for Mother to get his weekly paycheck, as she didn't trust him to bring it home after his usual night of drinking. On occasion, he would already be pretty inebriated. Our walk home wasn't very pleasant as Mother would be embarrassed and furious at him. It was on one of these trips downtown, after a successful collecting of the pay check, that we went shopping at Woolworths Store, and I got sick in the store. We walked home and my temperature went up very high, and I was told that I lost consciousness until the next afternoon. On the second day, I had a hallucination and told Mother that Daddy was in my room drinking a bottle of liquor. Mother took this as a hallucination, because she didn't think Daddy had completely lost his mind. My treatment for pneumonia was the usual treatment in those days, which was to put a mustard plaster on my chest. It felt as if Mother and/or Pastor Scalf were pouring hot water on my chest.

When we moved to the first house on Jones Street, it was only for a few months, until the second house was ready to move into. Papa went back to Georgia to spend a few months with Aunt Detty with plans to return as soon as we moved to 19 Jones Street. It was while at 6 Jones Street that I recall knowing when something bad would happen. Our next-door neighbors were the Abrahams. Mr. Sig Abraham worked in a store downtown. On this particular day, I had an awful foreboding all day that something bad was going to happen. Mr. Abraham was struck by a car as he got off the bus and was hospitalized with a broken leg. I was to have these premonitions many times as I was growing up. These feelings of dread and sadness were something I just accepted and thought of as something we all go through. Also, I thought it natural for me at bedtime to experience getting out of my body and being on the ceiling of the bedroom. I had this happen many times at 19 Jones Street. After age ten and moving to our next address, I don't recall having this happen again – that is, until the mid 70s in Cedar Rapids, Iowa. I'm sure my search for God and the meaning of life started at this young age, but I didn't understand it in those terms, and I would think of it as if there were a "secret garden" that I needed to find.

Mother must have been pretty intuitive, also, as she seemed to know when things had the potential to go wrong. Aunt Detty and her daughter, Alice, came from Georgia to visit for a few days. Aunt Detty's and Mother's cousin, Ludy, lived in Selma and came over to join in the visit. Ludy was the kind of person who would take seriously anything that was said to her. For instance, one night Aunt Detty and Ludy decided they would like to go see Missy, another cousin, who lived on the outskirts of Montgomery. Helen and I wanted to go with them, but Mother was opposed to our going but finally relented and let us go. Ludy was driving and Aunt Detty was in the front seat with her. I was in the middle of the back seat with Helen on one side and Alice on the other. As we got close to Missy's house, we had to cross some railroad tracks. We all saw that a train was approaching. Now, Aunt Detty could kid and say something she didn't really mean. On this occasion, she said, "Oh Ludy, go ahead and beat that train!" Ludy took her seriously and stepped on the gas. Well, we beat the train to the crossing, but only by a hair! I remember looking at Helen with her hand on the door handle on her side and at Alice ready to open the door on the other side. A divine intervention, if you please.

My home on Jones Street, as it looks today

Papa returned from Georgia when we moved over from 6 to 19 Jones Street. There was lots of gardening space, as it was the only house on that side of the street. Papa was a good gardener and would plant two lots next to the house with sweet potatoes, corn, beans, peas, okra, tomatoes and carrots. I could make a little spending money by gathering a basketful of vegetables and selling them to our neighbors. Papa was a carpenter, and he built a play house for me. It had two windows and a front porch, and it looked very good in front of the garage and facing our house. Papa also made stilts for me. He made my first pair when I was six years old. So now I had two pairs which I kept in my playhouse.

We lived two blocks from the grocery store, and Mother would be out of something and would send me to the store almost every day. Sometimes if I only had to carry one thing in the bag I would go on my stilts, which we called "Tom Walkers." On one of these trips to the grocery store, the meat market man, who had always been nice and friendly, asked me if I would like to see the walk-in refrigerator where the meat was kept. This was my first glimpse into a world of real ugliness as he shut the door and began to take liberties with my body. I resisted, and he quickly let me go. I walked home feeling ashamed and bewildered, but I certainly was not going to tell Mother. She never told me there were these kinds of people that I might meet up with, nor had I heard of this in the church. Eventually, I decided this man needed to be added to my prayer list, even though I didn't know his name. As long as I can remember, every night Mother had me on my knees praying: "Now I lay me down to sleep; I pray thee, Lord, my soul to keep. If I should die before I wake, I pray thee, Lord, my soul to take." To this I always added, "Bless Mother, Daddy, Helen, and Papa." As I began to have friends, I would add them to my prayer list. By the time the meat market man was added, I was on my knees a long time. Incidentally, this man did not return to the meat market after the above incident!

CHAPTER 3

⁻ THE STRINGS
OF MY LIFE ⁻

IN my eighth year the violin came into my life. I now remember how Mother decided to give me violin lessons. Our piano teacher, Mrs. Morrison, had two daughters, Stella and Louise, who played the violin and were taking lessons from Mrs. Fanny Marks Seibels. Mrs. Seibels was known as Montgomery's first lady of the violin, having studied in Berlin under the world-famous violinist Theodore Spiering. He invited her to return to America and become his assistant teacher in New York City. She also performed as a concert violinist in New York, Chicago, Berlin and London. I was thrilled to receive my first violin and to begin my violin lessons with Mrs. Seibels. She must have been in her early fifties, and I never heard her play the violin as she would no longer play because of the arthritic condition of her hands. I was eight years old when I began my lessons, and at eleven years, I was playing in my first symphony orchestra. I remember well the day Mother gave me my first violin. She warned me not to touch the pegs (that tune the violin). I tried to turn the pegs anyway and I broke a string! I guess I got a whipping for it.

Louise 15, Stella 13, Gene 11

After a few months of taking lessons, Louise, Stella, and I were playing in church every Sunday, which is what Mother's intention was. We also went to the TB Sanitarium as well as Kilby State Prison. As soon as we had finished playing at the Sanitarium, Stella and I would rush outside and spit a lot to avoid catching TB, we thought. Muriel Cottrell was my other best friend, who lived on nearby Cromwell Street. She and her mother went to the Tabernacle, where Muriel and I sang duets. She sang soprano, and I sang alto. We sang in a play at Goode Street School one night. Muriel wore black pants and a white shirt, and I wore a long dress.

We sang "Ramona." However, Muriel and I were much more interested in tap dancing than singing. So, that's how we spent much of our time – making up steps and trying to learn new steps. Of course, we had to do this behind Mother's back, as **she had warned me I would dance my way to hell**. I remember one day when Muriel was visiting me. We were using the Tom Walkers; however, the end of one of the pair she was using had been broken on the upper end and had a sharp point. Muriel fell, and the point pierced her upper right arm, requiring emergency medical attention. From time to time Mother would allow me to spend the night with Muriel. I liked to do this; however, I was unhappy the next morning when I was awake at my normal early hour, and Muriel and her family were all still asleep. This left me with the need for my morning coffee fix! By this time I had been drinking coffee for five years. I remember how missing my coffee would result in a bad headache!

My mother's extreme strictness and controlling parenting resulted in her misguided belief that she had the authority to dictate the path my life should take. Perhaps her strictness, on one hand, was a detriment to my learning in school. Her constant correcting me left me feeling that I could never do anything right; on the other hand, I believe I benefited from her toughness later, as I dealt with many difficulties in my life.

Nicky was a black-and-white terrier. He started following Helen to school and would wait for her to get out and follow her home. I think this is one case where the animal adopts his home, because after so long he would just stay at our house. Soon, there was no question about his being a member of the Shirley family. He always wanted to go with us wherever we went. We would have to lock him up to keep him from following us. At times, however, he would manage to slip out and attend church with us, lying at Mother's feet while she played the piano. Nicky remained with us a year after my first daughter, Carol, was born in 1946.

Gene, 1939

We moved again to a new neighborhood at 727 South Lawrence Street only three blocks away from Mrs. Seibels, when I was almost eleven years old. Our house was next door to a Seventh Day Adventist Church, which had previously been a hospital. It was a very spooky building, especially when the neighbor's big black dog would get into the basement and howl. In our back yard we had one fig, one pear and five pecan trees. I would climb the pear tree often and eat the fruit from the tree while sitting on the branches. My love for figs goes back to those childhood days. The house had a large open space underneath, where you could easily walk about. There was a large hole that I was to find out later that my future first husband, Dawson Parker, and his friend, Mike Richardson, had dug, hoping to make a swimming pool.

Dawson and his father and step-mother lived in the house behind us on McDonough Street. They had previously lived in our house on Lawrence Street. Mother's good friends for many years, Maebell, Douglas and Gladys Lee Williams lived next door to the Parkers. Mother would not allow me to associate with the Parkers as she had heard that they were worldly because of their smoking and drinking.

Mother continued sending me to the grocery store almost every day. I would take the shortcut through my backyard fence between the Parkers' and Williams' houses to the store on the corner of McDonough Street. Our house had three bedrooms, or four, if you consider where my bed was. It was a kitchen pantry that was large enough to put a cot in. Mother and Daddy were in one bedroom and Papa had a bedroom. Helen didn't have one, as she was sent to Toccoa Falls Bible Institute in Georgia to finish high school and go to college. Helen met Ed O'Neal, who was a student at the Bible College and her future husband. Our third bedroom was rented out to a lady and her daughter. I remember how the lady would try to hide her smoking from my mother. After a year, they moved out, and the room was rented to a young man who worked with Daddy at Tennille Furniture Store.

When I entered the seventh grade, I had to ride the bus, because the school was in Cloverdale about three or four miles from our house. I went to that school, as did Stella, which was outside our school district in order for us to play in Mrs. Seibels' school orchestra. Mrs. Seibels was conductor of the Montgomery Symphony Orchestra as well, where we also played. Every Saturday morning and Sunday afternoon we would go to orchestra rehearsals. The Symphony also played annually at the Montgomery Museum and the Blue and Gray Ball for The Daughters of the American Revolution.

Mrs. Fanny Marks Seibels and her string ensemble - "From Carolyn Voshell Collections, as published in Montgomery in the 20th Century by HPN Books"

The Cloverdale School Orchestra took a three-day trip to the University of Alabama at Tuscaloosa, which was around 100 miles from Montgomery. We rode the train – my first train ride. I thought I was quite grown up at eleven years of age, riding the train, staying in the university dormitory. I never forgot the bedtime snacks there. It was there that I had my first chocolate-covered graham crackers. I've had many over the years but never tasted any as good as those first ones. It was quite a thrill to be in a huge orchestra with kids from all over the state, and I was the youngest one in the orchestra. With all of those new wonderful experiences, I didn't even mind that Mother was a chaperone.

My friend, Muriel, and I were still trying to learn new tap dance steps, and I very much wanted a pair of real tap shoes, so I would walk to school and back to save bus money so I could buy taps to put on my shoes. My longing to have tap shoes must have clouded my thinking, because there was no way to hide them from Mother. So, Muriel's mother, being a lot more liberal than mine, I asked her to let me keep my tap shoes at her house. She agreed and, thus, the secret never got out to my mother.

One of the last times Papa and I sat on the back steps of our house, planning our escape, came from a whipping I got for asking Mother if I could go to church on Wednesday night without socks because my friends Muriel and Stella, who were going with us were not wearing socks. It was not really a "whipping" but, rather, a slap on the face.

I previously mentioned briefly the hospital-turned-church next door with the howling dog in the basement. The sanctuary was a long building with four large white pillars that went across the front of the church. Connected to the back of the sanctuary were four stories of rooms where the patients must have stayed. The ambulance would bring the patients to the basement where they would be taken to the upper floors by elevator. I was in the building many times as I was friends with the Seventh Day Adventist family who lived on the third floor. The father baked raisin bread every week, and I can still smell the wonderful aroma of the baking bread and, of course, it was delicious. This family moved to Selma. Mother allowed me to go visit them and stay for two or three days. I was eleven years old at the time. I certainly didn't know what the house next door would mean to me seven years later.

Our house had a front porch with rocking chairs where Papa would spend much of his days sitting and chewing his Brown's Mule tobacco. I idolized Papa, tobacco and all. In fact, my daughter, Carol, remembers very vividly, being told this story many, many times by my mother, that, as a toddler, when Papa would spit his tobacco juice over the porch railing, I would imitate him and do the same! It was on one of those days with Papa in his chair on the porch that a man walked up the steps and said to Papa, "Fuller Brush Man." Papa wasn't interested, unaware that the man was his son, Nick, who had been away in the Navy for many years. Papa didn't recognize him. Nick was a Chief Petty Officer and had been stationed in other countries for years. He had not seen any of his family since he joined the Navy at twenty years of age. Nick had his father's good looks and was an outgoing man. He had been married and divorced. We welcomed Nick, who seemed successful with his car and all the gifts he bestowed on us. My family never wanted for essential things, but we never had enough for the extras that other families seemed to enjoy.

Despite my sense of knowing whenever something bad was going to happen, I didn't have a clue about what was to transpire with Nick coming into my life. After his first visit, he would come to see us every time he was home on leave. Mother was his sister and Aunt Detty was his older sister who lived in Georgia. Nick would spend time with us and then go to Georgia to visit. My cousin Vera, who lived with Aunt Detty, had a baby daughter, Ginger. Mother was involved in her church activities and felt comfortable leaving me with Nick. It was at one of these times that I felt my world had fallen apart as he began to molest me. I felt trapped. No way could I tell Mother or anyone. Shortly afterwards, he bought me a shiny new yellow-and-blue bicycle from Sears, so I didn't tell my awful secret. I began believing the things he would tell me – things about how pretty I was and how much he loved me. I found out several years later that he had also molested Ginger.

He was sent to Key West for submarine duty, where he rented a house so Mother, Helen and I could stay for the summer. Mother didn't seem to notice that there was anything wrong with the attention that Nick paid to me or his constant, inappropriate displays of affection. By now, I was beginning to pick up annoyances that have bothered me to this day. I had zero tolerance for anyone making noise with chewing gum, especially popping it. I didn't like bad table manners, such as smacking food. Stella smacked her food, and Muriel could have won a gum-popping contest. I can still remember the startled look on Muriel's face when I yelled at her to please stop popping that gum! Another thing that was probably a worse annoyance was generated from Mother, who for as long as I can remember, had a habit of clearing her throat in a manner I have no way of describing. It would start with a noise in her throat and it would come out of her mouth as though she were going to spit something up. So, gradually over the years, up to my twelfth year, I must have come to my breaking point, as I began to stomp my foot on the floor automatically whenever she would do this (which was several times a day).

Another gum-popping incident took place in the Paramount Theater. Uncle Nick almost dragged me into my first movie at age twelve. The movie was The Sea Wolf, with John Garfield and Ida Lupino. Nick thought it was terrible that I had never been allowed to go to a movie. So, he and I were downtown one day, and he made me go into the theater. Mother's influence, at first, had me afraid to open my eyes in the theater, but I finally did, and I was hooked. I would start leaving school early to see a few minutes of a movie, which I paid for by not eating lunch. The incident at the Paramount happened when a man in front of me was making a lot of noise with his popcorn. I kicked the back of his seat – hard, which immediately scared me, thinking he might turn around and question me about why I had kicked his seat.

On one of Nick's visits we went to Georgia, leaving at dark. Albany is around 175 miles from Montgomery. I can't recall why we were traveling so late in the day, and especially why on earth we would be going in the Parkers' car, with Parker driving, and Mother in the front seat with him. It was a strange get-together in the car; however, Mother saw the opportunity for her and her brother, Nick, to get over to Albany to visit their sister, my Aunt Detty. Parker's wife, Barbara, Nick and I were in the back seat. Another odd thing was that we would be traveling on a stormy night, since Mother was very afraid of storms. She must have been scared out of her wits when Parker decided to start turning the car's headlights off and on as we rode down the highway.

As it turned out, there was a lot to be afraid of. When we arrived at Aunt Detty's around midnight, so did a tornado! I remember hearing it. So I knew from an early age that tornados do sound like trains. My aunt lived only a few blocks from downtown. The next morning Nick and I walked downtown and were shocked to see the buildings that were destroyed. I remember that the storm took twenty-three lives. The Parkers had continued on to Dawson, Georgia to stay with relatives, but that afternoon they returned to Albany for a much more subdued drive back to Montgomery.

CHAPTER 4

MY FATHER

CLARK Linden Shirley was my father. He was a gentle, mild-mannered, pipe-smoking and a very hard-working man. He worked at Frank Tennille Furniture Store six days a week, a half day on Wednesdays. His almost nightly drinking didn't keep him from going to work. But you could be sure he wouldn't be drinking on Sundays; however, Mother had no success in making him go to church. He took in extra work, refinishing furniture and re-upholstering sofas and chairs. This he did on Sundays and a few nights in the week when he hadn't been drinking. It was normal for our house to smell like varnish.

As long as I can remember, he worked at Tennille's, until Frank sold the store, and he had to go to work at another furniture store. Young Frank went to California and sang with the Bob Crosby Orchestra. His daughter, Toni, inherited his musical talent and was later to be known, with her husband as "Captain and Tennille." I used to look forward to going to Tennille's (as it was pronounced, with the emphasis on the first syllable) to visit Daddy in his workshop. He would take me around the store to see other employees. He had several nicknames for me, but most often he called me "Silly Kate."

Clark and Eunice Shirley in downtown Montgomery, Alabama

Daddy wasn't just a mild-mannered, hard-working man. Around fifty years of age, he quit drinking and started taking art lessons. When Mother and Daddy moved to Capitol Parkway in Capitol Heights, the shed in the back yard of their house became his studio. Eventually all members of the family – grandchildren and great grandchildren would have his paintings in their homes. He was also very good at art crafts, such as making wood jewelry boxes the size of a book, and painting meaningful pictures on the cover. He also made many other crafts with his paintings or photos on the cover. I am very proud of the paintings that hang on our walls along with the expensive *Wally Findlay Gallery* paintings I received years later.

He had a two-page story that was published in the local newspaper, "My Early Days with the Brassells," written when he was ninety three, shortly before he died at ninety four. He was fourteen or fifteen when he worked as a water boy in 1910 for the Wright brothers, Wilbur and Orville, who had their first flying school at the current Maxwell Field Air Force Base. According to Daddy, the Mobile and Ohio Railroad ran trains that would make several daily trips bringing people from all over the world to see them fly. The Wright Brothers would fly as high as a telephone pole, he said, circle around about a mile and then come down.

Eunice Pella Arnold Shirley, my mother, was a very pretty lady. In her senior years up to age ninety-seven, she was healthy and regal looking. She taught Sunday School and played the piano for church services. When I began my violin lessons, she began playing the violin by ear. She was talented but was tone deaf; therefore, her notes on the violin were most often out of tune.

After my father's death, she lived alone until she was ninety eight. At that time I sold my townhouse in Florida, and my son-in-law, Ray, went to Florida from Virginia to move me to Mother's apartment building in Montgomery, Alabama. Her health soon began to decline, and she agreed to move to Crowne Nursing Home. This I will write about later. Mother spent much of her time reading the Bible and telling me about God's love but more about the wrath of God, who had no tolerance for the poor mortals in what she called "their worldly ways."

In my early years, I would wonder why God had put all this rhythm in my bones, because **Mother had said I would dance my way to hell.** *Why* was each religious denomination in Christianity so sure that God had shown them the way, and left out the rest of God's creation? *How* could God answer my nightly prayers as I believed there must be hundreds and thousands praying at the same time? *Why* did some people in the church believe that only *they* knew the truth and yet could be so unkind to the black people? *Why* were some souls born poor, some rich, some crippled, while others were healthy? This didn't seem fair to me. After all, she had told me God created everyone equal.

While these were questions in my young years, in my early forties I had a desperate need to pursue them further. Mother had told me many times about her bargain with God – if God would give her a healthy baby, she would dedicate her baby to God. With all my questions concerning God, I was a little afraid of the wrath, fire and brimstone Mother talked about. My soul wisely guided me into knowing that God created every soul as well as all created things. I knew God was Love and was an ever-forgiving God.

The Capitol of Alabama is located on top of a hill facing Dexter Avenue. About ten blocks down is a large water fountain in the middle of the street. Dexter Avenue has become famous for Ebenezer Baptist Church, where Martin Luther King, Jr. was the pastor. It is located two blocks down the hill from the Capitol. Farther down the street is the famous Chris' Hot Dog Stand, established in 1917. The building is long and narrow and has newspapers and magazines in the front. The hot dogs were ordered at a take-out register and in this room there was a counter and to one side a separate small room with several booths. There was a jukebox at the end of the booths. It was in this room in 1940 that I saw my first jukebox that had moving people with music. If you visited or moved away from Montgomery and had been a customer and had eaten a Chris' hot dog, you would have to go back for another one. Uncle Nick had sold Montgomery Advertiser newspapers on Dexter Avenue as a teenager. He would always buy a hot dog when he finished selling his papers. Nick, Mother, Helen and I would make frequent trips to Chris' when he would visit us.

On the other side of the water fountain on Dexter Avenue was the J.C. Penney Store, where we would meet Daddy every Saturday night. The water fountain, according to Daddy was where Zelda Sayre, wife of F. Scott Fitzgerald, was known to have jumped in the fountain for a swim. On the other side of the street was Kress' "five and dime" store where I sold war bonds in a booth in front of the store. On the corner of Dexter and Perry was Woolworth's. I went to Woolworth's after one of my class-cutting days to see a movie. I surely didn't get by with it this time as I came face to face with my mother! I can't remember the outcome – it must have been too traumatic.

Stella, Mother, Gene

My twelfth and thirteenth years were pretty stressful trying to cope with my terrible secret. I remember vividly the many nights I would read the Bible, and this was not only because of Mother, but I felt great comfort in reading the Bible as the source for finding my "secret garden." Also engraved in my memory is the time I sat on a bus stop seat while waiting for the bus. I began to look at my hands, arms and legs and wonder how I got here and where I came from. Of course, I wasn't thinking about here and now. I was pondering, Where did this body come from and how did it get here? At this age, although I had always had experiences with knowing of things to happen and knowing that God existed, I was to find out the body was not my soul! My soul is who I really am.

During this period, I was still riding the bus to Cloverdale Jr. High School to play in the orchestra, and Muriel and I were still trying to learn new tap dance steps. I would spend as much time as possible in my hammock in the back yard trying to stay out of trouble with Mother.

CHAPTER 5

TOCCOA FALLS, GEORGIA

HELEN was still away in school at Toccoa Falls finishing high school and two years of college. Nick offered to pay my tuition at the same school. So, plans were made to send me there. I knew I would miss Mrs. Seibels and the orchestra, but mostly looked forward to going.

The new minister at the Tabernacle was Rev. Marsden, who replaced Rev. Scalf. Rev. Marsden had been instrumental in Mother's decision to send Helen to Toccoa. Ruth Marsden, his daughter, was the head of the music department at the school. Although she didn't teach violin, it was her decision to keep me from going to the State competition for music in Milledgeville, Georgia, in my second year. I had won first place in the regional competition in Gainesville. At the time, I thought she had made a terrible mistake, and I might add – I had many of the student body thinking the same. Years later, when I finally began to grow up, I realized she had been right not to allow me to go, because I hadn't practiced as I should have, even after her repeated warnings.

Toccoa Falls, Georgia - 186' high!

Rev. Marsden and his wife drove Mother and me to Toccoa Falls in September 1941. At that time, traveling through Atlanta was not as bad as the utter chaos of today, when you must go around or go through the city. We arrived at the Toccoa Falls campus around 8:00 p.m. I remember the ambience of the night as we unloaded the car. The crickets chirping, the crisp night air with street lights illuminating the campus, all of this seems fresh in my memory. My excitement for my new adventure was somewhat diminished by my leaving home for the first time.

My new home was a room in Stewart Hall, which was located directly across from the chapel and classroom building. The post office was down the hill from the chapel and Stewart Hall. The first morning I was awakened by the sun streaming through the trees into my room. After breakfast, I was taken to orientation for class schedules, followed by a tour of the campus. The campus and the falls were beautiful. Toccoa Falls is located in the foothills of the Blue Ridge Mountains. The falls are 186 feet high which is 26 feet higher than Niagara Falls. On the north side of the Chapel was a huge bell that would be rung at 6:30 a.m. as a wake up call and to dress for breakfast, and 10:00 p.m. for bedtime and lights out as well as ringing for classes, lunch and dinner. It also served as a fire alarm.

I don't recall much about the classes. I wasn't a good student (to my regret in later years). I **was** interested in music, and I did practice daily during my first year. However, I was fascinated with the falls and much preferred hiking to the top than paying attention to my books and classes.

After a few weeks I moved to LeTourneau Hall which was a fairly new building. The gym was on the main floor with music practice rooms on that same floor. On each end of the gym were two floors with 14 rooms for girls. Under the gym was the campus dining room. LeTourneau Hall was funded by R.G. LeTourneau, an internationally recognized industrialist. On June 06, 1944, the largest invasion force ever assembled moved onto the beaches of Normandy with an equally impressive display of machines and equipment, much of it built by this dedicated Christian layman. His company designed and built some of the world's most massive machinery, including earth movers, transporters, missile launchers, bridge builders and portable offshore drilling rigs. Mr. LeTourneau was a devout Christian and for many years he lived on ten percent of his income and gave ninety per cent to Christian work. I'll write more about Mr. LeTourneau, as in my second year of school at Toccoa Falls, I was privileged to live with his sister, Mrs. Newman, her husband and their daughter, Lorraine.

The high school students were often roommates with college students. My first roommates were one college student and two high school students who were my age. We had two bunk beds in a large room. Our room was on the second floor, and when you walked out of the room, you would be overlooking the gym. Kay Farrington was quite old to be a college student as she was in her thirties, and we all thought of her as an "old maid." After graduation, she stayed on as a staff member.

We had to be in our beds with lights out at 10:00 p.m. However, Kay was allowed to go to bed when she wanted to. She would often stay after 10 o'clock with Mrs. Helen M. Good, the house mother, in her apartment, which was located on the first floor. The three of us girls didn't like that, so we resorted to a prank, which was a pretty bad prank, if you disliked cats as much as Kay did. On one of her usual late nights, we put the house cat in her bed under the covers. The cat must have thought that it was a pretty cozy place to sleep, because it stayed there until Kay returned. She was very upset and yelled at us, but we pretended to be asleep.

Activities for the weekends were pretty routine but sometimes exciting. Saturday mornings were devoted to cleaning our rooms, washing our clothes and getting ready for the coming week. We were not supposed to have an iron in our rooms. However, we managed to effectively hide our iron from staff as they checked our rooms weekly. After lunch, we could socialize until the bell rang for us to go to our rooms for quiet time until the 3 o'clock bell would ring. Then the girls could go hiking to the falls. The boys had to go the opposite direction. The one time a girl and boy decided to meet in the hiking area they were caught. There may have been other couples that didn't get caught. No, I never tried it!

After dinner, while still sitting at the dining room tables, we had fifteen-minute devotions. I hesitate to think that I would do anything like the following: During one of those devotional times, I was sitting behind a fellow student, Don Scoggins. I sprinkled some pepper into the palm of my hand, tapped him on the shoulder, he turned around, and I blew the pepper into his face. I don't remember that I was punished for this act. After dinner, there was always a half-hour social period. On Saturday nights, we had fun times in the gym, cakewalks and, of course, there was snipe hunting! First-year students had never heard of snipe hunting, so we usually were eager to go. We were given large bags and told after we had hiked a good distance into the hills that the other hikers (who knew what snipes were) would go in different directions in order to cause the snipes to run to us, and we would be able to catch them in our bags. Fortunately, while I excitedly hiked up the mountain to catch my first snipe, one member of the group explained that there was no such thing as a snipe. The ones with the bags would be left holding them, while the rest of the students returned to the campus. I'm sure some of the staff stayed back to rescue them. It must have been scary sitting there in the dark, especially if you began thinking about the campus rumor that an old hermit lived in the mountains.

One night after returning to our rooms from dinner, several of the students who lived in LeTourneau Hall, discovered some of their clothes were cut up into shreds. We were all upset and scared. The rumor was that the old man who lived in the mountains had somehow gotten into the girls' rooms and cut up their clothes. Mr. Paul Kirk, who was the assistant principal, looked and acted more like a tough policeman or detective and, I might add, we were all scared of him, soon found that the one responsible for cutting the clothes was a student in the building. I'm sure, at the very least, she was kicked out of school.

Sunday, December 07, 1941 turned out to be the most "infamous day" of my 85 years and "for all Americans," as stated by our president, Franklin D. Roosevelt. Our Sunday, that day, had been the usual, going to church, lunch and afternoon hiking. Later in the evening, all students and staff were summoned to the Chapel, where Mr. Kelly Barnes, the superintendent, was to talk to us, which had us speculating as to why we were there. We were soon in sobs and tears as Mr. Barnes told us Pearl Harbor had been attacked. The fact that we were away from home and our families caused fear and near panic in all of us.

President Roosevelt declared war on December 08, 1941. While our minds and thoughts were fearful of the future, we were comforted a little by knowing we would be going home for Christmas for 10 days. On the night before our Christmas vacation, some of the students congregated on the steps of LeTourneau Hall, and we sang Christmas carols. I was to think of that night over the years as being very inspiring and magical.

The next day, I left for Montgomery on a Greyhound bus. As I waited for the boarding of the bus, I overheard a conversation that was to bother me for years. A lady was saying, "Every bone in my body hurts." I thought what a terrible thing to happen, and I surely hoped it didn't happen to me. I don't recall much about the 10 days at home, but I'm sure I was glad to see my family and our dog, Nicky.

The second semester was a return to the routine of school – study, hiking and church. I became more involved with playing the violin at dinners and other events. One thing that was new for me was that there was quite a snow storm which was rather unusual for Northern Georgia. For me, it was a great experience, since I had never seen snow before.

Occasionally, we were allowed to go on a bus trip with a date. Of course, we were well chaperoned. I had begun to take notice of the opposite sex, and I had my first boyfriend. His name was Jack. We had only been able to see each other for a half hour after lunch and dinner, so when we had the opportunity to go on a bus trip to Atlanta, we were eager to go. We were allowed to go to a movie. I don't remember the name of the movie, probably because I was distracted by my first kiss! And my second kiss was on the bus returning to school.

CHAPTER 6

RETURN
TO MONTGOMERY

SCHOOL was out in May, and I stayed at home the next school year. I don't recall why I didn't return to Toccoa. It could have been that my grades were barely passing or maybe because of the war. Had Mother been able to see what was to transpire that year, she would have sent me to Timbuktu.

The war became much more real to me at home. Montgomery had two air force bases: Maxwell Field and Gunter Field. On weekends, downtown Montgomery was crowded with cadets. Everyone was very patriotic and supported the war. No one seemed to mind the rationing of tobacco, gas, tires and sugar, and it was impossible to buy nylon stockings.

Papa had gone to California to stay a few months with Uncle Eugene. Uncle Nick was sent to the Panama Canal for submarine duty. I went back to my violin lessons with Mrs. Seibels and orchestra practice every Saturday morning and Sunday afternoon. Mother started sending me to the grocery store almost every day. (I wondered what she did when I was away at school.) As I have mentioned, my route to the store was to go the shortcut which was between the Parkers' and Williams' houses. Oftentimes, Dawson Parker and his best friend, Mike Richardson, would be in Dawson's backyard or off on their motor scooters. Although I had known Dawson for two years as a friend, our friendship had suddenly developed into my first love. His stepmother, Barbara, encouraged us to see each other; however, Mother would never allow me to see Dawson or to associate with his family. Barbara was a red-headed lady with a very vindictive side to her, if you dared to offend her. Chester, Dawson's father, who was always referred to by his surname, was known to have girlfriends on the side. When Barbara found out about one of his girlfriends, not only did she and Parker get into physical fights, the girlfriend was certain to get her punishment. An example that I later learned about is that she put snakes in the girlfriend's house and threatened to do her bodily harm. Also, she would have someone put sugar in her car's gas tank. Dawson didn't approve of her behavior, but he loved her, and she was very good to him. I don't believe he knew for a long time some of the things she was doing. It was several years later that he and I would discover a very shocking fact about her.

Mother had been right about not allowing me to associate with the Parker family, but she was wrong about Dawson. He was a good student, and he spent a lot of his leisure time making model airplanes, as he wanted to be an Air Force pilot, which he did later become.

I began to spend more time in my hammock in the backyard, as it gave me the opportunity to see Dawson. He and his friends often played ball in his backyard. Muriel and I were in the yard one day, and I stepped on a board with a rusty nail in it. The nail went all the way through my foot. Dawson was there to pull the nail out. I believe that was the beginning of our budding romance. Mother didn't take me to the doctor as some of her friends told her she should do. As a result of having received no medical attention, I began having ugly sores on my legs which lasted for months.

When school started in September, I attended Baldwin Jr. High School which was within walking distance of my house. Baldwin was very close to downtown Montgomery, and I would occasionally leave school early to go to a movie. I did not stay very long at the movie so I could get home without getting into trouble. The one exception was the time I came face-to-face with Mother in Woolworth's store after the movie.

There were a few boys, mostly from church, that Mother began to allow me to "date" for such things as church activities, picnics at Oak Park, and I was allowed to go to football games in the fall, but I was not interested in anyone, except Dawson. When football season started, Ray Bozeman, who was on Mother's approval list (and who happened to be Dawson's friend) would come to the house to take me to the ball games; however, Dawson would be waiting around the corner to take me to the game. This went on all football season, and I became good at concealing my true activities from Mother.

CHAPTER 7

MY FIRST
MARRIAGE

DAWSON'S mother, Barbara, encouraged our romance. And, in fact, in February 1943, a few days before my fifteenth birthday, she and her friend took Dawson and me to Wetumpka, where we were married by a Justice of the Peace. That evening, Mother allowed me to spend the night with Shane Benford, whose mother was Mother's cousin. We called her Aunt Helen. I had borrowed brown high-heeled shoes from my friend, Stella (that belonged to her mother) and, of course, her mother didn't know it. I was trying to look eighteen – old enough to get married without Mother's permission. After we were married, I went back to Aunt Helen's to spend the rest of the night. I don't recall where she thought I had been, but I'm sure she had no idea what I had done. The next morning I went home.

I was back in school the next week. I don't remember what our plans were in revealing our marriage, but on Friday of that week, all of this was resolved. I had written to Nadia Moore, a friend at Toccoa Falls. In my letter, I wrote the details of my slipping out to see Dawson. What happened at school that Friday is forever engraved in my mind. I was sitting in class, and, all of a sudden, I *knew* I had left the letter at home and I *knew* Mother had read it, and believe me when I came home from school, there was hell to pay! The following day, she was still telling me of her plans for me, such as how she was going to escort me to school and pick me up after school. I got up from the table, went into my bedroom, put as many things in my purse as possible and walked out the door. Since Dawson and his family had moved two or three miles away to Panama Street a few months earlier, my first stop was around the corner on Perry Street to Mrs. Seibels' home. Mrs. Seibels was shocked at my news, and when I asked her to call Mother to tell her I was now married, she refused. So I then went to Mabel Williams' home with the same request. She didn't hesitate to call, and Mother acted like this was the end of the world. In fact, she told me she would rather see me dead than to be in the Parker family. Daddy came home early from work drunk. Papa was very upset. The next day I moved to Panama Street with Dawson.

Dawson was in school and had an early morning paper route. He had plans to join the Air Force to become a pilot as soon as possible. Dawson's room – our room now – had model airplanes all over the room. There was also a shotgun hanging across the wall above his bed.

I spent my days at home with Barbara trying to be a housewife and learning to cook. I tried making biscuits, which turned out to be a complete disaster. I also spent time with Nancy Arnold, a distant cousin on Mother's side. She lived one block away from the Parkers. She would come over, and we would dance to Woodchopper's Ball. She was a good dancer and really loved to dance. A few months later she got married, and she and her husband spent their honeymoon in South Carolina. On their way home, she was killed in an automobile accident.

Barbara had an operation and was in the hospital for a week. Parker would stay out most all night taking advantage of her being gone. Dawson would leave the house every morning at 5:00 a.m. for his paper route. One morning, Parker came in after Dawson had left and tried to rape me. I fought him off, and he left me with the threat that if I told Dawson he would shoot me with the gun hanging above our bed. I told Dawson as soon as he walked in. Parker tried to make good on his threat. Dawson fought with him and finally got the gun away from him. Barbara came home from the hospital later that day. I don't believe she ever knew what happened, but Dawson never again went on his paper route alone. I went with him.

Dawson was called to the Air Force in May, and was accepted as a Cadet. About the same time, Parker, who was a career Master Sergeant in the Air Force, was transferred to Chanute AFB in Illinois. Barbara wanted me to go with them. I refused, which meant I had to go back home with hopes of eventually joining Dawson. But you didn't cross Barbara! She was upset with me for not going to Chanute with them, so she somehow, without my knowledge, was able to get a divorce! (I found out later that she had a lot of political clout.)

Chapter 8

Return
To Toccoa Falls

So, in the summer of 1943, I was living back at home with Mother, in misery, when she decided I should return to Toccoa Falls. This time I did not live on campus but was invited to live with the Newmans. Lorraine Newman, who was a niece of R. G. Le Tourneau, was the best friend of my sister, Helen, and, a few months later, served as maid of honor at Helen's December wedding. When Lorraine's parents offered their home to me, Mother was happy to accept. Perhaps the school administrators thought it would be better for me not to stay on campus, since I had been married. No doubt, Mother thought I needed closer supervision. I liked the Newmans and liked living in their home. The home was made entirely of steel, and was located on top of a large hill, which was very close to LeTourneau plant. I would walk down the hill and through the woods to catch the bus for the five-mile ride to the campus. The Newmans treated me like family and even allowed me to have girlfriends stay with me on the weekends. The LeTourneau plant was a huge factory that built earth-moving equipment, such as Tournapulls, scrapers, cranes, rooters and rollers. Mr. LeTourneau owned the local radio station WRLC (later changed to WLET) and several airplanes.

I was invited to go for a plane ride in one of the small planes. I had never been in a plane before, but I was determined to go, in spite of my fears. I will always remember walking from the house through the woods to the air field. I was pretty sure I might not come back alive! I don't remember being so afraid after we were airborne. While flying, the pilot, Mr. Green, said to me, "I could hold your hand and you couldn't do anything about it!" Helen and Ed's first home was in LeTourneau Trailer Park, which was where several Toccoa Falls married students were housed. The trailers were very nice, and they were also constructed of steel.

Living off campus, I didn't play the violin very much. I did practice at school, and I much preferred that to my school work. Dawson and I continued to write to each other. He graduated and received his wings and commission as Lieutenant in March 1944. He sent me money to come to Keesler Field in Mississippi for his graduation. Shockingly, Mother and the school gave their permission for me to go! I then left the Newmans' home. Although I had enjoyed living with them, I regretted not being able to take part in most of the school activities.

CHAPTER 9

HOME
FOR THE SUMMER

MONTGOMERY, as I have mentioned, was very crowded with cadets from Maxwell and Gunter Field air bases. Montgomery businesses had almost more than they could handle. On the weekends, when the cadets were allowed off base, the restaurants would be overflowing with them and some of the families that would visit them. I was able to get a job as a waitress in the coffee shop of Montgomery's leading hotel, the Jefferson Davis. The summer months were filled with my work and making plans to re-marry Dawson.

Montgomery would soon become the temporary home of Glenn Miller and his family while he was stationed at Maxwell Field. The big band music is still my favorite. That summer, I had several experiences that would be an important part of my memories. One day at work on my fifteen-minute break, I noticed a door that went upstairs near the kitchen. I didn't realize it then, but the stairs would lead me to the ballroom. When I opened the door, I thought I was in heaven. I was hearing the most beautiful music I had ever heard. The Ray McKinley Orchestra was playing, and I had never heard a big band playing live before. I suppose they were rehearsing for a dance at one of the air bases.

I was to meet several people while working there who would be important to me. Mr. Earl Andrews had an office in the building next to the hotel. He would come over for coffee, and when I mentioned to him that I was home for the summer from Toccoa Falls, he said, "Dr. Forrest is a good friend of mine!" Dr. Richard A. Forrest was the Founder and President of Toccoa Falls Bible College. Mr. Andrews, who was the president of the Kiwanis club, asked me to play for the Kiwanis luncheon. He encouraged me to pursue my music and wanted to help me obtain a scholarship to Juilliard Conservatory of Music.

A dentist from next door would come into the coffee shop for coffee. One day I told him I had never been to a dentist. Mother just hadn't thought it necessary. The dentist was astounded and wanted me to come to his office and let him examine my teeth. After checking my teeth, he was astounded again because I had **not one** cavity or bad condition in my mouth.

WSFA, one of Montgomery's radio stations, was located on the second floor of the hotel. Mr. Caldwell Stewart, who was a well-known pianist in Montgomery, worked at the station. He would often come in for coffee with two or three friends and sit at the counter. He and I had previously talked about my playing the violin with him, and I wanted to set a time for us to play. One

29

afternoon he came into the shop with a group of friends and while serving them coffee, I asked, "Mr. Stewart, when can you play with me?" To my humiliation, he and his friends all laughed. I was very embarrassed when I realized how my question had sounded.

Dawson was sent to Germany a few months after graduation. When I had gone to Keesler Field for his graduation, I had been happy for him that Barbara had bought him his first car, a new blue convertible. I had believed that we would be married before he went overseas. Mother was even reluctantly helping me with wedding plans, as she believed that once you were married, you stayed married, no matter what. Well, my plans for becoming the wife of Lt. Dawson Parker with a brand new convertible came crashing down when he finally told me we would have to wait until he returned from overseas. Barbara had given him the car with his promise that we wouldn't be married before he went overseas. My happy plans had turned into heartbreak and despair. The song, "I'll never smile again" says it all. My job at the *Jeff Davis Coffee Shop* helped with my unhappiness, and the tips and wages were a help in preparing for my return to Toccoa Falls in September (1944).

CHAPTER 10

RETURN
TO TOCCOA FALLS ... AGAIN

MY sister, Helen, and her husband, Ed O'Neal, were in their last year of college and living in the steel trailer near the Newmans. I went back to the campus and LeTourneau Hall. I was working a few hours a week as a waitress in LeTourneau Hall dining room. I suppose my job at the coffee shop helped me get the coveted job of dining room server.

My room was on the third floor, and I had three new roommates. We were all high school students. Pat Tingley was the oldest. Her father was a well-known minister in Birmingham, Alabama. Pat and I would often race down the steps from the third floor to the second floor. We must have sounded like a herd of stampeding cattle. We managed to find our way to other mischief. One night, we decided to light sparklers in our room. A blanket caught fire which sent us scrambling to put the fire out. By some miracle, we didn't get caught. Going back to the Tingleys, I must mention that Pat's sisters, Ruthie and Alice Mae, were also close friends. In fact, I maintain regular telephone conversations today with Alice Mae, who lives in Grass Valley, California.

Several music students had entered the regional music competition to be held in Pearce Auditorium at Brenau College, today Brenau University, in Gainesville, Georgia. The first-place winners of their instruments would go to the state competition in Milledgeville, Georgia. What should have been a happy experience was mixed with two embarrassing moments. The competition was held in the college auditorium full of people. A few minutes before I was to go on the stage to play my violin selection, I discovered the soles on my shoes had come loose. My nervousness about playing was bad enough, but now I had to walk to the center of the stage with flapping soles on my shoes! The Toccoa Falls students were sitting together waiting for their turn to perform. My previously mentioned friend, Don, was next with his trumpet selection. We had been sitting next to each other, but when I returned to my seat, I hadn't noticed that Don had moved over a seat. So I proceeded to sit in his lap. The happy part of this experience was that I won first place!

The state competition in Milledgeville was to be held later that school year. Having won first place in the regional contest I was eligible to participate. Miss Ruth Marsden, head of the music department, began to monitor my practicing for the state competition. After her repeated warnings about my not practicing as I should, she finally told me I could not go to the state contest.

31

I thought she was being unfair to me; after all, I had won first place in the regional competition.

Earl Hall at Toccoa Falls – High School Classroom Building

As for my classroom participation, this consisted of my just being present in the classroom, as my mind was elsewhere, and my teachers did nothing to get me involved in my education. I did notice a boy in my English class named Richard Richey and saw him from time to time in the canteen. I'll have more to say about him later on!

My life outside the classroom was more interesting in our social activities. On Saturdays, I would hike to the falls with friends, or I would go alone, hiking with my radio to the top of a hill overlooking the campus, which was my favorite thing to do. I would lie in the sun and listen to my big band orchestras with Glenn Miller, Benny Goodman, Tommy Dorsey and Artie Shaw. Dawson and I continued to write to each other, even though he had broken my heart when he chose the car instead of me. He wanted us to re-marry when he returned home. I was very worried about his safety as he was a fighter pilot against the Germans.

The latest fashion fad of 1944 was the broomstick skirt. In spite of my low self-esteem, I thought I looked exceptional in my yellow skirt. They were called broomstick skirts because there were tiny pleats all around the waist band. It required no ironing after washing as it would be wrapped around a broom handle (or stick) to dry. It seemed to be back in style in the department stores of 2006. Thank goodness, today we have the washer and dryer, which would certainly have been a luxury in 1944.

My disappointment of not going to the state competition diminished somewhat when I was asked to go on a tour when school was out. Alma Henderson, a college student, Margaret Morgensen, a staff member, and I would be representing Toccoa Falls Bible College. We went to Kings Mountain, Charlotte and Lumberton, North Carolina, Macon and Savannah, Georgia and Jacksonville, Florida.

Dr. Forrest drove us to Kings Mountain. We were there two weeks. I was to play the violin for the nightly services conducted by Billy Graham and his friend, Torrey Johnson. Billy Graham had graduated from Florida Bible Institute (now, Trinity College of Florida) in 1940 and Wheaton College in 1943 and was already becoming well-known as an evangelist. His wife, Ruth, was with him, and they were expecting their first child, Virginia.

Alma, Margaret and I were driven from Kings Mountain to Charlotte by the Chief of Police of Charlotte in his car with the siren turned on. Billy Graham was the speaker for the *Kiwanis Club* luncheon. I played the violin accompanied by Alma on the piano. The one thing which stands out about Charlotte was that I had the impression that someone tried to get into our hotel room that night.

The camp site at Kings Mountain consisted of rustic cabins, dining room and kitchen and a chapel where nightly services were held. After breakfast, we went to Bible study. The rest of the day we were free to go hiking, play soft ball, throw horse shoes or go horse back riding. I had never ridden or even been close to a horse. I decided that could be a fun thing to do. A couple of my newly made friends and I mounted our horses for what I mistakenly thought would be my first fun ride on a horse. My horse had other ideas as he trotted along with my friends for a mile or so, then suddenly turned and galloped back to the barn with me hanging on for dear life! I was sore all over from my wild horse ride. I was supposed to play the violin that night. I went to Chapel late and tried to slip into the service undetected, but Mr. Johnson noticed me and announced my late arrival to the congregation.

From Kings Mountain, we continued our tour to Lumberton, North Carolina. We were there for a youth seminar. I can't remember ever being more miserable from the heat, which must have dulled my memory, because that's about all I do remember about Lumberton. Oh yes, I remember one very embarrassing thing. We were attending a youth meeting at a church, and I noticed this good-looking young man. I had been looking at him with interest; before I found out he was the minister of the church which was sponsoring the youth seminar.

From Lumberton, we were driven to Macon, Georgia. Billy Graham was the guest speaker at the Kiwanis Club luncheon. I played the violin, and Alma played the piano. From our overnight stay in Macon, we traveled to Savannah, Georgia. The private residence in which we were given hospitality was located at 11 West Charlton Street, diagonally from Madison Square, in the famous historic district of the city. We attended and played at a week-long youth rally. An event, as though it were carved in stone in my memory, occurred on a hot summer, Sunday afternoon. I walked several blocks to make a purchase at a drug store, located on the intersection of Bull Street and East Perry Street and across from Chippewa Square. On my way back, a couple of sailors in uniform were approaching me. All at once, one of them grabbed the front of my dress and ripped it open. The buttons flew off, exposing my bra! I ran up the Bull Street steps of the DeSoto Hilton Hotel where guests were seated in rocking chairs on the porch. I quickly sat down in an empty rocker next to a man who undoubtedly saw the incident; however, he made no effort to express concern or to offer protection. The sailors went on their merry way. I sat there a while and, then, went back to the home where we were staying.

From Savannah, we went on a fun trip to Jacksonville, Florida. Alma, Margaret and I bought some costume rings at the beautiful white sandy beach. It was while we were in Jacksonville on 28 July 1945 that a B-25 bomber crashed into the 79th floor of the Empire State Building in New York City. We were walking in the famous Japanese garden when the news reached us. I have current contact with Alma who is now 93 years of age and lives in Athens, Georgia. It was great to see her at Homecoming in October 2007, when the centennial of Toccoa Falls College was celebrated. Alma continues with a ministry she and her late husband, George Henderson, started for students at the University of Georgia. Alma and George graduated from Toccoa Falls Bible College in 1946. That same year she attended the Toccoa Falls Flying School. She and George went to Africa with a Baptist foreign mission board. Margaret traveled with us on our summer tour and kept an eye on us on behalf of Toccoa Falls. When the tour was over, we returned to the school to pack and go to our respective homes.

CHAPTER 11

RETURN
TO ALABAMA

MY parents had moved from 727 Lawrence Street to 28 West Jeff Davis. Helen and Ed had just graduated from college and were leading revival services in North Alabama by holding meetings in a tent. They invited me to join them and play my violin in their services. I made the trip by Greyhound bus. Of course, Mother was pleased with this development, because she felt that my participation in their ministry would help to develop my musical ability and, at the same time, keep me on "the straight and narrow way." Ed was able to get time on a radio station in a larger, nearby town. So, my part in their ministry was playing the violin in their nightly services and weekly on the radio. Three experiences linger in my memory. First: A car was lent to Ed; however, he did not yet know how to drive! One day, Helen and I were with him on the way to the radio station, and he was trying to get up a hill; however, he was unable to control it, allowing it to roll backwards and cause some minor damage to the rear of the car. Second: It was while I was with them that I fell in love with Heinz 57 Sauce. That love continues to this day! Third: We stayed in the home of a lady from the group meeting in the tent. One day, she told me that I was pretty and reminded her of her sister. However, she added, "But you're not quite as pretty as she is!" After the tent meetings, Ed was called to pastor a church in Calera, Alabama, some twenty miles south of Birmingham.

Following the tent meetings with Helen and Ed, I worked again in the *Jeff Davis Coffee Shop* for a brief period of time. The son of Carling Dinkler (founder of the Dinkler Hotels of the Southeast), Carling Dinkler, Jr. was a warrant officer at Maxwell Field who would come by the coffee shop. As we got acquainted, he told me that he could get me a job at the Officer's Club on base. I was subsequently hired as cashier. A memory which stands out is that someone left the top off a salt shaker, and I poured all of the salt on my eggs!

About two months after I went to Maxwell Field, Carling Dinkler, Jr. arranged a new job for me as bookkeeper at Gunter Field (big joke, to think that I could do that job!) Anyhow, I went to Gunter Field but, within a month, I developed tonsillitis which resulted in surgery to remove my tonsils and losing my job at Gunter. While I was there, an inebriated airman fell into the empty swimming pool and was seriously injured.

As a rule, families were nice to the military, due to the fact that it was patriotic to support our armed forces. The United Service Organization enlisted young ladies to meet and entertain servicemen. Also, there were social programs when live orchestras performed at Maxwell and Gunter Fields. I suppose Mother's motive was to be patriotic; however, it was mostly to give her a good way to keep an eye on me. It seems strange as I write this that she went several times to these social gatherings at Maxwell Field. Between my new job, which I'll write about next, and these events, I met a few servicemen. Over the years I collected a drawer full of letters that I was planning to keep, but Mother eventually managed to get rid of them. I remember how proud Mother was when I came to a service at the Tabernacle with a date, Lt. Kenneth Nign. I think she believed I would soon find a new husband, which was contrary to her belief that it would be a sin for me to marry again. I think she probably believed that God would understand my not going back to Dawson. Ken and I were somewhat serious, but soon he was sent to another air base. After exchanging a few letters, that relationship ended.

After recuperating from the tonsillectomy, I went to work at Art's Music Shop in downtown Montgomery. My good friend, Stella, and I had gone there often down through the years to get violin supplies; e.g., strings, resin, pegs, etc. My main job at the shop was to prepare and mail invoices to customers and to wait on people who came into the store. One customer who was in arrears with his account was the well-known country singer, the late Hank Williams, Sr. The city was still inundated with servicemen, many of whom came into the store to make purchases or just to browse. One day, a group of them came in and two of them asked me for my telephone number. One of them called and said he was going to Jamestown, New York, his home, and wanted a date with me when he returned. His name was Lt. Markus Albertsson but quickly became just Mark. Two weeks later, he returned to his assignment as a fighter pilot at Craig Field in Selma, Alabama. We double dated the first time we went out together. The other couple drove us to a cemetery where we went around in circles for a while. The other girl and I were scared due to being in a cemetery at night!

CHAPTER 12

MY SECOND
MARRIAGE

MARK had made a pencil sketch of a female figure. I showed it to Mr. Andrews, who had previously encouraged me to think of going to Juilliard Conservatory of Music in New York. He was a friend of Dr. Forrest at Toccoa Falls. Mr. Andrews exclaimed that Mark had genuine talent with his sketching and should pursue it. He also said that Mark might be a good catch for me as a husband.

Mark and I fell victims of infatuation immediately. Following that date, he asked me to go with him on the bus to Craig Field to pick up something he needed. Mother gave her permission for me to go with him. On the bus he asked me to marry him! Of course, Mother was supportive of this move, feeling that I needed to settle down and have a family. She and Mae Belle Williams made the arrangements for us to get married at the Montgomery Court House on January 03, 1946. During the ceremony I bit off a hangnail on my left thumb. Infection set in immediately and I had to go to the emergency room at St. Margaret's Hospital that night. It was necessary to remove the nail. Now, sixty-seven years later my nail has finally returned to a normal shape and size. My daughter, Carol, has the only wedding gift I received, a silver dish.

We spent that night at the Jeff Davis Hotel. The next day we went to Selma to look for an apartment. We found a room to use temporarily while we looked. It was quite a shock to realize that the room was located next door to the house where I had visited several years before with the aforementioned Seventh Day Adventists who lived on Lawrence Street in Montgomery. Housing was very difficult to find in those years due to the war situation. We finally located a large apartment on the second floor of a big Southern mansion with typical white columns in front. It was located about a half mile from the bus stop. Most airmen who lived off base did not have cars. The owner of the house was an older man whose wife had passed away a short time before. His son and daughter-in-law lived with him downstairs. Right after we moved in, the daughter-in-law went to the hospital to give birth to her first child. I shall never forget that at the bottom of the stairs there was a pretty table with a picture of the owner's late wife in a nice 8 x 10 frame. The strange thing for me was that every time I went upstairs and glanced at the picture, all I could see was a skeleton! So, every time I went upstairs I would move the picture to a different angle so that I would not have a clear view of it. Somehow, it kept getting moved back to its former position. No doubt, it was the lady's husband, who probably wondered how her picture kept getting moved.

Less than a week later, we went to a cafeteria in downtown Selma. After we had our meal and went to the cashier to pay our bill, Mark introduced me to several of his fellow pilots who had eaten there, also. We then went to a grocery store and made our purchases. When we were about half way from the bus stop to our apartment, Mark threw the two bags of groceries he was carrying on the ground and accused me of having flirted with the other pilots. I had not done anything of the kind! When we were back in the apartment, he hit me for the first time! I thought, "What in the world have I gotten myself into?" That first blow was the first in a long story of mistreatment. My low self-esteem dropped even lower. He was a genius in many ways: art, music, anything of a mechanical nature; on the other hand, he thought he had the right to abuse me, because he had married me. So, I was nothing more to him than a sexual object! When he would hit me over and over, he would then beg for my forgiveness and make me promise not to leave him. I would promise what he wanted, because I was afraid not to! Within a month, when I realized that I had missed my period, I knew my problem was even greater.

Mark arranged for me to play my violin at the Officer's Club on base, which I did, even though I was pregnant. On the way home I suffered a migraine headache, the only one I remember ever having, and it was a killer! Constantly, he would make me play my violin at home, whether I wanted to or not, and he would accompany me with his trumpet. I had to give the impression of wanting to play for him, whether I really did or not; otherwise, I would be in for further mistreatment. Mother and Daddy came over to visit us in Selma a couple of times. Mark took pictures with a camera he had made and developed them in the apartment. I have pictures today which he took of my parents at that time. He made me pose often for pictures that would be called "glamour" shots today; however, if they didn't turn out according to his expectations, I would get the blame and the punishment.

While he was on duty at Craig Field, I would sometimes catch the bus and go to town for shopping. One day, just as I was going to get on the bus, a fighter plane came very low and "buzzed" the bus, causing everyone to be frightened. I knew immediately that it was Mark! He knew I would be catching the bus at that moment and had timed his move perfectly. If he had been reported, he certainly would have received a reprimand, perhaps worse, for such behavior. Another day, I went to Craig Field, because he wanted to take me up for my second plane ride. The pilots would talk about the acrobatics they often did when they were aloft. Due to my pregnancy, I was not subjected to that kind of flight, which would have terrified me to no end. It turned out to be a short and normal flight.

Mark received his discharge from the service in May 1946, following which we moved to Montgomery to live with my mother and father on West Jeff Davis. I was making regular visits to the obstetrician, and the pregnancy developed normally. I listened to the big band music a lot, almost willing that my love for it would be picked up by my baby. In effect, Carol is very talented musically, especially as a tap dancer and pianist. One song that I played over and over was "Moonlight in Vermont" by Bunny Barrigan and his orchestra. It was the very first music she heard after her birth. Instead of coming home the next day, as the custom is today, I stayed in the hospital a week and came home in an ambulance.

Daddy was drinking a lot in those days. He would come home, and Mother would wait until he would drop off to sleep; then, she would search him to see if he had brought a bottle home with him, which he sometimes would do. She would hide his bottle at first. Later, Mark saw this as an opportunity for him to have a weekend drink. On one occasion, he discovered that the bottle contained water rather than liquor, because Mother had replaced the liquor with water! I had not told my parents about the way my husband was mistreating me physically, mentally, emotionally and every other way possible. We lived upstairs, but they didn't catch on. He knew better than to hit me when they were at home, especially to not leave any marks which would identify him as the offender. I think he tried to curb his anger at such times. He obtained employment as an artist at the Polled Hereford Magazine. I would take his lunch, and we would go to Oak Park to eat and to look at the animals in the zoo, especially the monkeys. A family friend from the church, Miss Pearl Ray, warned me that if I didn't quit going to see the monkeys, I was going to "mark" my baby.

Chapter 13

My First
Baby

CAROL was born at St. Margaret's Hospital on September 29, 1946. When I first saw her, after a prolonged period of labor, I was shocked when I saw her very pointed head and remembered what Pearl had said; however, Carol developed very normally and was a beautiful baby. In fact, in her college years in Iowa she was selected by the school to participate in the Miss Iowa Falls Competition, in which she won first place in the bathing suit contest!

We stayed upstairs at my parents' home for two or three months. I would wash diapers by hand and put them on a rope on pulleys outside our window. When Carol was about a month old, Mr. Hiram Herbert, the publisher of the Polled Hereford Magazine, was planning to move the business to Louisville, Kentucky and wanted Mark to relocate and continue working for him as art editor. I appeared on the cover of one of the issues. Of course, I had to pose for the picture. Mr. Herbert was very good to us. He even paid for our plane fare to Jamestown, New York, to visit Mark's family. Mark made a trip to Louisville with Mr. Herbert. Mother and Daddy were away at the time. I was alone and had the impression that someone was attempting to break into the house. Being scared, I called Mike, Dawson's best friend. He came over and found nothing.

Barbara Parker called me and said she had a letter from Dawson for me, which he had sent from Germany. Upon learning that I had re-married, he was very upset and asked me how I could marry someone else, when I "belonged" to him. From that time on, Barbara believed that I belonged to her son, so she tried in every way possible to get me to leave Mark. Dawson even sent a really pretty dress from Germany for me. Of course, I was now married to Mark and had a beautiful baby girl. Barbara would call me from time to time during the next years. She was very unhappy about the news that Dawson had married an Air Force nurse named Juanita. When Dawson and his wife came to Montgomery the first time, Barbara ordered her out of her house, feeling that I should be back with Dawson. She hated Juanita and wanted to break up their marriage.

Although we slept upstairs at my parents' home, we did our cooking in Mother's kitchen downstairs. We paid rent; however, we supplied our own food. Mother carefully marked her milk, so as to know whether or not we had taken any of it. Mark could not understand this, and it angered him greatly. So, we found a room on Perry Street, directly across from Mrs. Seibels, my childhood violin teacher. It was a large two-story house in which six couples lived and shared one kitchen. It was while living at this house that Mark and I were walking down Perry Street, at which time he lost his temper and hit me on my left breast with his fist! A large lump formed very quickly, which resulted in my second surgery.

In spite of Mark's jealousy, we decided that I should apply for the carhop position which was being offered at the *Parkmore Drive-in* on the Atlanta Highway. He would stay with Carol at night while I was at work. Mr. Herbert decided not to move to Louisville, so Mark continued working at the magazine and, also, did free-lance art work at Paragon Press. We kept his art materials and Carol's baby supplies in our room. Somehow, the boric acid and the turpentine were in identical bottles. One day, my eyes were very irritated, so I decided to put the boric acid I used for Carol in my eyes. I mistakenly put Mark's turpentine in both eyes, which caused terrible burning, and I was unable to see for several minutes. A couple who lived in the house took me to a doctor's office downtown. The doctor proceeded to put milk in my eyes, which proved to be the appropriate remedy. There was no pain, and my eyes were clearer than they had ever been!

After a few months on Perry Street, we moved to an apartment on Pleasant Avenue. We had the whole upstairs and were able to rent out one of the rooms. A year after the previous trip to Jamestown, we went again, this time by train, for Mark's younger brother's wedding. Anders and Mary had a lovely ceremony. Mark had one of his mood changes on the return trip. He accused me of being overfriendly with his older brother, Bruno. Returning home on the train with our daughter, Carol, and really not knowing just what to expect from Mark, caused me to be fearful of what might happen before we got home. I was glad to get home without mishap.

Barbara Parker was a red-headed, vindictive person; however, I did not know that she was a well-known abortionist on a nationwide basis. She had the cooperation of several well-known doctors and would be alerted by public authorities when investigations were getting too close for comfort. Her husband, Parker, had been transferred from Chanute AFB in Illinois back to Maxwell Field in Montgomery. They had moved from their home on Panama Street to a home on South Perry Street, two blocks from the Governor's Mansion. The house was up a long driveway and was practically hidden, which was an advantage to Barbara for her illegal practice.

Mr. Herbert moved his business to an office building on Bibb Street. With more space than before, he placed Mark in a larger office than he had at the previous location, although he continued his free-lance work at Paragon Press. I would leave Carol with Mother and go downtown to take Mark's dinner to him, due to his having to work late. Now that Carol was no longer a small baby, Mother began to show affection and willingness to look after her. So, I didn't hesitate to leave her with her grandmother.

With Mark's income at that time, we decided to purchase a home at 2031 Johnson Street in Ridgecrest Subdivision on the south side of Fairview Avenue.

Although the houses in that area were new, they were very small. The one we chose was next to the railroad track. Right after we moved there, Mr. Ed Wise of Paragon Press called me and said he would like to hire Mark on a full-time basis but that he needed an assurance from me that I could get him to arrive for work on a regular basis. You see, during his free-lance work at Paragon Press, Mr. Wise had learned of Mark's temperament and his desire to drop whatever he was doing and go fishing at Lake Jordan or shoot a game of pool, whenever the notion would strike him. I told Mr. Wise that I would do my best to get Mark off to work on time. We started saving money to buy a car and kept it hidden in a closet. Somehow, it got misplaced, I suppose it was my fault, and I thought sure my goose was cooked. However, we found the money, and everything was all right. We bought a beautiful, used, green Cadillac convertible. Of course, in addition to going to his work, the car gave Mark a way to get to the pool hall and to the lake more frequently than before. His pool buddy, Johnny Veich, would often go with us on weekends. We would go trolling in rough water. This frightened me, because I had never learned to swim. However, we stopped fishing so much and began water skiing. Can you imagine that? Here I couldn't swim, and now I'm being pulled across the lake on skis. I enjoyed these outings for the most part; however, on one such occasion, we went from one part of the lake to another and for some reason, Mark lost his temper and started yelling and banging his fist on the dash. This was in the presence of Carol and Johnny, and they didn't know what to think!

Mark's mother came down from Jamestown, New York for annual visits of two or three months. She was Polish, spoke broken English and was also the object of her son's temper and ill treatment, as was I. On one occasion, we were driving down Fairview Avenue and, for some reason, he lost his temper with her and ordered her out of the car! He drove away and left her on the street. After a few blocks, he went back and picked her up, probably realizing the bad consequences the incident could cause for him.

We had two German shepherds, Fritz and Toby. Mark decided to be their trainer, so he spent a degree of his time with them, trying to get them to heel on command. They would go in the car with us. One day, Fritz took his usual position in the car with a paw on Mark's left shoulder. As we turned a corner, Fritz fell out of the open convertible! He quickly recovered and got back in the car. The news about Toby is more tragic. As I stated previously, the house was located very close to the railroad tracks. One day, Toby got out of the yard and was struck by the train and killed. This was a shock and made all of us very sad.

Mark would occasionally drop me off at the NCO Club at Maxwell Field to play Bingo. Bill Kollister, a warrant officer, was in charge of the club. He had been a pool hall friend of Mark's. We had met his wife and become friends; therefore, I was invited to play Bingo on Friday nights. Two things stand out very vividly in my mind. The first was when I took a friend named Mary Ann with me for her very first Bingo game. She needed instructions on how to play and asked me to pick up her Bingo card, which I did; however, I went to pick out my card, trying to find a winner. At the last minute, I picked up a card for her. Guess what? She won the five-hundred dollar jackpot with that card! The other thing was when Barbara Parker, who would come to play Bingo, also, looked at me from where she sat across the table from me and said, "Gene, you are pregnant!" At that time, I had no reason to believe what she said, but I came to find out shortly that she knew what she was talking about. I hadn't missed a period yet, so … she must have seen it in my eyes! Within a very short time, I missed a period and went to Dr. Perry for a checkup. He confirmed that I was indeed pregnant!

In spite of all the misery I was going through, I still wanted to make things better. For instance, I always searched for some way to promote Mark's art work. He once painted a portrait of then Governor Tom Folsom, Sr., which I personally delivered to the Governor's Mansion on Perry Street. I took it on myself to try to get Mark up in the mornings and off to his work, wherever he happened to be working at the moment. This was sometimes a very unpleasant task, especially when it resulted in his hitting me.

Mark was reared in a Roman Catholic background, his mother being very dedicated to her religious convictions. He thought it was his responsibility to get me to convert to his church, although he was not a practicing Catholic himself. We went to a local priest. After hearing of my short, previous marriage when I was only fourteen years of age, he turned us down without further ado. Mark believed that if we wrote to the bishop in Mobile, I might still be accepted. We did so, and the reply was a firm "No!" These negative responses from the hierarchy secretly enraged me. How can they have the audacity to blatantly judge a person, feeling that they have authority to condemn the soul, when the God I knew was love, mercy, grace and forgiveness? This brought me back to the days on Lawrence Street when, not from my mother's influence but, rather, from deep within me, I went back to my pondering and wanting to know answers. This led me to read the Bible, searching for a way to reach my *"Secret Garden."* Oftentimes in church, I was sure the preacher was singling me out; so, I would either hide behind someone's back or behind a post or, sometimes, go to the altar to be saved.

To put it bluntly, Mark was both physically and sexually abusive. From the beginning of our marriage, I sank deeper and deeper into a low self-esteem. Not only did I have to put up with his abuse, I really didn't know what to do to get out of it. Mother believed that the only reason for having sex was to bear children and that sex for any other reason was dirty and bad. My first question about sex was when I was about eight or nine years of age. It was not answered, but I did get a whipping for asking about it! In the midst of all my bad experiences, I still knew that God was with me, though at times I could see that several of my friends were getting good husbands and things were going well for them. I seemed to be the only one who was in the mess I was in. Although I had questions, I never quit knowing that God was omniscient (all knowing), omnipresent (in all places at all times) and omnipotent (all powerful). In spite of everything, *I knew that I was a child of God!*

Chapter 14

My Second Baby

Mark's mother came on one of her visits when I was eight months into my second pregnancy. She wanted to help out at this particular time. I got permission from a factory on Birmingham Highway to make and deliver sandwiches to their employees in order to get some extra money. Mother Bukowski helped me in this endeavor. If Mark didn't have work at home, he could be found at the pool hall. When I felt the beginning of labor pains, I reached him by telephone and told him so. He tried to tell me that they weren't often enough, so he just didn't come home. At 10 o'clock that night, I called a taxi and went to the Professional Center Hospital, where I went through hours of hard labor. Finally getting home and finding that I was gone, Mark was very upset. I heard later that he took the dogs out and walked them all over the neighborhood. I had my son, Steve, on September 27, 1952. He weighed eight pounds and ten ounces and was a handsome and healthy baby. Mark came to the hospital the next day with his mother. He started blaming me for not getting him home in time to take me to the hospital. It was there that he learned that our two mothers had planned a party for Carol's sixth birthday, September 29. This made him so angry that he slapped his mother on the face. Her response was not due to any harm she had suffered but the fact that he had actually slapped his own mother. She said, "Son, God will make you pay for this!"

Mark showed me a feature article in either Time or Life magazine, I don't remember which, about the newly discovered method of breast augmentation by way of sponge implants. He said he wanted me to get that done, since he was constantly having me pose for his paintings and photographs. After all the pressure and mistreatment I had suffered from him, my state of mind was such that I was unable to think it through and consider the possibility of negative results from having an untried procedure performed on my breasts. I think I was the second patient for this operation. Someone came from Florida to visit me in the hospital who was contemplating having the same procedure done. I came through the surgery without complications; however, within a year the sponges would move and form hard balls in different areas of my breasts. The surgeon had said he would put in the implants at no cost to me, but I soon found out that this was not true, and he began billing me! So, I went to see my friend, Judge Eugene Loe, who, when he heard about my situation, said, "You ought to sue that doctor, but, do you know what? You're the craziest person I've ever known!" Let it suffice to say at this point that the doctor did not get his money. I will have something more to say about the implants when I move to Cedar Rapids, Iowa.

The house on Johnson was rather isolated at the end of the street next to the railroad track. One night, when Steve was still a young baby, Mark was at the pool hall, and Steve and I were sleeping on the bed. I awakened to see that someone was trying to get in at the bedroom window. I heard a train coming and, at that specific moment, a delivery man from Western Union rang the doorbell. I gladly opened the door for him. The telegram was to advise us that Mark's mother and brother, Bruno, were coming to visit us. Nothing more was seen of the intruder. *I believe beyond any shadow of doubt that God intervened that night and saved Steve and me from imminent danger!*

Helen and Ed came for their first visit at that address while they were still at the church in Calera. We failed to tell them that the railroad track was so close to the house and that a train would be going through in the night. They were rudely awakened at midnight by the rumble of the wheels and the shrill sound of the whistle of a freight train! Ed said, "I thought the world was coming to an end."

When Steve was eight months old, he had a bad cold but had no fever; however, I felt uneasy and took him to the doctor's office at Jackson Hospital on Forrest Avenue. The waiting room was full of people when I checked in. When I sat down a nurse came to me very quickly and said, "Your baby is turning blue!" So, he was admitted to the hospital, where he stayed several days with pneumonia. He recovered with no ill effects. This was the same hospital where Carol had her tonsils removed.

I have made some negative comments about Barbara Parker, but she revealed a more positive side to herself from time to time. For instance, I was at home one night with the children, and Carol had a nosebleed. I didn't know what to do when my efforts failed to stop the bleeding. So, I called Barbara and told her about the situation. She immediately got in her car and came over to Johnson Street. She knew exactly what to do! I was thankful for her help in that time of need. While Barbara wanted me to go back to Dawson, at the same time she was friendly to Mark. Parker, Barbara's husband, loved to fish. They had a cabin on Lake Martin. This appealed to Mark, so we would all go to the lake occasionally. We trolled a lot, but in the spring of the year you could "jump" fish. For those who are reading this and don't know what jump fishing is, let me explain. You can believe it or not. Most people I have told about this choose not to believe it. For instance, at a later date, when I told my friend, Judge Loe, that I had been jump fishing, he said, "I hope you don't ever come before me in court. I don't believe it!" You see, when the crappies are spawning, you paddle along the shore with your motor off. The fish actually jump out of the water and into the boat. Believe it or not! On another occasion up there, I got into poison ivy and spent several days getting over it.

We always needed additional funds; therefore, Mark was in agreement that I look for employment. It must be said that, no matter what I did, his jealousy would come to the surface. At the beginning of our marriage I thought that his jealous rages were due to his loving me so much, but I soon realized that this was nothing more than his wanting to possess what he thought of as "his property." On one occasion, we walked out of his office at Paragon Press, and a young man coming down the street in our direction was looking at me with what Mark thought was an inappropriate stare. He proceeded to stop the fellow and say to him, "Would you like to meet my wife?" Rather than get involved in an altercation, the man went on his way down the sidewalk. This is just one example of the way in which normal life situations would bruise his ego and cause him to react in a way that had made me into a non-person. I was afraid to look up or talk to other people for fear of his reaction. Bill Kollister needed a hat check girl at the NCO Club at Maxwell Field and offered me the position. One night, Bill came up to me and said, "Mark is standing outside watching you!" Mark picked me up when I got off work and, instead of taking me home, he drove down a deserted road, stopped and threatened me with a pistol. I was scared to death and surprised, because I didn't know he even had a gun. It must have been his jealous rage, due to the attention I was given by the guests, as he observed through the window in the door of the NCO Club.

I got a job at Hollywood Candy Company on the Northeast side of Montgomery, close to the train station. I can only recall how the candy passed in front of me on a conveyor belt. I also remember that I would take a bus to the train station and then walk down the tracks to get to work. Someone told me about an opening at Merrill, Lynch, Pierce, Finner and Beane, today known simply as Merrill Lynch. My job was in a large assembly room in which investors would sit, talk, smoke, drink coffee and watch the stock market ticker tape. I had to transfer major ups and downs of the market onto a large chalkboard, as they would be dictated to me verbally by a supervisor. While working at the *Jeff Davis Coffee Shop* years before, I wrote previously about my visit to the dentist who invited me to let him check my teeth, at which time he found no problems whatsoever. Now, in the midst of my job of marking the stock market board, I suddenly knew what a terrible toothache was! I had to leave my work and go to a nearby dentist's office on Court Square to have a cavity filled.

While still living on Johnson Street, Mark continued going to the pool hall and the lake and, I learned, having affairs with various women. I didn't believe that I could even mention the word "divorce," but, somehow, we began talking about it, and he agreed to consult with a lawyer friend of his. As the legal proceedings went forward, I rented an apartment on Court Street, which was about three blocks from my parents' home on Jeff Davis. Of course, Carol was now in school or with my mother. Pearl, mentioned earlier, lived directly behind me on Elizabeth Street. She was my solution for a baby sitter for Steve, while I was at work. This "old maid" would often say, "Stevie Boy is the sweetest child I've ever seen!" One day while I was on my off day from work, Steve and I were taking a nap. He got up, saw the open door to the kitchen, and also saw … the gas stove! While I was asleep, he turned on all of the gas jets. I suddenly awakened, realized the danger, and turned off the gas. Again I say, "But God …"; i.e., *God intervened and saved our lives!*

CHAPTER 15

THE RANCH

I HEARD about a job opening at *The Ranch*, a restaurant which was mentioned three years in a row in McCall's magazine for best food and service in the United States. I applied for the position of cashier, because I had heard that their cashier was leaving. I quickly noticed that the waitresses were making great money through their tips. So, I guess I begged them to let me be a waitress. Although I had worked in the dining room at boarding school in Georgia and at the *Jeff Davis Coffee Shop* in Montgomery, my experience was not sufficient for the service provided by *The Ranch*. Thus, they gave me two weeks of special training at two tables in the front dining room, which was known as the Breakfast Room. My income increased as a result of the generous tips of customers. The employees and even the owner, Mr. Henry McGowan, kidded me due to the fact that, one day, I called in to tell them I would be late to work because my house was on fire! I remember that the fire trucks came and put out the fire with minimal damage to the house. Several months later, I began to think that it was a real hassle to go back and forth to get coffee for customers. There were only two waitresses in the Breakfast Room and each had six tables to serve. At my suggestion they put a hotplate with coffee in that room. Mr. McGowan not only kidded me now about my house being on fire, but he added that I wanted the coffee available in the Breakfast Room, because I was too lazy to walk back and forth to the kitchen to get it! We did not use trays to take food to the tables but, rather, we had to learn to balance several plates in each hand and arm. The exception was when the order was for *The Ranch's* famous "Fish Boat" (seafood platter), which consisted of all kinds of seafood served on a wood plank on the platter with a mast and sail, indicating that it was a boat. We could not possibly carry more than one platter in each hand! It was there that I learned to open swinging doors with my hips.

I had three good friends among the waitresses, Quinn, Lois and Ruby. Quinn was very pretty, but she had dental problems. Mr. McGowan liked her so much that he paid the bill for her dentures. She had three children and was living with two of them, Brenda and Jim. Quinn's personality would shift from being very happy to withdrawn and depressed. I made an effort to help her. She finally married a man named Dick Rawls. He was from a well-to-do family in Chicago. In Montgomery, he had a large chicken farm on the Birmingham Highway and a bar downtown on Commerce Street, called Quinn's. They bought a nice home, but fairly soon, Quinn was unhappy in that situation. Her two children were friends with Carol and Steve. I'll say more about Quinn later, because she was in and out of my life until she passed away in 1997.

Lois was an attractive brunette who dated a lot of officers from the air bases. She would be petrified when thunder and lightning occurred. No matter what was going on, she would go straight to the waitress serving station and get under the table and stay there until the storm was over! Ruby was married to an alcoholic, Nathan. She had four children and lived around the corner from me on Court Street and Finley Avenue. She was a good friend and had a lot to do with my future life, as did I with hers. One weekend, Steve and I went to her home so that we could go to a Halloween party at her daughter Beverly's school. Of course, Carol was staying with my mother for the weekend, as usual. Nathan came home intoxicated after being out all night and went to bed. So, Ruby, Steve and I went downtown to go shopping. We had come out of J. C. Penney's and heard the fire trucks going out Court Street, not occurring to us that they were on their way to Ruby's house. Undoubtedly, trying to light a cigarette in a drunken stupor, Nathan set himself and the house on fire. He was critically burned and died a few days later! The house was damaged but not destroyed.

CHAPTER 16

HANK WILLIAMS, SR.

With my violin at 25 years of age

I GOT up one day and took my violin to WCOV Radio Station on Court Square in downtown Montgomery. I auditioned with Walt Shepura, radio announcer and talent agent, and he hired me on the spot to play on a weekly television show as twin fiddler with Freddie Veich. All of the musicians on the show were members of Hank Williams, Sr.'s original band, known as "The Drifting Cowboys." Hank died January 01, 1953. I would never have thought I would be playing hillbilly music, but I had become familiar with the songs Hank had written. By then, I really liked his music. I played with them for a year, at which time their contract with the station ended. A short time later, the band went to the Alabama State Fair, which was held in Dothan that year. We played nightly for a week. We also played in a school auditorium in Prattville. I then went to Birmingham a couple of times to play on television with Walt Shepura as my agent. Mark was in the background all along, seeking to control me, as usual, and thinking that I would perhaps have the opportunity to go to Nashville which, in itself, could be of benefit to him.

CHAPTER 17

OVER ... BUT NOT OVER!

THE divorce decree was granted on March 05, 1954 and stated that I would have custody of the children. Mark was required to give me eighty dollars a month for child support, which was not forthcoming, and that he would be allowed to visit once a week. The case went back to court on March 06, 1959, at which time Mark gave me total custody of the children with no rights to visitation, relieving him completely of child support and making him the sole owner of the house on Johnson Street. This was an arrangement reached between Mark's lawyer friend and the judge. During most of the time between these two decrees, I lived on the second floor of a two-story apartment house belonging to Barbara Parker, located at 1436 Perry Street and was next to the driveway going into her home, where she carried on her illegal business, referred to previously. Although her son, Dawson, now had four children with his wife, Juanita, Barbara continued to urge me to wait for Dawson while she made every effort possible to break up their marriage, which was on the skids at that time.

One evening, Ruby Todd and another waitress friend came over to my apartment, at which time we had the company of three gentlemen we had come to know at the restaurant. As the evening progressed and we were having a nice social visit, Barbara came in and sat down with us. It was obvious that she was not pleased with the company we had; however, she didn't say anything negative at that time. She soon got up and left the apartment. The visitors left, and the children and I went to bed. We were awakened early the next morning by several black women who were packing all of our belongings. Barbara had let them in. We had to get out of the apartment immediately! We went a few blocks away to Ruby's apartment, where she lived with her four children, one of whom was Wanda, a good friend of Carol's. We stayed there a couple of days, until I found an apartment on Finley Avenue, right around the corner from Barbara's house on Perry Street. Mark moved in and, once again, sought to control our lives! It was as if the divorce decree had not been issued. He would give some of his time to Carol and Steve, going with us to the lake, taking pictures, playing with them, etc. However, he was the same domineering character, while I continued to be a non-entity and deeply afraid of him! After a few months of the same old assault and battery, I awakened one morning with the inner conviction that I had to get out and away from Mark, before he got home at 5 p.m. Carol, Steve and I packed everything and were gone when he came home to an empty apartment. We found a place to live on Sayre Street, right across from the grammar school Carol would be attending.

CHAPTER 18

THE RIVIERA

By this time, I had left my work at *The Ranch* and had been hired as a waitress right across the highway at the Greek *Riviera Restaurant*. I had to learn tray service as opposed to the serving method previously described at *The Ranch*. At about the same time, a German lady, named Tina, who was married to a U. S. serviceman, had made up her mind that she was going to be the hostess at the *Riviera*. It took a couple of weeks of her persistence before Nick, one of the owners, gave in and hired her. She was a tiny, well proportioned and extremely full-busted lady who spoke with a slight German accent. She was a real drawing card for customers! This made Nick realize that he had made the right decision. As well as being well liked by tourists, it was not unusual for politicians, including Governor John Patterson, to eat at the restaurant several times a week.

On a very busy night at the restaurant, I received a call from Barbara Parker. She gave me the shocking news that Dawson had been rescued from the Hudson River where the military plane he was piloting had crashed. Sensing that I was in shock, she added that he had not been injured. This was his second plane crash!

I was given special recognition as an outstanding waitress; however, one very busy evening I spoiled that idea. I came out of the kitchen with a loaded tray on my uplifted left hand and reached the table I was serving. As I lowered the tray to put it on the serving table, it slipped out of my hand and fell to the floor with a crash. Of course, this incident totally humiliated me. In spite of my urge to run out of the dining room crying, somehow I pulled myself together and finished my shift!

One of the waitresses, Dolores Williams, was a special friend of mine. She was married to Joseph and they had two children. She and Joe, as her husband was known, had a happy marriage at the beginning. This changed when their older child in some way came into contact with a live wire in their back yard and was electrocuted. Burdened with this terrible loss, their marriage deteriorated to the point that she went her way, and Joe went his way. She rented an apartment in the Ridgecrest Subdivision. Trying to get away from Mark, the children and I spent a night with her. A friend, who had been visiting Dolores, left a lighted cigarette behind when he left the apartment that night. I was awakened at daybreak by loud knocking on the front door. A man going by had noticed smoke coming from the house, called the Fire Department and warned us of the danger. The fire was quickly extinguished without extensive damage to the house.

About a year later, Dolores revealed a side of herself that I had not known. She called me from the Montgomery County Jail, saying that she had been arrested on the charge of being a kleptomaniac which, of course, she denied. They accused her of taking an item of clothing from a department store, even though she had one exactly like it at home. I was outraged, believing that she could not be guilty of such an offense. So, I called my good friend, Judge Loe, and explained the problem, feeling he would do something about it. A short time later, he called me back and said, "Gene, your friend is guilty. She has a record of having done this same thing before. The law will take its course with her, but you should know more about your friends before you intervene on their behalf." Later on, I tried to get help for someone else and Judge Loe sternly told me, "You stop trying to practice law in my court!" Dolores went back to Joe, and they continued to live in the same house for the sake of their son, Jimmy. Several years later, on a visit home from Iowa to see my mother and daddy, I naturally went to see Dolores. I knew she had not been well, but I was shocked when I saw her physical condition. When I left her home and was leaving Montgomery, I felt a deep sadness, knowing that I would never see her again.

My children's companion, Martha Peck

It was at this time that Martha Peck, a black lady I had known from *The Ranch*, came to do housekeeping and to take care of the children while I was at work. Not only was she a good worker, but she was my friend. Carol and Steve were crazy about her. I only had to pay her ten dollars a week, which was about average wages for work in that day. In the section of this book relating to my early childhood, I stated that I had questions and doubts of a spiritual nature based on my conviction that God not only created all things but, also, all people, regardless of their color. Therefore, I knew that prejudice against the blacks was wrong. For me, the Civil Rights Movement brought these thoughts more into focus than ever before in my life. Maybe I should have been afraid, but my determination to overcome racial obstacles caused me to be friendly and open to blacks. For instance, Martha loved to go fishing. She had no transportation; therefore, if her friends didn't invite her, she would ask me to take her to nearby ponds and lakes. On a couple of occasions, she had black ladies with her. So, there I was, driving them through the city, not feeling at all afraid. Also, Martha loved to dance. She was a great dancer and, often, she would invite me to her home to dance with her and her lady friends to black rock and the blues on 78 rpm records. Carol enjoyed going along. One day, she brought home a note from school, advising me of some minor infraction of the rules. While I was at work, Martha marched across the street to the school and, in no time flat, she had straightened out the problem. She even went to Iowa to visit me in the 1970s. We went on together to visit Carol in Wisconsin. We went directly there, but we had a late start on the return trip; so, we stopped at a motel but were turned away, because she was black! Martha and I remained good friends until her death in 1999.

CHAPTER 19

THE HOLIDAY INN

A NEW motel and restaurant opened a mile south of *The Ranch* and the *Riviera*. Waitress friends from both of these restaurants and I began working at the *Holiday Inn*, probably thinking that due to the tourist trade, we would make more money in tips. Quinn's children, Brenda and Tom, were visiting Carol and Steve for the day. It seemed that I could not get away from Mark, no matter where I moved. He had returned and moved himself in with us once again! He went to the lake early that morning. I had fixed lunch for the children and myself, when he returned, earlier than I thought he would. Although we had finished eating, there was plenty of food left for him; however, he went into one of his rages, because I didn't get up and heat his food. He locked the children out of the house and proceeded to beat me up! From the depths of my being, I didn't see how I could keep going like this.

While working at the *Holiday Inn*, I went back to playing my violin in Mrs. Seibels' orchestra. She celebrated her symphony anniversary at the Whitley Hotel. We were in formal attire. With my working that day at the restaurant and then playing at the hotel that evening, I was especially tired and needed rest. Carol was at my parents' home and Steve was asleep. When I walked into the apartment and into the bedroom, there was Mark, nude, sitting on the bed and, obviously, waiting for me. In my exhausted state of mind and body and from deep within my soul, I said to myself, "I cannot endure this any longer, even though I have no solution for taking care of my kids. Something has to happen!"

Right after this incident, Papa (my grandfather) passed away in Albany, Georgia. I felt that I had to go to the funeral. It was then that I made a decision, although others might judge me differently for what I did. You see, there was a wealthy businessman, Mr. J. C. Jones, who ate frequently at the restaurant, especially for breakfast. He had been trying to get me to date him. Up to that point, I hadn't even considered it. When he learned that my grandfather had died and that I needed to go to Georgia, he offered to take Steve and me to the funeral. On that trip, he said he would give me a year-old Ford automobile and place it in front of my parents' home. Also, he said he would locate an apartment for the children and me. I accepted his offer, and he kept his word with a nice apartment with a swimming pool on Fairview Avenue.

CHAPTER 20

TRIP TO NEW YORK

A LITTLE less than a year later, my sister, Helen, wrote to me from New York. By this time, her husband, Ed, was no longer pastor of a church but, rather, was serving as a chaplain at the air base in Plattsburg, New York. They invited me to visit them, thinking that I could find employment in their area. The night before we left, Mark came over to say good-by to the children. He sat there in the apartment for a couple of hours without saying a word. He had a strange look on his face. He finally left, and I learned later that he had called Mr. Jones and asked him to come to a certain place for a meeting of the two of them. It did not take place, as J. C. refused to meet him. Apparently, Mark had in mind to do him bodily harm due to J. C.'s attentiveness to me. So, the next morning, the first day of September 1957, for my very first trip driving outside of the city limits, I left with my children and drove from Montgomery, Alabama to Upper State, New York.

In Northern Alabama, we kept seeing signs for Lookout Mountain, Tennessee. I didn't need too much begging from Carol to stop for the scenic view of five states. I was a little leery to cross the narrow bridge near the top! Our first night on the road we stayed in a motel in North Carolina. The next morning we discovered winged termites on the ceiling, on the bed and on the floor. When I checked out, I asked the desk clerk if they made an additional charge for the bugs! The next stop of interest was Luray Caverns in Shenandoah National Park in Northern Virginia. If I had known about the low temperature in the caverns, we would have all worn our sweaters. In spite of having to carry Steve, who was four years old at the time, we were in awe of the beauty of the cave. After spending another night in a motel, this time without bedbugs, we left early in the morning in our black Ford and finally arrived in Keeseville, where Helen and Ed were awaiting our arrival.

They had bought a nice three-bedroom home. I immediately enrolled Carol in the Keeseville Grammar School. She has fond memories of that school, especially when she took a music test along with the whole school and earned the top score! Helen and Ed took us in their car on a ferry across Lake Champlain to Burlington, Vermont. This was my first ferry trip, which I enjoyed very much. We drove around for a while and then returned to Keeseville. My children, Carol and Steve, as well as Helen and Ed's children, Peggy and Danny, all enjoyed our visit to Santa's Workshop at North Pole, New York. One weekend, we visited an awesome place called Ausable Chasm.

I went to an interview for a job at the Officers' Club on the air base. Although my memory generally serves me well, I cannot for the life of me give the reason why I did not accept the position or why we did not stay more than a month before heading back to Alabama. Maybe I was just homesick! On the way south, I remember stopping for lunch in Williamsburg, Virginia. We were impressed with the many historic buildings and monuments in the area. Upon reaching Montgomery, we went directly to the apartment on Fairview Avenue, which J. C. Jones had maintained for us with our furniture and personal belongings.

CHAPTER 21

A NEW FRIEND

I RETURNED to one of my first places of employment, the *Jeff Davis Coffee Shop* and stayed there about a month. While there, I met a customer, Mr. Tom Moore, who impressed me as being like the tourists who stayed at the Jeff Davis Hotel; however, I soon learned that he was from Marion County, Alabama. His father was the well-known sheriff of that county, whose racial prejudice made life miserable for the blacks of that area. Tom was strikingly handsome, had brown eyes, dark brown hair and wore a mustache. He was some fifteen years older than I and had been in combat in World War II in Germany.

I received a call from the manager of the *Holiday Inn*, who heard that I was back in town. He wanted me to take the early-morning shift at the restaurant. While working there again, Tom called and asked me for a date. He picked me up and took me to the first tavern I had ever entered. It was called Gaither's Tavern and was fairly close to my apartment on Fairview Avenue. When we went in, I saw only the bartender and one lady sitting at the bar. Tom and I sat in a booth for about half an hour, talking and getting acquainted. We decided to leave and had reached the door when the woman at the bar, Edith, jumped up, ran to the door and tried to grab me! It turned out that she and Tom had been dating for some time. I was in quite a state of shock over the incident.

I was in for a greater shock the next day at work. The manager took me aside and said he received a call from a woman who said that I was dating her sister's husband and that they had several children. Later that day, before I got off work, two women came into the restaurant, sat down and asked for me. They were Rebecca and Susan, sisters of Edith, who accused me of attempting to break up their sister's marriage with Tom. They warned me that Edith could be very violent and that I should stay away from Tom. I quickly learned that their tale was not true, that Tom had dated Edith in the past, but he was not married to her and had no children with her. Edith herself started calling me and warning me over and over to stay away from Tom.

About a month after all of this began, one day I stepped out of my front door as a convertible pulled up in front of my apartment, and there was Edith behind the wheel! She was somewhat friendly and said, "Gene, get in." So, I went in and got my purse and got in the car with her. We rode around and stopped to have a *Coke* and to talk. We became friends, and she never bothered me again. When the sisters learned that I had gone for a ride with Edith, they were shocked. They were no longer belligerent, and Rebecca and I became good friends.

I dated Tom a few times after that. He was a nice guy; however, he had a severe drinking problem. It probably was related to his war experiences. We went back to Gaither's Tavern one weekend and found it crowded. We noticed that Edith was sitting nearby with a group of people. Tom needed to go to the restroom. When he returned to our booth, he exclaimed, "Sweetie, she cut me!" He had a superficial cut across his neck. As he walked by Edith's table, she had jumped up and attacked him. We decided the best thing to do was to leave.

I wrote earlier about my good friend from childhood, Nell Wilson. She married Jack Hill. They had two girls, Vicky and Debby. Complications in their marriage led to divorce. They suffered a tragic loss, when Debby was killed in an automobile accident on Jefferson Street, along with several of her classmates. Jack committed suicide one year to the day after the accident. Nell and I, being divorcees, began to double date. One man she dated was known as Sam; in fact, he had a used car lot on Bell Street, called Sam's Used Cars. It turned out that Sam and Tom were friends. Nell knew about Tom's involvement with Edith and the roughnecks at Gaither's Tavern and elsewhere around the city. She admonished me and said, "Gene, you shouldn't associate with that crowd!"

So far, in the journey of my soul, my self-esteem had been badly bruised over and over. Deep within myself I *knew* that God was love but, at the same time, I had two children to care for, and I really didn't have a solution for my problems. Furthermore, I did not have answers to my early-childhood questions, about which I yearned to have satisfaction: *Where did my musical abilities come from so early in life? Why did some people experience a seemingly happy and smooth life and, yet, mine was rocky and rough?* I did realize that some people were worse off than I. The fact that I could see some people happy, others rich, others healthy but, on the other hand, others who were sad, poor, crippled or sick, just didn't add up to my concept of God as having made all His creation equal.

Another thing about me is that I always had a very forgiving spirit, especially if the offender told me that he or she was sorry and asked for my forgiveness. I would forgive and forget! Mother would often say to me, "Gene, I just can't understand you. You have no pride." I can honestly say that I had, and still have to this day, compassion and empathy for the underdogs of life. It could be said, however, that my forgiving attitude helped to lead me into further complications in my life, such as my third marriage. Without that marriage, however, I would not have my wonderful, talented daughter, Jacqueline Kimberly Winn.

On one occasion, Tom and I went swimming at the Millbrook Gravel Pit. There was a hill behind us and, all of a sudden, a dog barked. We turned around and saw a fox terrier looking from the top of the hill with only his head showing and his ears standing erect. He was staring directly at me! I called him, and he came to me and acted very friendly; however, he was not at all friendly to Tom. So, Tom said, "Sweetie, why don't you take the dog with you? He doesn't even have a collar." Due to his friendliness and being a duplicate of our dog, Nicky, which died years before, I decided to adopt him. He got in the car without any problem, and I took him home with me. I named him Toby, after the German shepherd which was hit by the train.

Due to the fact that I was dating Tom, and J. C. Jones didn't like him or his father, all of them being from Marion County, it became necessary for me to find another place to live. I found an apartment nearby but still on Fairview Avenue. A short time later, I was notified by the manager that pets were not allowed in the apartments. So, I found an apartment on South Street near Mother, where the rent was cheaper, and I could keep Toby. I tried to get him to leave. He would go away for a while but would then return to me. Finally, the week that I was to move, Rebecca came to visit me. As we were standing by her car, Toby showed up! I told him he had to leave but that he could come back on Friday, because we were going to move and he could go with us. I wasn't sure that would happen, but he showed up again as we were moving, so we took him with us! I normally worked the day shift at the *Holiday Inn* but, occasionally, I would be assigned to the night shift. In the latter case, I would arrive home about 10 p.m.

One night, when I got home, Carol and Steve were asleep, and I couldn't get them to come to the door. For some reason, I didn't have my key with me. I had not gotten to know the neighbors yet, so I walked a long block to the nearest pay telephone on Jeff Davis and called Carol. I was walking quite briskly and was not afraid, because Toby was trotting along by my side and would bark from time to time. I had the feeling he was escorting and protecting me that night! A few months later, my friend, Rebecca, came to see me one day at noon. When I opened the door, she said, "Gene, your dog is black and white, isn't he?" I replied, "Yes, he is." She pointed to the street and said, "Well, he's been hit by a truck!" Carol, Steve and I were heartbroken over Toby's death.

I was working the morning shift at the *Holiday Inn* and got off at 2 o'clock. I went to the service station on Mobile Highway, about a block from my work, to get gas. I had a friend who owned the station, so I always bought my gas from him. Being the only one there when I arrived, he began to fill my tank. He stopped very quickly and came to my window and said, "You must have an enemy. Somebody put sugar in your gas tank!" This normally ruins an engine. I was in a real predicament, because I needed my car. I knew that Mark was good at car repairs, so I called him and told him what had happened. He had the car towed to his home on Johnson Street. He had it in running condition in a couple of days. Within a week, someone who was in a position to know told me that Barbara had paid someone to put the sugar in my gas tank.

Although Mark had no legal right to visit the children, I strongly believed that the children had only one father and one mother, that they loved their father and, no matter what had happened to me, he loved them. Therefore, I allowed him to take them, I thought, to the house on Johnson Street, which was their first home. One Saturday, in the middle of the afternoon, my mother called and in her typically sarcastic tone of voice, she said, "Well, do you know where your children are?" I replied, "Yes. Mark has them at his house." Mother then said, "No, they're not there. Carol is lying in the Emergency Room at St. Margaret's Hospital." I ran to the car, went by and picked up my mother and rushed to the hospital. Very quickly, while en route, Mother said, "Well, I don't think she's all that bad off." I think she was trying to get me to slow down. I was shocked when I saw Carol's face, for it had been cut open in an automobile accident and seventy-six stitches had been taken. A nurse took me by the arm, thinking I was on the verge of fainting. Mark had taken the children and had left them with his current girlfriend's daughter, who was fifteen years of age, about the same age of Carol at the time. A teenaged boy came by to see them and took them for a ride with a fourteen-year-old girl at the wheel. The boy had beer in the car. Steve was standing in front of Mark's girlfriend's house and saw what happened. When the girl circled the block and attempted to stop in front of the house, instead of stepping on the brake pedal, she pushed the accelerator pedal to the floor! The car crashed into a tree, and Carol was thrown into the windshield. The windshield was broken from the impact and Carol's face severely lacerated. The car belonged to the boy's father, who turned out to be Colonel Paul Tibbets, the pilot of the Enola Gay plane which dropped the atomic bomb on Hiroshima, Japan, bringing World War II to an end. Mr. Morris Dees, who was just beginning his law practice, was waiting for me at the hospital. He took Carol's case to court. Paul Tibbets, a war hero, was able to come out of the case by only paying Carol's hospital expenses. He would not have gotten away with such a light sentence today, due to the fact that his son had allowed under-aged girls to drive. Mr. Dees later became the founder and chief trial counsel for the Southern Poverty Law Center.

CHAPTER 22

THE BLUE
BONNET INN

DUE to my low income employment and no child support from the children's father, I qualified for an apartment in the Government Housing Project on Bell Street. My friend, Nell Hill, called me and asked if I would work the night shift at the *Blue Bonnet Inn* on Narrow Lane Road. It was located on the south side of Montgomery outside the city limits, while I was living on the north side of the city, looking down on the Alabama River. I decided to go to work there, and it turned out to be enjoyable for me, except for the long ride home late at night. If I saw a car which seemed to be following me, I would swing by the downtown police station and park there, which would cause the person, or persons, following me to continue on their way. One night, however, and it stands out very vividly in my mind, I was really tired. When I stopped at the red light just before the Bell Street Bridge, I glanced at the truck in the lane next to me and saw three men who were trying to get my attention. It aggravated me, because I was tired and wanted to get home.

After crossing the bridge, there was a service station. I drove to the far side of the station and parked, hoping that those men would keep going and leave me alone. After a minute or so, a man in uniform came to my car. He looked like an employee at the station. He said, "Can I help you, Ma'am?" I told him I was just sitting there for a minute. He replied, "But, Ma'am, you have a flat tire." I said, "Well, I live very close to here and, besides, I don't have any money to fix it." To my surprise, he opened my door, pushed me over, got behind the wheel, started my car and drove onto the street. Again, *God intervened on my behalf.* I reached over and snatched the keys out of the ignition switch and, in the same motion, threw them out of the window on my side of the car. When I did that, he hit me on the shoulder, at the same time seeming to realize that he was in a bad situation in a public place. He jumped out and ran back to his friends. I got out quickly and ran down between two houses. All of a sudden, I realized that there was a fence surrounding the houses, and I couldn't get out that way. By then, I was close to the next street corner, so I went to the corner house and knocked on the door. A man opened the door and, hearing of my predicament, called the police. When they arrived, I explained my situation to them. Believe it or not, they were able to locate my keys where I had thrown them from the car! Thus, well after midnight, I arrived home to my worried children.

I explained to them what had happened. Then, thoroughly exhausted but happy to be safe at home, I went to bed.

Rufus Gibson, a nineteen-year-old muscular fellow who lived in the next building from us, came over one afternoon. Carol and Steve liked him a lot. They started horsing around in the living room. I was standing there looking at them when, all of a sudden, Rufus lifted Carol up in the air and brought her down quickly, not intending to hit her head on the floor, but that's what happened! I knew immediately that something was wrong, so I got her into the car. Rufus drove with Steve up front with him, while I held Carol in my arms in the back seat. We went straight to the Emergency Room at Professional Center Hospital. I was afraid she would throw up, which would have indicated a really serious problem. This fear became a reality, just as we arrived at the hospital, for she did throw up. After the medical examination, I was told she had a skull fracture and had to be admitted. She came out of that ordeal with no negative results. Rufus felt badly about what had happened, feeling guilty and responsible for the accident.

Although I have said that Rufus was a nice young man, he was very different from his brother, Sonny Gibson. Sonny was quite involved with the "roughnecks" I referred to previously. So, when he heard about the problem I had on my way home from work with the three men who tried to pick me up, he and his cohorts really got upset. When I described what the fellow looked like who got into my car and the kind of truck he and his friends were driving, Sonny believed he knew who they were. So, he asked me to go with him and a friend of his in an effort to find and identify these men. I'm sure of this, if we had located them, Sonny and his friend would have taken care of them. I was unable to point them out. I never saw them again, but I have never forgotten how near I came to either being killed or going through a horrible experience at their hands. Even though my life didn't seem to be improving to a great extent, I must say, *God was with me in one event after another!*

CHAPTER 23

MY THIRD MARRIAGE

MY friend, Bill Kollister, had been discharged from military service and had opened a club next door to the Veterans of Foreign Wars on Catoma Street. I was still working at the *Blue Bonnet Inn*, which was very difficult for me due to the distance to and from work. A telephone call from Bill asking me to come to work at his new club seemed to be the answer! I did enjoy the juke box music; e.g., Ray Charles, Benny Goodman, Les Brown and others. Although I always felt safe with Bill on the scene, sensing that he was my protector, I soon realized that perhaps this was not the place I *wanted* to be nor was it where I *should* be. One night, a tall, good-looking fellow came in, wearing a cowboy hat, and sat at the bar. We started talking, got acquainted, had a few dates, and the next thing I knew … I was Mrs. Jack Winn!

I did not know that Jack was an alcoholic, until it was too late. To him, he had to have his liquor one way or another! If this meant he had to write bad checks, he would do so without thinking twice. He would occasionally work for his friend, Bobby, who had a small furniture repair shop. One day, Jack did not come home. The next morning, I called Bobby, and he told me that Jack had been arrested on a bad check charge. I had not been working since my marriage to Jack; therefore, I could not continue to live in the project on Bell Street. Whereas Mother would not keep Steve when he was younger, she now saw him as old enough so as not to cause her any problems, and she felt he was in need of her influence toward church attendance. So, the three of us moved in with my parents on Jeff Davis.

A short time later, Jack was released from jail and went back to his work with Bobby. He begged for my forgiveness, saying he had found an apartment on Caroline Street. Things went fairly well for a few days, until he went on one of his drinking binges. Carol's boyfriend was visiting her one afternoon. They were playing Monopoly in the living room downstairs. I was upstairs thinking, "Well, things have gone OK, at least for a few days." At that instant, Jack burst into my room in a jealous rage, accusing me of flirting with someone down the street. Before I could open my mouth, he started beating on me. I screamed, causing Carol's friend to come running. When he came in the room, Jack hit him in the face. Neighbors, who heard the commotion, called the police. Very quickly, Jack left the house. After this terrible afternoon, and realizing that he might return, I took Carol and Steve and found a room for the night in a cheap motel.

CHAPTER 24

MY THIRD
BABY

ALL of a sudden, I realized I was really in a pickle. I had missed my period, and I was pregnant! Jack's boss, Bobby, must have told him that I had moved to my parents' home. So, he called me from the jail. I answered him on the upstairs phone. I told him about my condition, not realizing that Mother was listening on the downstairs phone. He said he was happy over the news, but I couldn't understand how this could be possible, when he couldn't hold down a job or pay bills or leave the booze alone and, for now, he was in jail! Mother was furious! In a loud and angry voice, she stated, "I am going to take Carol and Steve away from you!" Pointing my finger at her, my quick reply was, "You'll take Carol and Steve from me over my dead body!" Years later, Mother confessed to me that she was proud of me for standing up to her the way I did that day.

Jack was finally released from jail, but he knew better than to come to my parents' home. I got a job working at a small restaurant on Mt. Meigs Road. One day, Jack showed up at the restaurant. He said he had just been to a doctor and was told he didn't have long to live. He wanted me to give him thirty dollars to have a test done. I wasn't quite that stupid so as to fall for his game. I knew he wanted money for liquor. He didn't return to bother me at work. A short time later, I learned that he had gone to court on the bad check charge. Since it was not his first offense of this nature, he was convicted and sentenced to serve time at Elmore County Prison. While he was incarcerated, the time came for my baby to be born. Because I was living with my parents, I was not eligible for welfare, the State feeling that my parents were able and should assist me. I was able to get some help by going to St. Jude's Catholic Hospital for the delivery. I reached the hospital at 8 p.m., labor pains already having started, and my third child was born two hours later on October 03, 1963! I left the hospital with my new baby the next morning with Jack's sister, Betty, who lived in Millbrook, north of Montgomery. Jack had two wonderful sisters, Betty and Ann, who were sympathetic, knowing what I had been through with their brother. I stayed in Betty's home for five weeks. My sister and her husband had moved from New York to the University of Iowa in Iowa City, where Ed was working on his PhD. Helen and Mother had talked about my situation. Helen was happy for us to live with them temporarily.

Although Mother was not too happy about having a disruptive, crying baby in her home, she accepted the fact that I needed to be where all my things were located, in order to be ready to move to Iowa as soon as possible. I can't remember what kind of car I had at the time, but one thing is clear in my mind. It used oil, to the extent that I had to check the oil level every two hundred miles or so. Probably through his sisters, Jack learned that I was leaving with the children for Iowa. The day before we were ready to leave, Betty called and asked me to come to her home before I left town. So, I stopped my packing momentarily and drove out to Millbrook to see what she wanted. To my surprise, Jack was there, totally sober, and begged me to let him go with us. He felt he needed a new place to start over. I felt that he was being sincere with me, and he certainly needed a new lease on life. Also, my forgiving nature led me to agree to his making the trip with us. At the same time, I was concerned about my old car and the possibility of getting stranded with it along the way. A neighbor friend of my mother gave me twenty dollars to help on the trip. Her gift brought my total of cash on hand to thirty dollars! We left the next day, November 18, 1963, as planned, and without Mother's knowing that Jack was going with us.

CHAPTER 25

MOVE
TO IOWA

THE trip went fairly well. Jack stayed sober, but he was obviously suffering from alcohol withdrawal symptoms. I had to stop from time to time, because he was nauseated and had to vomit. Also, my mind was burdened with not knowing how Helen and Ed were going to accept my bringing Jack up there, when the purpose of the move was to leave Alabama and get away from him. When we did arrive in Iowa City late the next day, I stopped and called her from a pay telephone and tried to plead his case. I'm sure they were shocked, but they didn't turn us away, for which I was thankful. They were living in a rented two-story house. They let us use two bedrooms upstairs. Kim slept in a dresser drawer in the room I was in! With the five of us and the four of them, the house was pretty-well filled!

Within a couple of days, Jack began searching for employment. He had been a steeplejack, so it was not surprising that he got a job repairing roofs with a construction company in Davenport, Iowa. He took my car with him for transportation. Late that first night, he came home without the car, which he had sold in order to buy liquor and, now, he was totally inebriated! Helen and Ed told me firmly not to let in him, so I refused to unlock the door. This made him furious. He proceeded to climb to the second floor and force his way through the window of the corner bedroom where Kim and I were staying. He went straight downstairs, where he and Ed had an argument, which led to Jack's punching Ed in the nose. Helen cried out, "Look what he's done to my husband. He's given him a bloody nose!" We called the police immediately. Jack was aware of this and quickly left the house. It didn't take the police long to find him walking down the street. They arrested him and took him to jail. He had a court hearing a few days later, at which time Ed testified against him. When he left the house, he took with him a walking stick, as though it were to defend himself against Jack. The judge sentenced Jack to three months in jail.

CONGRESS INN

WITHIN a few days, I found a job in the restaurant of the *Congress Inn*, an upscale motel on the outskirts of Iowa City. The owner/manager was Bob Anderson. His parents were part owners and were on the premises much of the time. Realizing that I was new in the city and was now without a car, they would give me a ride home after work. After I had worked there three weeks or so, they were taking me home after work on a Sunday afternoon. I asked them to just drop me off in town, close to the courthouse. I had Jack's cigarettes, which he had left in the house. Soft-hearted me, I decided to take them to him in the jail. I think Mr. and Mrs. Anderson saw me go into the jail and wondered what I was up to. They were members of more than one civic organization and were well acquainted with city officials, so it was not difficult for them to find out what I was doing at the city jail. They did not think any less of me but, rather, they tried to help me. Consequently, they talked to the Chief of Police and, as a result, Jack was released from jail and was given a bus ticket to some destination unknown to me. The police escorted him to the bus station with the admonition that he was to *never* return to the State of Iowa! He did return years later. I will write about that at the appropriate time.

The tips were good at the restaurant. In fact, I still have a misprinted dollar bill that I've always hoped would turn out to be valuable. Something that I've always remembered as being humorous was that, one day, after the lunch hour was over, I commented to the hostess that I had to go to the restroom. Her reply was, "Why, Gene, why didn't you do that before you got here?" At first, I thought she was serious, then I realized she was just kidding me! I was so excited when I received my first paycheck from the *Congress Inn*, because it allowed me to go to Good Will to get some much-needed school clothes for Carol and Steve and a decent change of clothes for me. It was very disconcerting when I arrived home to have Ed present me with an itemized bill of my share of household expenses, including rent, power, water and food. This upset me greatly, but I soon realized that I was responsible to pay my just debts. I accepted this as a valuable realization that each human being must make his/her own way in life with all of its duties and obligations!

CHAPTER 26

CEDAR RAPIDS
- THE TOWN HOUSE

JUST after Christmas of 1963, Ed received a call to pastor a small Congregational Church in Cedar Rapids, Iowa. He and Helen purchased a nice split-level home at 1412 Seminole Avenue. Naturally, I had to move with them in order to have a place to live and to continue to have Helen as Kim's baby sitter. Bob Anderson from the *Congress Inn* had a friend, Mr. Gerald Spresser, who managed the *Town House Motel* in Cedar Rapids. Bob called Gerald and told him about me. Gerald replied by saying that he had an opening for a competent hostess in his Officers' Club. I was thrilled to know that I had a good job waiting for me when I arrived in Cedar Rapids.

The *Town House* was a huge luxury facility, complete with a large dining room, coffee shop, two separate bars, Officers' Club, conference rooms and a golf course. In addition to the tourist trade, Collins Radio housed their out-of-town clients there, including astronauts. In fact, astronaut Lt. Col. Edward H. White stayed there some time before the fatal Apollo space craft flash fire during a launch pad test on January 27, 1967.

My background of having been trained at *The Ranch* in Montgomery, well-known nationwide for its food and service, prepared me for this new employment as well as for future jobs I would have in this same field. After working for a week or so in the Officers' Club, Mr. Spresser called me into his office and asked for my opinion on the quality of the service being provided by the waitresses. I hesitated to answer him, but I had to be truthful; so, I told him about several things they were neglecting. I guess I must have impressed him with my knowledge of food service, because he offered me the position of General Hostess, which included the supervision of the total staff involved in food and beverage at the *Town House*. I was even given my own private office! I was elated, but said nothing for a couple of weeks, waiting until the current General Hostess, whose position I would be taking, had left.

During those two weeks, I continued working at the Officers' Club. I heard over and over the question, "I wonder who Mr. Spresser is planning to hire as General Hostess?" After hearing this for two or three days, I finally told them, "I know who it is." Of course, they all wanted to know, "Who is it?" I said, "I've been given the job." I already knew they didn't like me very much, being from the Deep South and being a new arrival in their town. I had no way to know the trauma my getting the position was going to cause them. They immediately went to Mr. Spresser's office and expressed their disappointment that one of them did not get the position.

My balloon of joy soon burst, when I realized the attitude being taken by the waitresses as a result of my being so new and, yet, being given this position over them. I learned that Mr. Spresser told them in no uncertain terms that there would be a waitress training class, beginning the next week which would be given by Mrs. Winn. He added that they *would* attend or, to the contrary, they would punch the time clock and not return to work! Knowing they didn't like me and being very sensitive to the thoughts and feelings I was picking up, as well as having to teach a course for waitresses, something which I had never done, almost overwhelmed me and made me somewhat unsure of myself. The classes took place, as Mr. Spresser had scheduled them, and things calmed down after a few months. The most antagonistic waitress was Connie Tischer. I will write more about her later on. I was able to get Carol a job in the *Coffee Shop*.

An interesting aspect of my new position was that Collins Radio not only had their clients stay at the *Town House* but also provided special programs for them. For instance, well-known singers, such as The Ink Spots, The Four Lads and others would provide entertainment. A unique feature, as far as I personally was concerned, was when Collins Radio provided a large bus to transport their clients to dinner at one of the Amana Colonies. The bus was provided at the cocktail hour, and who do you suppose was the hostess on board to serve their drinks? Right, yours truly! It was sort of fun, but also tricky, to handle the mixing and serving of drinks with the bus in motion. I don't remember spilling a single drink on a guest!

The children and I always attended Helen and Ed's church. We would then go out for Sunday Brunch. Kim was a beautiful baby with dark, curly hair and crystal-clear blue eyes. The church people would crowd around to make over her, but she didn't like that kind of attention and would let out a piercing scream, as though to say, "Leave me alone!" Carol was then a sophomore in high school, and Steve was in the fourth grade. Of course, Helen and Ed's children were in school, also.

I had never had the experience of driving on snow and ice. When my first ice storm came, I took all the children to school one day without mishap. However, on my return trip alone, the first thing I knew I was headed in the opposite direction! It takes me a little time to learn things, such as you don't put your foot on the brake pedal when you are driving on ice. Would you believe it? The same thing happened again! I finally got it, and I had no more experiences of that specific nature. However, one day, when Kim was in the first grade, I dropped her off at school before returning home. I was going down an incline and soon had to turn right at the corner. The only thing straight ahead was the lake. Again, I was on ice and driving slowly. The problem this time was not in the braking procedure but, rather, I was unable to steer to make the right turn. At that moment, a young lady was crossing the intersection in her car. I had no other option, except to hit her. The damage to her car was minor. When the police arrived, the young lady was irate, because I had hit her car. The policeman spoke to her, rather sternly, and said, "Miss, if you had not been here at that precise moment, this lady would have gone directly into the lake!"

Carol was chosen to be in a play at school. She and I were very happy about it; however, Helen and Ed thought it was immoral, because it would include dancing. This led to a big argument between Ed and me, due to the fact that our opinions on morality were very different. He said he wanted the book he had given to Carol returned to him immediately, and he added, "Your children are not going to amount to anything." In the middle of the confrontation, I put my hand on the living room wall, and he ordered me sharply, "Take your hand off my wall!" Naturally, I was really upset. When I got to work I told Mr. Spresser about the incident. He told me right away that I should move to the *Town House* until I could find a place for us to live.

I soon found a house very close to the motel on Blair's Ferry Road and made the move. I had to enroll Carol and Steve in the Marion, Iowa schools, due to the fact that the house was in a different school district than where we lived previously. It was a ranch-style home with extra space, so I rented a room to two young ladies who were beauticians. One of them had a German shepherd, so we were all happy to have them move in along with their dog. Several months after moving there, a tornado hit Cedar Rapids. It didn't do any structural damage to the house, but we did awaken the next morning not being able to see out due to fallen trees which had covered the windows.

Mr. Art Rankin, who was KCRG-TV's Farm News Director in Cedar Rapids and a frequent customer at the *Town House Restaurant*, took a special liking to me. While I was not at all attracted in the same way he was, the idea of someone having an interest in helping me provide for my children caused me to have some serious thoughts about the situation. In the meantime, my brother-in-law, Ed, received a call to a large Congregational Church in Los Angeles, which resulted in their house on Seminole Avenue being put up for sale. Art stepped forward to help them by buying the house; however, *he had the deed made out to me!* After a cocktail party to which he invited the staff of the TV station for the purpose of meeting me, Art proposed the following: marriage, a trip around the world; the gift of a motel which was for sale on the outskirts of Anamosa, 20 miles east of Cedar Rapids, which he wanted me to manage. I simply could not bring myself to accept his proposal. However, I must add that I was very grateful for his letters early in 1965 on Carol's behalf to Ellsworth College in Iowa Falls. She earned her associate of arts degree from Ellsworth two years later.

I must point out that we did move into the house on Seminole. I managed to go to Montgomery once a year to visit my parents. On one such occasion, Art learned that I was going and, shortly thereafter, he decided he would go down, also, and try to get an interview with Governor George Wallace. He was able to do this, surprisingly, through Alabama State College, a black school in Montgomery, today known as Alabama State University. I drove my car, and Art flew down while I was there. He was able to meet my parents at that time. He invited me to accompany him to the interview at the governor's office at the Capitol. While I held Kim in my arms, the governor gave her an auto-graphed picture of himself, on which she promptly began to chew. The governor remarked, "That's all right, Sweetheart. You're not the first one to chew on me!"

Things were going relatively smoothly at the *Town House*, and I was thankful for my job which provided me with a little sense of security and the ability to provide for my family. The food service manager was transferred on short notice to another motel. This created the urgent need for someone to take his place on a temporary basis, until a qualified person could be found to take the position on a permanent basis. Mr. Spresser called Mr. Verlin Sedrel, who was very well known in the Cedar Rapids area as simply "Stretch." He established and for many years operated a motel and restaurant, known as the *Cedrel Supper Club*, on Highway 30. He had recently sold his business and, thus, was available to accept Mr. Stresser's invitation to come and fill the vacant position. I remember very clearly the first day Stretch was on the job. That was the day my hand got caught in the elevator door! Stretch rushed to put ice on my hand, which kept it from swelling and probably caused me to recover more quickly.

CHAPTER 27

THE MONTROSE
HOTEL

AFTER two months as temporary food service manager at the *Town House*, Stretch and his wife, Iz (Isabel), leased the *Montrose Hotel Food and Beverage Services*. He asked me to come with them and be their catering service manager. I accepted and felt that it was a promotion for me. I was responsible to make the weekly menu and to schedule the civic affairs which were held there on a regular basis. My move to the *Montrose* was a real step upwards in my life. Although I had received training in the food and beverage field, I now had the responsibility of being a catering manager. This gave me valuable experience in a new facet of work which I had not previously experienced. Also, it greatly enhanced my low self-esteem. After all, I was now able to dine on a tablecloth with real silverware, listen to live piano music and be served, rather than being the server.

A health problem I had experienced for some time became more severe, in that the sponge breast implants I had received some fourteen years previously began to bother me more and more. The implants would move around, forming knots in my breasts. For some reason, I wasn't overly concerned about potential damage to my health; rather, it was the discomfort of the knots which bothered me. In the late fall of 1966, I made an appointment with a specialist on Third Avenue in Cedar Rapids. He scheduled a date to remove the implants at Mercy Hospital. Although he never revealed his private thoughts about the situation, I'm pretty sure he must have been thinking, *"What in the world was she thinking to have had this done to herself?"* The operation was successful with no ill effects. After a year, the owner of the *Montrose* refused to renew Stretch's lease, probably due to his seeing more money being made by Stretch than he had envisioned. With this development, I had to do something immediately.

CHAPTER 28

THE ROOSEVELT HOTEL

ALTHOUGH no position had been advertised, I went over to the *Roosevelt Hotel* on First Avenue and talked to the manager, Mr. Kennedy. He offered me the job of hostess in the *Gaslamp Dining Room.* I accepted, and he had me fitted for two formal, off-the-shoulder velvet gowns, one was red, the other black. He instructed the seamstress to give me two push-ups, to be inserted in my strapless bra. Obviously, he wanted me to look more voluptuous! While working there, Carol brought Ray, her future husband, from Iowa Falls to meet me. He was teaching English at Ellsworth College. Carol had a work scholarship at the college and was Ray's secretary.

CHAPTER 29

THE ARMAR BALLROOM

Armar Ballroom, Cedar Rapids, Iowa

AFTER working at the *Gaslamp* for eight months, Stretch was asked by Mr. Lou Feldman to be a partner at *Armar Ballroom*, which Stretch declined; however, Mr. Feldman was in agreement to lease the ballroom to Stretch. Thus, Stretch was now in a position to ask me to transfer to the ballroom as manager. The *Armar*, located at 641 Marion Boulevard in Marion, Iowa, had the space and facilities to accommodate 100 to 3,000 people. It opened in 1947 with Harry James and his orchestra. The functions of the ballroom included bowling banquets, luncheons, church fund raising, special showings, company meetings, conventions, wedding dances and fashion shows. I had two offices as well as an apartment for Steve, Kim and me. My responsibilities at the ballroom involved booking all of the parties, Wednesday and Saturday night dances, booking and paying all of the bands and providing staff supervision.

The Dave Dighton Band at the Armar

The most popular country western dances featured The Dave Dighton Band. To this day, I have the accounting books showing the dates, bands contracted and paid from 1967 until the ballroom closed on December 31, 1976. Also, I would go out to surrounding towns and place posters advertising coming attractions. I had the privilege of having contacts with Senator Ted Kennedy, Senator Joe Biden, Iowa Senator John Culver, New York Governor Nelson Rockefeller, Carol Channing, Bobby Uncer, Joan Kennedy, Alan Funt and many others.

Early in 1967, I made my second visit back to Montgomery from Iowa. Stretch and Iz had friends in Fort Lauderdale and dropped the children and me off in Montgomery on their way to Florida. My mother always wanted me to visit all of her friends; however, I managed to see some of mine as well. One of them was Toresa with whom I had worked at the *Riviera*. During the past few years she had become quite dependent on the bottle. I went to visit her and found her gravely ill. I shall never forget the sadness I felt as we left Montgomery on our return trip to Iowa. Toresa passed away in September 1967. Another friend was Quinn Rawls, with whom I worked at *The Ranch*. I stayed in touch with her periodically through the years, especially when I started going back to Montgomery on a yearly basis. She, also, had a drinking problem.

CHAPTER 30

CAROL'S MARRIAGE

Carol and Ray's wedding day

AT the end of Carol's two-year program at Ellsworth College, she and Ray announced their engagement. By then, Helen and Ed had returned from California and were serving a church in Marshalltown, Iowa. Carol and Ray were married on August 19, 1967 at St. Matthew's Catholic Church in Cedar Rapids. Ed had a part in the ceremony. Due to my being manager, the ballroom was available for the reception. Relatives and friends from out of town joined local friends, thus making quite a large crowd. We had live music with one of the regular bands at the ballroom. Ray's mother and other relatives attended the wedding. His brother, Tom, was best man. At Carol's request, her father, Mark, came up to Cedar Rapids from Montgomery and gave her away. Kim and another little girl her age were the flower girls. Stretch and I worked hard to set up the tables and serve the guests. Carol and Ray left on their honeymoon after the reception and went to Spirit Lake, Iowa. I met Ray's mother, Josie, at the wedding. She stayed with Kim and me in our apartment at the ballroom. I really got along well with her, especially due to her dancing ability. After the newlyweds left, Josie and I had our ball upstairs in the apartment, where we danced into the wee hours! When Carol and Ray returned from their honeymoon, Ray had been given a position as English professor at Briar Cliff College in Sioux City, Iowa. Carol planned to attend Morningside College across town, where she had received a small theater scholarship.

CHAPTER 31

MY SURGERY

TOWARD the end of October 1967, I began to have irregular periods which were not normal for me. I had been told about a German gynecologist in Marion, who was going to retire the next year. I decided to go to him, since he was close to the ballroom. The blood test resulted in my being scheduled for surgery the next day at Mercy Hospital. I began to bleed excessively, which no doubt caused me to go into shock during surgery. My uterus and left ovary were removed. Carol came over and took Kim to Sioux City while I recovered. I became quite concerned, thinking I was going to die, following the doctor's statement that I had cancer and he had rushed me into surgery to save my life. I suppose I became a hypochondriac, because I began to visit different doctors for their opinion on my condition. As a matter of fact, I went back to the surgeon who had removed my breast implants. He told me after my second visit to see him, "You did not have cancer! I checked your chart at Mercy Hospital. What you had could have become malignant." Of course, I was relieved at his diagnosis; however, I soon had some very negative thoughts about the doctor who had performed the hysterectomy, rushing me into the operating room for a surgery that maybe I didn't really need.

Following recuperation, things were going relatively smoothly in my work at the ballroom. In addition to the responsibilities previously mentioned, I had to go downstairs, get out the coconut oil and pop the popcorn, calculating the amount by the attendance expected for the next function. I had no problems in this little chore, except when hot oil would splatter and burn my hands. I did not enjoy having to activate the air conditioning system! I had to go into a large, sort of scary, room filled with pipes, compressors and other related equipment. I would have to bend over and stretch across an open drainage pit in order to prime the pump and be able to turn on the system.

CHAPTER 32

MORE ABOUT
THE ARMAR

THE *Armar Ballroom* was noted as being sort of a "spooky" place in and of itself. Although Kim, Steve and I were the only people living in the building, I never felt afraid. Steve told me on one occasion, "We don't have to worry about anyone breaking in, because they would be afraid due to the ballroom's reputation of being 'haunted'." This reputation had no negative effect on the thousands of faithful *Armar* patrons.

My daughter, Kim – May 1970

As Kim grew older at the ballroom, she had little opportunity for playmates. The exceptions were Julie and Sherrie Adams, who were three years older and one year younger than Kim, respectively. They lived next door to the ballroom with their parents, Sandy and Loyal Adams, in what was known to the public in Cedar Rapids and surrounding areas as Cemar Acres. Attractions in that area included a Ferris wheel, a skating rink and rides for children, although the amusement park was gone by the time I came on the scene. The grandmother of Julie and Sherrie, Clista McElhinney, was Miss Health USA of 1933 at the Chicago World's Fair, when she was sixteen years of age. We became good friends and, every May, as long as I was at the ballroom, we would go out in the woods and gather mushrooms. Clista's husband, Donald, was an avid collector of antique *Victrolas*; i.e., phonographs.

On February 01, 1968, Stretch and I were sitting in the office doing some bookkeeping, when a taxi drove up, and a huge man (365 lbs.) came in. He told the driver to wait for him. He talked with us for a couple of hours. His name was Tiny Hill, who at that time had a well-known big band, and he wanted bookings at the ballroom. We were happy to accommodate him and had him for numerous occasions. Tiny took a special interest in me. When he heard that I was going to California for a visit, he contacted the Lawrence Welk Show. I received a very nice letter from Mr. Welk himself, saying that Tiny Hill was a friend of his, but that he regretted that the show would be taped previously for the dates I planned to be in California and that he and his musicians would be out of the state at that time. Another memory from 1968 relates to Mr. Alan Funt of Candid Camera. At one of our receptions at the ballroom, Senator John C. Culver (Senator Ted Kennedy's college roommate) was honored, with performing artist, Carol Channing, and guest speaker, Mrs. Edward (Joan) Kennedy.

Armar Ballroom, settings for 3,000 people

I have always liked rocks, gems and pretty stones, so I would be thrilled when the ballroom would be booked for a two or three-day show by rock collectors. On one occasion we had a convention which was  booked by race car drivers. The drivers would be busy arranging their cars on the dance floor; therefore, I only had to check in with them from time to time to see if they needed anything. After doing so one day, I had an unexpected and frightening experience. Kim and I had gone down to the ballroom and then returned to our apartment upstairs. We were greeted by a big animal standing on its hind legs right in front of our apartment door! In a single glance at that creature, it only took a second for me to grab Kim by the arm and fly downstairs for help. I told everybody about the situation, and who do you think went up to rescue us? It was none other than the well-known race car driver, Bobby Uncer! He came back quickly, because he recognized that it was a raccoon. The other drivers kidded him, saying he was supposed to be tough and not afraid of anything. Someone called the Humane Society, especially thinking that the raccoon might be rabid. They caught it and took it away.

CHAPTER 33

ANNUAL TRIP
TO ALABAMA

WE had not yet made our annual trip to Alabama. Although Carol was six months into her first pregnancy, she decided to make the trip with us. Near St. Louis, we stopped to check into a motel. The manager told us he only had one room left for the four of us. He escorted us to the room. We couldn't believe it! It turned out to be the Miss America Suite. He said he would charge us the normal room rate. This suite left a lasting impression on me due to the egg crates (foam mattresses) on the beds. I had never had such a restful night's sleep. From then on, wherever I've gone, I've had to have my own egg crate along with me!

The next day was Sunday, and we continued on our way south. We needed gasoline and had trouble finding a station that was open. We were relieved to finally find one. We paid the attendant and continued our trip. Our relief soon turned to dismay when I glanced at the gas gauge and saw that it was on empty. The attendant just pocketed our money and put no gas in the tank. This discovery scared us and really made me angry. We finally found another station which was open. I paid close attention as the gas was put in. I probably told the attendant about our previous experience. I wanted to call the police about it, but we needed to continue on our way.

Mother and Daddy had moved across the street on Jeff Davis, and it was considered to be a historic site. It had a servants' house in the rear. On the corner vacant lot, Daddy had his garden. In fact, their house was located at the exact bus stop corner where I had my very meaningful experience as a child, wondering *Where did I come from?*

There was another memorable road incident on our return trip home. We were driving along the interstate and heard, even *felt*, what sounded like gunshot. Again, this was during that time of racial strife in our country. We were still in *The South* and suddenly became aware of the fact that our car was displaying license plates from *The North*. We pulled over to the shoulder and nervously (bravely!) got out of the car to investigate, thinking that quite possibly someone could have shot at us. Carol and I found ourselves kneeling on the ground at the rear of the car peering underneath, where we saw the culprit. It was one of those bungee-like, rubber straps with a metal hook on it, something that seems to litter the highways all across the country, possibly falling off trucks. Satisfied that we had found the source, we stood up, still nervous, and I handed Carol a rock I had picked up while kneeling on the ground and said, "Here." She took the rock and looked at me, like "Well, why are you handing me this rock?" Then we broke out laughing, pretty much all the way home. To this day, I keep picking up rocks!

CHAPTER 34

MY FIRST
GRANDSON

THE outstanding event of 1968 was the birth of my grandson, Tom, on October 14. An hour before his birth, I decided to go shopping at the Hy-Vee Supermarket. Just before I got there, I had to go into a church parking lot, due to the fact that I was crying uncontrollably! This was very unusual for me, and I found myself wondering what in the world was happening! I continued on my shopping errand. When I returned to the ballroom, walking into my apartment, my telephone was ringing. It was a call from Ray, announcing to me that I had a grandson who had just been born! He was born at 12:45 p.m., exactly the time when I had to stop the car to get control of myself from the crying episode.

CHAPTER 35

CHRISTMAS 1968

QUINN, referred to previously, brought my parents to Cedar Rapids for Christmas 1968. Happy holidays were enjoyed; however, I must say that this was possible in spite of the circumstances under which Quinn brought my parents from Alabama. The night before they left, she went to her husband's bar in downtown Montgomery, at which time, in his absence, she helped herself to the till and several bottles of liquor. I knew she had a drinking problem, but I didn't know she would be under the influence on the trip to Iowa. Thank God, they arrived without mishap! She and her daughter, Ginny, stayed for a couple of months, to the extent I had to call her husband, Dick, and ask for his help. Her drinking was causing me a problem in my work at the ballroom. He came soon and took Quinn and Ginny home.

CHAPTER 36

DEPRESSION

DURING the holidays I had a severe bout with depression. It affected me to the extent that I refused to come downstairs and join the family in the Christmas celebration. However, I was able to do my work, knowing that I had a great job and three wonderful children and, yet, I realized that this depression was something that I had not experienced to this extent. I went to my doctor at the time and asked him what in the world was wrong with me. His answer was, "You're fine and in good health! You may be going through something resulting from your hysterectomy." The problem increased and seemed to hit me the hardest in the late afternoons. I didn't have a clue as to what was wrong with me, but I was soon to find out some answers. As a matter of fact, they revolved around some of my early childhood ponderings.

One day, the thought came to me, "If I could get a college education, perhaps that would be what I need." I had ample time, since my ballroom responsibilities only involved Wednesday, Friday and Saturday nights. So, I checked with Kirkwood College and decided I would begin with English Literature and a couple of other subjects. I called Carol and told her what I was doing. She suggested a list of books she thought I should read. On my first trip in search of those books, I came across one book which really caught my attention. It was Edgar Cayce's Reader One, which increased my search and love of discovering truth. Some things seemed strange, at first, but opened the door to that *Secret Garden* I had longed for since my childhood. I became so enthralled with what I was discovering that I read many related books. *All of a sudden, I realized that I was coming out of my depression!*

CHAPTER 37

A NEW
AWARENESS

CAYCE was born on a farm in Hopkinsville, Kentucky on March 18, 1877. He was known as the "Sleeping Prophet." During periods of sleep, he was able to diagnose illnesses, often in people he had never met, and, then, he would prescribe treatment. He never received medical training, yet God used him as an instrument to heal thousands of people who had tried conventional medicine without success. In June 1954, the University of Chicago held him in sufficient esteem to allow his life and work as the basis for a doctoral thesis. Cayce displayed powers of perception which seemed to extend beyond the range of the five senses. At six or seven years of age he told his parents that he could see and talk to visions. Later, by sleeping with his head on his school books, he developed some form of photographic memory, which helped him to advance rapidly in school. One of his books opened the door to deep meditation in my life. I would lie down with my eyes completely covered so that no light could penetrate; then, I would totally relax my body by taking deep breaths. When I achieved that deep level of relaxation, known as the alpha state, I would be very much awake but would not be able to sense my body. With each deep breath, I would know, as I had never known before, that " ... peace of God which transcends all understanding ... " and " ... will guard your hearts and your minds ... " (Philippians 4:7 NIV). In my heart and soul, I know that this was what I had been searching for so long! As I have continued the regular practice of meditation, I can honestly say that I have never returned to that deep depression, which I had experienced previously.

Kim and I went to church on Sunday mornings on a regular basis. On one of such occasions, although I cannot remember the name of the church, I do recall the way it looked on the inside. I was quite startled when the minister began his sermon to see over his head, about two feet in height, a bright yellow question mark! This confirmed deep within my being that I had found what I had been looking for all my life. In Edgar Cayce's books, I had read that he had founded an Association for Research and Enlightenment (A.R.E.) in Virginia Beach, Virginia. I had a deep conviction that I needed to go there. It was about time for my vacation trip to Alabama (June 1969), so I asked Helen to go with me.

CHAPTER 38

VIRGINIA BEACH

WE drove to Virginia Beach, where we spent the night at the Association's beachfront motel. I had a very enjoyable time the next day at the library, although Helen refused to enter the A. R. E. facilities, thinking that the whole establishment was contrary to her beliefs. While in the library, I met Shirley Winston, who was previously a Metropolitan Opera singer but had now dedicated her life to working and writing at the Association. She was friendly and open to my sharing with her the new life before me as a result of my reading some of Cayce's books. She asked me where I was from, to which I responded that I was from Montgomery, Alabama. We immediately bonded, especially when she said that, prior to her vocal career, she had studied violin with Fanny Marks Seibels. I have said previously that Mrs. Seibels was my violin instructor when I was a child and young adolescent. In Mrs. Seibels' autobiography, *"Wishes Are Horses"* (1958), she states, "Shirley Winston is now a grand opera star. For several years she was a member of the New England Opera Company, but six months ago she signed a contract with the New York City Opera Company. When interviewed, she told the reporters that her inspiration had come from her first music teacher, Fanny Marks Seibels of Montgomery, Alabama." During the course of our long conversation that day, Shirley and I discussed the subject of reincarnation. I told her that I now lived in Cedar Rapids, Iowa, and wondered if there was a church there which included it in their belief system. She immediately referred me to the Reverend Mabel Swanson, minister at Unity Church in Cedar Rapids. During later years, Shirley wrote a couple of books. I maintained correspondence and telephone communication with her through the years. She remained at the A. R. E. until her death.

CHAPTER 39

ANNUAL TRIP TO MONTGOMERY

WE left Virginia Beach early the next morning, headed for Montgomery. Our intention was to go directly there; however, since Helen and I both attended school at Toccoa Falls Institute, we decided it would be nice to stop there for a while, giving Kim a chance to see the beautiful falls and taking a picture of her at its foot. "Toccoa" in the Cherokee Indian language is pronounced, "Tocco-ah" and means "The Beautiful." We spent that night at the Carlin Dinkler Hotel in downtown Atlanta. After we checked in, we went to Morrison's Cafeteria, which was located close to the hotel. As we walked back to the Dinkler, I spotted a bookstore. At that point in my life's journey, I took every opportunity to look for books which I felt were relevant for me. We were toward the back of the store and stopped at a table and picked up a couple of books. Helen and I realized at the same instant that we had brought Kim and ourselves into a pornographic bookstore! We dropped those books and got out of that store in a hurry.

We completed our trip to Montgomery the next morning and found my parents' new home on Capitol Parkway. Betty Cripple, who was Jack's sister, came to the hospital six years previously and took newborn baby Kim and me to her home for several weeks. When I told Betty then of my plans for moving to Iowa, she said, "Well, I guess I'll never see Kim again!" I promised her that I would always bring Kim to see her whenever I came back. I faithfully did this, believing that it was vitally important for Kim to know that she had a real father and that she needed to know him and his family. While there, I visited Barbara Parker briefly without anything special being said between us. Steve was spending this summer with his father and, of course, we saw him while we were there. After a week in Montgomery, Helen, Kim and I had an uneventful trip back to Cedar Rapids.

CHAPTER 40

A REMARRIAGE ...
ALMOST

SHORTLY after returning to work, I received a call from Barbara, saying that Dawson was visiting her from Mississippi and wanted to speak to me. He now had four children and was divorced from Juanita. When Barbara came back on the line, she said she wanted to drive out with Dawson to visit me. He was now retired as an Air Force major and had a good job in sales. I agreed to their visit, and they arrived a short time later. I suppose his age and weight showed on my face. His first comment was, "Gene, you don't like the way I look!" They stayed for a few days, Barbara with me at the ballroom and Dawson at the *Town House*. Both of them began talking about re-marriage taking place between Dawson and me. I suppose the idea of an active father for Kim and Steve and his financial security made me think seriously about it.

Immediately after his return to Mississippi, he began calling and writing to further pursue the subject. Also, he wanted to come for another visit. So, he flew up around the first of August 1969. It was a brief visit, but we did drive over to Sioux City so that he could meet Carol and Ray and their new baby, Tom. He, Steve and Kim had a mutual attraction. Thus, I began to think that Dawson's proposal could be a good thing for the children and me. We began to make plans and, of course, I had to advise Stretch that I would be leaving the ballroom. Dawson lived with his older son, Patrick, in the Richelieu Apartments in Pass Christian, Mississippi, facing the Gulf of Mexico. His former wife and the other three children lived in their home nearby. I had planned to move about the middle of August, so I began packing and making arrangements. Dawson had given me money for the rental of a moving van.

My plans went awry due to hurricane Camille which hit the coast on August 17-18. Evacuation orders were given to all coastal residents, so Dawson went to Montgomery and stayed with his parents. I was shocked when I picked up the Cedar Rapids Gazette and read the headlines, *"Richelieu Apartments swept into the Gulf."* From Dawson's letters, I was familiar with those apartments. The article stated that the residents were having a drinking party when the hurricane struck. I found out later that this was not true. A couple of weeks later, Dawson talked with the lone survivor of the apartments who remained behind. He had managed to escape by swimming off of the third floor balcony and by clinging to a tree until he could be rescued. All the other remaining residents perished! They had been asked by the owner to help move furniture to the third floor.

Dawson flew to Cedar Rapids and drove my car on the trip. My mother accepted this new relationship, because she felt that a person's first marriage was the only right one in the sight of God. We visited my parents and then went to Dawson's home to spend the night. We left the next day, picking up Steve at his father's home and headed for Biloxi. Dawson had rented a new apartment with a swimming pool for the children and me. Much earlier that same year, I had a very vivid dream in which I saw this same apartment and pool while they were under construction. The dream was so real that I had gotten out of bed and written it down.

The children and I drove from Biloxi to the Richelieu property, the buildings of which were totally destroyed. As we walked around, I found a silver teaspoon, which I use today at almost every meal. We had only spent a short time there, when I had an urgent feeling that, for some reason, we should go back to our apartment. We arrived just in time to see my Uncle Nick and his wife, Catherine, as they were leaving our front door. I had no idea they would be visiting from California en route to Montgomery. You will remember that I wrote previously about the uncle who molested my cousin, Ginger, and me in our childhood. I must reiterate here that to not forgive causes damage to one's soul. God says, "*Do not judge, or you too will be judged.*" I sincerely and deeply believe that forgiveness is all inclusive; i.e., the perpetrator is to be forgiven regardless of the circumstances.

I began to think, *What have I done after all these years?* Dawson had been mistreated as a child; however, he was a family person and loved his children very much. They were not in agreement with his leaving their mother. After the hurricane, they needed and demanded a lot of help from their father. I needed the security offered by Dawson, but I didn't need his children with all their requests for assistance.

I came to the conclusion that what I really needed to do was go back to Cedar Rapids, if Stretch would let me return to the ballroom. I called him, and he agreed. I told Dawson I wanted to go back, and that I needed a thousand dollars for the move. He agreed to this change in plans and gave me the money. A few hours later, Barbara called me and said, "Gene, this is Barbara Parker. I'll kill you, or I'll have you killed for what you've done to my son!" I hung up the phone thinking she just might follow through on her threat.

The moving van left with the furniture, and Steve and I loaded the car. We left early the next morning, reaching Memphis, Tennessee by evening, where we spent the night in a luxury motel. I had been thinking all day that I had never wanted a person to be upset and angry with me. So, I decided to call Barbara and try to reason with her. She didn't answer the call. I found out, after arriving in Cedar Rapids, that Barbara had suffered a stroke that very day that I tried to reach her. She was not discovered until the next day, which means she was probably lying on the floor when I was trying to reach her. She recovered from the stroke with certain physical impairments. On my next visit to Montgomery a year later, I went to see her. She didn't show any hostility toward me and even tried to get me to move back and take care of her. I must point out that in the midst of all of this time of trial and adjustment, I continued my daily practice of reading and meditation.

CHAPTER 41

BACK
TO THE ARMAR

WE moved back into the apartment at the ballroom on October 01, 1969. Our furniture arrived in good condition, and we quickly got settled. Stretch had been good enough to do my work while I was gone. In fact, it was as if I had just been gone on a long vacation! True, I had taken all my belongings, but now the children and I were back, pretty much as if we had never left.

Shirley Winston, of the Association for Research and Enlightenment at Virginia Beach, had referred me to Mabel Swanson, minister at the Unity Church on Second Avenue in Cedar Rapids. I called Mabel and asked her rather bluntly if her church doctrine embraced a belief in reincarnation. She did not seem surprised at all and immediately responded, "We certainly do. You are cordially invited to come and attend one of our services." Kim and I were there the following Sunday. This began a relationship which lasted about eight years, that is, until her death. She was about seventy-five years of age when I met her.

The church building was quite impressive to me in that it was an old three-story mansion near downtown Cedar Rapids. During a period of thirty years Mabel proved herself to be an astute business woman and purchased almost a city block of valuable property. I invited Mabel and her assistant minister, Elizabeth, to come to my apartment at the ballroom for Thanksgiving Dinner (1969). I served the meal at one o'clock. We enjoyed our dinner, but we were much more interested in our conversation which lasted all afternoon, until it was time to eat again! Kim and I attended Unity on a regular basis for the next three years. One day, Mabel invited me and eight others from the church to return on a Sunday afternoon to listen to a tape by Joel Goldsmith, the founder of The Infinite Way. With the reading I had done of Edgar Cayce and others, my personal meditation and, now, with the Goldsmith tapes, I *knew* I was getting answers to those questions and ponderings my soul had longed for since childhood.

Mabel was diagnosed with having breast cancer when she was fifty years of age. In a personal conversation with me, she told me that upon receiving this verdict, she had gone home and entered into meditation, knowing that God was the only power and that He could heal her, if it was His will. She lived almost thirty years cancer free! It returned several months before her death. You could see that she was in severe pain as she stood in the pulpit and delivered her messages. Shortly before her death, I visited her in her upstairs apartment at the church. Her gown was open sufficiently so that I could see that, apparently, her breasts had been eaten away by the cancer. She was determined to live by her beliefs and refused medications and medical attention.

CHAPTER 42

MY FIRST
GRANDDAUGHTER

I WAS having lunch in my apartment on New Year's Eve 1969. I knew that Carol was expecting her baby at any time, but halfway through my meal I felt the urgency to call her. She quickly said, "I can't talk now. I'm on the way to the hospital!" My granddaughter, Suzanne Marie, was born at 5:30 p.m., December 31, 1969. I was now the proud grandmother of two wonderful children, Tom and Suzy. Ray had completed his teaching year at Briar Cliff College in Sioux City and had taken a position on the faculty at the University of Wisconsin in Eau Claire. Kim and I were very eager to see the new baby, so we went for a visit in January 1970. Steve would have liked to have gone with us, but he couldn't afford to miss a week at school. I promised him that we would go in the summer, so that he could see his niece. While there, I continued my daily reading and meditation. Of course, I talked with Carol and Ray about this development in my life and the positive benefits that I felt I was getting from it. They didn't express any opposition to what I was doing. I'm sure they wondered why I was spending so much time in the bathroom. Well, I had no physical problems; however, the privacy along with the mirrors allowed me to concentrate on seeing my aura. An aura is luminous radiation of colors which emanates from the body. Everyone has an aura! I learned later that certain gifted people could observe auras quite easily.

We left Eau Claire the middle of the afternoon a week later to return to Cedar Rapids. After crossing the state line into Iowa, the weather began to deteriorate and became a blizzard, reaching the point that I could see no other cars on the highway. Besides, the snow obliterated the lanes. I didn't dare stop on the side of the road, so I continued on, saying over and over, "My Father and I are one. My Father and I are one," and I kept on saying it. Finally, I was exhausted and, although not far from Cedar Rapids, I stopped at a motel in Center Point, thinking I was too tired to continue, only to find out that there was no room available! So, I got back in the car, and we made it home to the ballroom, *deeply grateful for another divine intervention.*

In addition to my regular work responsibilities and my reading and meditation, I made regular visits to the bookstores in search of books on related subjects. In the early 1970s, you didn't start a conversation with just anyone about the realm of the metaphysical! I was so impressed with Edgar Cayce's Reader One, and yet naïve at the same time, that I felt I should talk with some minister to share what I had discovered. So, I called a local Lutheran church and made an appointment for a couple of days later. The minister greeted me cordially, but when I related my story to him and gave him a copy of the book, asking him to read it, he said I could leave it, but that he really didn't have time for it. I interpreted this as meaning that he was not interested and was brushing me off.

I had just been reading where Cayce had said that it was possible to go into meditation and have another person do your bidding; however, he said, "Don't do it, because you're taking away that person's God-given free will." Well, I went home and went into meditation, feeling that I could will that minister to read the book. I had my eyes covered so no light could enter. The result was that I opened my "Third Eye." I didn't know there was such a thing at that time. Immediately, I saw a huge statue of Venus. I could not understand the significance of seeing the Roman goddess of love and beauty, but my Third Eye was clearly opened. Dr. Douglas Baker, in his book, "The Opening of The Third Eye" (1977, p. 71), states, "The Third Eye is, in fact, an organ that emerges with the spiritual growth of the integrated personality." Shortly after this experience, I had an appointment with an ophthalmologist. I asked if he knew that we all had a Third Eye. His response was similar to that of the Lutheran minister. I decided that, in the future, I would not approach people on this subject, unless they opened the door for discussion.

So far, Mabel Swanson was the only person I could talk to about my experiences. I really wanted to talk to someone who might have had, or had read about, experiences similar to mine. Mabel told me about a friend of hers who attended a Tuesday evening group meeting in a private home. She was sure the group would give me a warm welcome. It was at that first meeting in Southwest Cedar Rapids that I met Hazel Hopper. She was a very elegant eighty-year-old lady, very stylish and with nicely manicured nails. She and I became instant friends. She was quite interested in hearing of my experiences. Later on, I told her I was very interested in Joel Goldsmith's tapes and writings. She said, "Why, Gene, you are a very old soul!" I had never heard of an "old soul" and much less of a "very old soul." She explained that this is a soul who has reincarnated many times. I heard this expression over and over, as I continued to read and study in this new field of interest.

Kitty looking at Carol

Kim wanted a cat. It didn't take much to convince me that we needed a cat. Stretch went with Kim and me to the Humane Society. A staff member took us to a room filled with cages and, there, we found our cat. Actually, she was a kitten from a fairly new-born litter. This one special feline seemed to be saying, "Please take me home with you!" So, we adopted her and named her "Kitty." A year after we got her, I designed a carpeted house which included the litter box. We called it "Kitty's Kan." Also, I came up with the idea of a special feeding house, called "Kitty's Kafé." She was a part of our family for seventeen years. It was a heart-breaking experience when she died; however, she had a very special graveside ceremony, officiated by movie actress, Joanne Dru, who was the leading lady with John Wayne, Burt Lancaster, Errol Flynn and many others. Joanne's houseman dug a deep hole, afterwards placing a large concrete cover over it. It was located just below the balcony of my apartment in Beverly Hills.

CHAPTER 43

TRIP
TO CALIFORNIA

ED was no longer in the ministry. He was now a certified realtor. They were living in Whittier, California. Helen had been writing me and telling me about all of the interesting places she had visited and encouraged me to come out for a visit. So, the children and I decided to go for two weeks. We drove our green Plymouth, leaving in June 1970. Steve had gotten his license and was a good driver, so he was a big help on the trip. Of course, Kitty made the trip with us. At one of our stops we took her into a restaurant with us, due to the extreme heat. The restaurant wasn't very crowded, but we were still able to take her in with us undetected! We made the trip in three days, arriving in Whittier late at night on the third day.

Helen had prepared a great itinerary for us, which included Disneyland, Universal Studios, Sea World and Knott's Berry Farm. On subsequent trips to California, I always had to go back to the fried chicken restaurant at Knott's Berry Farm, which, I do believe, served the most delicious fried chicken and biscuits I have ever eaten! I visited my friend, Alice Mae Tingley Shafer, who lived in Anaheim. We had gone to high school together in Toccoa Falls, Georgia. We were both good friends with Nadia Moore Sims, who was also a student at the same school. We visited her in her home in Fallbrook. This is the same Nadia I wrote about earlier, to whom I had written a letter which was discovered by my mother while I was away at school. In it, I gave details of how I slipped out of the house to meet secretly with Dawson Parker. Another visit I made was to see my Uncle Eugene and Aunt Dorothy in Mission Viejo. One would think that with all the places Helen had arranged for us to visit that I would have been satisfied. Such was not the case!

I had seen an advertisement in a local paper announcing a lecture to be given by Anthony Norvell. The subject was "The Million Dollar Secret which lies hidden within you." Of course, you know that really caught my attention, and I just had to go. Even though the lecture was in the evening, and I was not at all familiar with the freeways and streets of Los Angeles, I was able to find my way to Wilshire Boulevard, where the lecture was to be given. I felt fortunate to be able to speak personally to Mr. Norvell, in view of the large audience. Our conversation had to do with age. When I told him how old I was, he seemed very impressed and said, "You surely don't look your age!" The nightmare began on our return to Whittier. Somehow, I took a wrong exit and found that we were in Watts in South Central Los Angeles. Of course, this was five years after the race riots there, but they were relatively fresh in people's minds. I realized that I was in a bad spot by having taken myself and my children into that area. We were finally able to find our way back to the 605 and the exit to Whittier. What a relief!

Helen and Ed had a very nice town home, but Kitty must have thought we had deserted her. Helen had a dog, Dusty, and a cat named Boots. So, Kitty had to be closed up in our bedroom while we were sightseeing. Even on our last day in California, we didn't stay home. We went to Hollywood! I suppose that is the normal thing to do if you visit Los Angeles. We went to Grauman's Chinese Theatre and saw the "Who's Who" of Hollywood superstars, with the footprints, handprints and autographs in the legendary cement of Clark Gable, Marilyn Monroe, Tommy Stewart, Shirley Temple, John Wayne, Elizabeth Taylor and many, many more. They claim some two million visitors a year! On the next corner, as we waited for the traffic light to change, I looked down at my feet and saw a quarter. I immediately bent over to pick it up and was chagrined to find that it was embedded in the sidewalk! I'm sure that thousands of people have had the same experience.

I suppose Kim and I were a little star struck. Right down the street from Grauman's Chinese Theatre I noticed a talent agent's studio. Kim was a very pretty seven-year-old, so we went into Columbia Casting on Hollywood Boulevard. After a short wait, we were called in for an initial interview. We were then told that they would call us for a second interview. We had a good, safe trip home and a fun time at Circus Circus in Las Vegas on the way. I couldn't resist putting a few nickels and quarters in the slots. Of course, Kim and Steve had never seen anything like this. They had to stay outside of the ropes, but they kept their eyes on me and all the action that was going on. I don't remember winning anything. I did receive a letter from the talent agent some time later, saying I should contact their office for the promised second interview. Of course, when the letter was received, we were in Iowa. So, Kim missed her chance to become a big Hollywood star!

CHAPTER 44

RETURN
TO CEDAR RAPIDS

STEVE returned to his work at the golf course, and Kim went back to play with Julie and Sherry and, of course, I was working once again at the ballroom. I continued my reading and meditation. I watched very little television, but I did like Monty Hall's Let's Make a Deal! I tried not to miss a day, because Helen had invited us to return to California the following year. I had a plan that I hoped would help me to become a contestant on the show. Consequently, for months I would record the date and the winning door. My plan was to design a "flapper" dress, which was a favorite in the 1920s, known for prohibition, gangsters and, of course, The Charleston. I designed the dress and took it to a seamstress. It was made of light blue satin with a band just below the waist. From this band I attached ribbons which reached to the hem of the dress. On each ribbon was printed the number of a winning door and its respective date. My goal was to impress the show managers. When we returned to California the next year, I was not chosen to participate, but I did have a lengthy conversation after the show with the announcer, Jay Stewart. He really seemed to be impressed with my dress!

Kim, Steve and I went to Eau Claire that summer (July 1970), so that Steve could meet his niece, Suzy. For some reason, I suppose Carol asked me, I took my violin on the trip. Ray's colleague, Will Jennings, was working on the side playing his guitar in night spots. He and his wife, Carole, lived in a little house in the country with their cat, Mimsey. One day while we were there, Carol and Carole went shopping, and I stayed behind to play my violin with Will's guitar accompaniment. Little did I ever suspect that in the 1980s and 1990s he would win two Oscars as a songwriter, one for An Officer and a Gentlemen ("Up Where We Belong") and the other, Titanic ("My Heart Will Go On"). In addition to these, he was awarded numerous Grammies and Golden Globe Awards. We played until late that night, when the girls returned from their shopping. We had a great visit in Eau Claire. Steve and Kim had a nephew, Tom, and now, they had a niece, Suzy. And, of course, I was again a happy grandmother!

The following February, on my usual visit to Killian's Department Store, I couldn't find what I was looking for, so I went over to Montgomery Ward. On the first floor, among knick knacks on a sale table, to my surprise there was a crystal ball. Even at the sale price, it was still pretty expensive. I *knew* it was mine, and I just *had* to have it! The 4½ inch ball was made in Italy, and the base was crafted in Spain of wood from *Madera de Aliso* (alder wood). I made the purchase and could hardly wait to get home with my new acquisition. Mixed with my excitement was the feeling of guilt for having spent that much money. I read the instructions on the art of crystal gazing and attempted to put them into practice. The crystal would become cloudy rather than clear. After trying for several days and getting red eyed in the process, I was still happy I had it, but I put it among my other curios. I will write more about the crystal ball later.

I continued my reading, meditating and listening to the Joel Goldsmith tapes. I had started a collection of Joel's tapes, buying one a month until I had a total of seventy tapes. One afternoon, I was reading one of Edgar Cayce's books. Suddenly, I was seeing pinpoints of light everywhere! I shut my eyes, and I could still see those multitudes of very small but bright lights. On another occasion, when I was reading at night, I turned my eyes away from the book when, lo and behold, the whole page was visible to me up on the wall in my bedroom. These experiences caused me to realize that, indeed, there is great value in meditation.

Now that Kim was approaching eight years of age, I thought she could benefit from taking music lessons. I already had a Baldwin piano, so I located a piano teacher whose name was Cleo Shanklin. She was a grandmother from Tennessee who taught piano in the Marion school system. Both of us being from the South, we naturally had good rapport with each other. The current tag on the front of my car expresses what we felt back then: "American by birth – Southern by the grace of God." Kim took lessons for a year or so but showed no real interest in continuing. During this period of time, Cleo and I had a growing relationship and became very good friends. I shared with her my interest in meditation, metaphysics and the books I was reading. While she showed no particular interest in pursuing the subject for herself, she said, "Well, I'm going to have to introduce you to a teacher at school who talks like you do." So far, I had hardly anyone to share with, so I urged Cleo to call and set up a time when her teacher friend and I could meet. She did this, and I met Leone Geary the next day, when she came to my apartment. I had three friends at this point who shared a mutual interest with me, Mabel Swanson, Hazel Hopper and Leone Geary.

Chapter 45

My Son Goes
To Vietnam

STEVE had always displayed a talent for rhythm. He was forever drumming on tables, chairs or whatever. His father, who played the drums in local bands in Montgomery, sent him a Ludwig drum set. I was happy that he had the drums, but I wasn't thrilled about loud music and drumming in the apartment. The solution to the problem was a small apartment on the first floor, located directly in front of the stairs to our apartment. It had not been occupied for over a year. So, Steve had a good place to practice his drums when he wasn't in school or working at the golf course. I had begun to have feelings of accomplishment and satisfaction, finally, after my years of struggle. I had three beautiful children, a son-in-law, two grandchildren and a good job. In addition, I had begun to find some of the answers in my life-long spiritual journey.

Steve joined the U. S. Navy Reserve in June 1971 and was called to active duty in October of that same year. He was given a ten-day leave and came home for Christmas in his seaman's uniform. Of course, I was very proud of him. He was a radioman seaman apprentice and received his certificate of completion in San Diego, California on May 12, 1972. He was sent to the Philippines and to Vietnam on the USS Hancock (CVA-19). I began to know the fear and dread of a mother who sees her son or daughter go off to war.

My son, Steve

Chapter 46

Kim's Eighth Birthday

Kim and I missed Steve very much, but I do not remember that I was ever afraid with just the two of us living in the huge ballroom building. This was amazing, due to the fact that the ballroom was beginning to get the reputation of being haunted. On a recent trip to Cedar Rapids, I was told that the popular current belief was that even the restaurant which now stands where the ballroom was located is *haunted*! Both Kim and I had reason to believe it back then. I went through many strange happenings, to which there were witnesses. I do not remember being afraid of any of them, with the exception of one about which I will write later. Oh yes, we were apprehensive about Kim's bedroom. I had bought squares of carpet for the floor, which I put down myself. I bought white French Provincial furniture for her. I must say that I was quite proud of my decorating abilities. Her room adjoined mine, and it paralleled the big ballroom neon sign just outside the bedroom windows. Kim loved toy horses and had quite a collection of them. They were about eight inches high and twelve inches long. We placed them on the window ledge the full length of the room. One afternoon, my good friend, Dolores, and her daughter, Joanie, who was Kim's age, came to visit us. We were all sitting in the living room when, suddenly, we heard a loud noise coming from Kim's room. So, the four of us ran to her room and saw that two of the horses had fallen to the floor. We were amazed to see that each of them was sitting upright with its legs grasping one of the bed posts at the foot of the bed! On another occasion, other friends were visiting. The bathroom was at the end of the hall with no windows. I had left shampoo, conditioner, lotion, soap and soap dish around the edge of the tub. Again, there was a loud noise, this time from the bathroom. We ran back there ... and found everything in the middle of the tub!

I planned a party for Kim in the ballroom party room on her eighth birthday, October 03, 1971. All of her schoolmates were invited. I thought it was a huge success, and I'm sure Kim thought so, also, with all the presents she received. She was really impressed when she saw her name and "Happy Birthday" in big letters on the ballroom marquee. I continued having her parties there for the next several years.

Stretch gave Kim a real pony, which we kept at his ranch. Kim and Tracy, Stretch's grandson, spent many happy days riding their ponies together. Stretch and Iz, along with their daughter-in-law, RuthAnn, knew of my love for okra, a true Southern dish. So, they planted a couple of rows for me in their garden. I was quite eager to pick my first batch, only to find out that you do not pick okra without gloves. Yankees, who are not familiar with this delicacy, need to know that the raw vegetable is a slender, ribbed, green pod with thistle-like fuzz. When cooked, it can be eaten alone, with tomatoes or in soup, but my favorite way is to slice the pods, season and cover them with corn meal and deep fry them. Yummy!

CHAPTER 47

SPIRITUAL GROWTH

MY books, tapes and friends helped me to overcome my fears stemming from my son's being overseas during the war with Vietnam. I will write more about Hazel Hopper later on; however, I must say at this point that, although she lived on the other side of Cedar Rapids, we talked several times a week by telephone. She knew how to give me the encouragement I needed at that particular time. My new friend, Leone Geary, lived in Marion, very close to the ballroom. She came to visit me several times a week. She knew a good bit about subjects that I was just beginning to read and study. She had pursued her metaphysical studies for several years before I met her. All my life I had vivid dreams, some of which I puzzled over, yet at the same time believing they had a meaning and a reason to be discovered in the pursuit of the journey of one's soul. For instance, in March 1969, I dreamt of an apartment building under construction. It had a fence around the pool. When dreams were very clear and fresh, I would take notice and immediately know that something important was involved. In the instance of the apartment building, I did not find out the significance of the dream until I arrived in Biloxi, Mississippi following Hurricane Camille (August 1969). The apartment Dawson had rented for Kim, Steve and me was the exact apartment building and grounds which appeared in my dream in Cedar Rapids!

I subsequently had several dreams of equal significance. This led me to develop what was published as Gene Winn's Dream Log, which was accepted by many people and proved to help them in the interpretation of their dreams. Before retiring, you must speak to your subconscious, stating that you want to remember your dreams. This must be done on a regular basis; otherwise, the results will be less valuable. Immediately, upon awakening from a dream, things you want to remember must be checked off in the log; e.g., dates, people, places. This will enable you to bring back the dream so that you can give it more thought with clearer interpretation.

I later worked with Zolar's Encyclopedia and Dictionary of Dreams. An example of this was when I received a call from my friend, Lucille Yeater, who wanted to know what I thought of her dream of the preceding night. She had left her car at the shop for repairs the day before and her husband, Dave, took her to work and planned to pick her up. She had dreamt the night before that, as she waited outside her office for him to pick her up, she saw him driving toward her. Suddenly, a mail truck hit his car and knocked it into the ditch. She seemed very upset about the dream and wanted my opinion on it. I told her I didn't think it was a bad dream and that I would call her later with my interpretation. I consulted my *Zolar's* and told her it was not a negative dream at all but rather, quite positive, in that Dave would be receiving an inheritance right away. She probably thought I didn't know what I was talking about, and even I wondered why I told her what I did. The very next day Lucille called me and was very excited as she told me that Dave had received an inheritance in the mail that very day from a relative. I had met Lucille at a class to which Hazel had invited me.

Lucille was a devout Catholic but had turned her back on religion. Her son was killed in a motorcycle accident in California, and she blamed God for it and was deeply depressed. When she began to understand that God does not do things to His children, rather that the Father loves us, she began to come out of her depression. With the free will God has given every soul, we make our own choices in life. Very often, God gets the blame for our mistakes and sorrows through which we pass in our journey. She and her husband, Dave, would occasionally work for me at the ballroom on weekends, she as cashier and he as bartender.

The biggest night of the year at the ballroom was the New Year's Eve dance. After spending a nice Christmas with Carol and Ray and my grandchildren, Kim and I had to rush back to Cedar Rapids. It took a lot of work to coordinate reservations. This required setting up tables and the hiring of extra staff. This year (December 1971), the popular band Do's and Don'ts had been booked for the occasion. Everything worked out perfectly, and the ballroom was filled to capacity (3,000).

CHAPTER 48

1972 KIRKWOOD COMMUNITY COLLEGE - CARLETON COLLEGE

KIRKWOOD Community College sent out their usual course offerings for the new semester, beginning January 1972. The astrology class caught my eye, since I knew very little on the subject. I signed up and paid my tuition fee and waited eagerly for the first class. I had no clue or intuitive feelings about the person I was about to meet. This marked the beginning of a long and close friendship with Jessie Nagle. She was the astrology teacher at Kirkwood. She taught evening adult classes, and I signed up for her beginning class. Since astrology is a very complex subject ('way above my head!), I requested supplemental private lessons at my apartment, which "cemented" our relationship. She was a dedicated, enthusiastic teacher, and we "connected" at the soul level immediately. I was very impressed with Jessie's teaching. During the second week, Leone joined the class. I had good reason to believe that I would not be able to make an astrology chart. I was fascinated with what I was learning. With Jessie's extra help, I was finally able to do a few charts. I met another dear friend in my first class with Jessie, Beryl Farland. Our friendship continued until her death on March 15, 2006.

Jessie Nagle, my very best Cedar Rapids friend

I discovered Jessie had a talent for psychometry (the ability to receive vibrations from inanimate objects), which she displayed time and again. When she arrived at my apartment, Kim was playing on the floor with my crystal ball. Jessie said, "Oh, I've always wanted to look into a ball like that." I quickly decided that she wouldn't see anything, since I had tried and failed. We decided to wait until the close of the class. She then took the ball into my bedroom, read the instructions and turned off the lights with only the lights from the living room reaching the bedroom. I went to the kitchen to get a glass of water. Jessie called and said, "Gene, get some paper and write this down!" To my utter amazement, she was able to "see" in my crystal ball the face of my old, black friend, Martha, who worked for me in Montgomery and, also, the famed dinner bell and waterfall at Toccoa Falls Institute in Georgia, where I went to school (and about which I had not told her anything!).

Jessie and I found that we both had an unquenchable thirst for spiritual and metaphysical information. We gathered an enviable collection of books on the subject. At the annual Friends of the Library Book Sale, held on October 01 each year by the Cedar Rapids Public Library, it became a competitive "game" to see who would get there first to have her choice of the multitude of books sold at ridiculous prices (35¢ or 50¢ each). I was amazed at the diversity of Jessie's accomplishments. Besides being a legal secretary at a large law firm, she was an expert swimmer with a synchronized team, The Aquarelles, which was inducted into the Swimming Hall of Fame in Fort Lauderdale, Florida, in 1969. She was the "guest lecturer" on astrology twice on the cruise ship Norway in the Caribbean. She also became a certified graphologist (hand-writing analyst) after a two-year series of lessons. In earlier years, she was the bowling coach for the junior bowling league and actively participated in national bowling tournaments with her own team. She did a 13-week series of "mini lessons" on television on her own show, The Astrologers' Corner, at the request of the TV station and, also, wrote a weekly column for a newspaper. She was a popular lecturer at local clubs and conventions. She touched the lives of many people, and we kept in touch down through the years. Jessie retired and lived a quiet life at her home in Cedar Rapids until her death on February 15, 2010.

Along with my attempts to understand the charts, my meditations and readings, I stayed busy with my responsibilities at the ballroom. I had booked several top-name bands for 1972. The first was Russ Morgan's band for the Cedar Rapids Zoological Society on May 23. The band was led by Jack Morgan, following his father's death in 1969. Russ has a star on the Hollywood Walk of Fame. Just prior to the Zoological ball, I went into the "spooky" room, as we had come to call Kim's bedroom after the horse incident, referred to earlier. I must add that Kim would no longer sleep in that room! Upon entering the room, I heard the sound of whistling, although it wasn't a tune per se; rather, it was more up and down notes. At the intermission during the ball, I was extremely interested in speaking to Jack Morgan for a moment. To my amazement, he came down from the band area and walked in my direction. I took advantage of the opportunity to speak to him. I said, "Jack, you're going to think I'm crazy, but I would like to know if your father had the habit of whistling around the house." Well, he looked a little surprised and replied, "Yes, he did, but he never whistled a tune. He would just go up and down the scale." I guess I just didn't have the nerve to tell him why I had asked the question about his father. This was one more incident in my life which made me realize that when the soul passes from the human body it continues to exist.

I received a program schedule for an annual national retreat of Spiritual Frontiers Fellowship, to be held at Carleton College in Northfield, Minnesota in July 1972. I called Leone and asked her how I happened to get this information. She said she had no idea. We decided, almost immediately, that we were both going to attend. Leone made the trip by bus. My friend, Lucille, had always wanted me to leave Kitty with her, and this was the opportunity. Evidently, Kitty was not at all pleased about this. When I told her good-by and closed Lucille's front door, she was sitting in the bay window with a look which said, "Please don't leave me here!" When I returned from my trip, Lucille told me she had not seen Kitty all the time I was gone. She stayed out of sight under the bed. So, she left her food and litter box in the bedroom for her. I had to drive to Waseca, Minnesota in order to leave Kim with Carol and Ray. Since my last reference to their being in Eau Claire, Wisconsin, Ray had accepted a teaching position at the University of Minnesota in Waseca. That night, I had a very clear dream in which I was traveling to Carleton College; however, my route was detoured due to a parade with animals, clowns and floats. It was forty miles from Waseca to Northfield, when, lo and behold, my dream materialized! There was the parade, just as I had seen it in my dream, causing me somewhat of a delay in reaching the campus. Northfield was the location of the most daring attempt to date of the infamous Jesse James to rob a bank, which was the First National Bank on September 07, 1876. Also, Carleton College was the scene of one of the first "streaking" incidents (running naked for a short distance in a public place), which occurred on the stage of the campus auditorium.

Spiritual Frontiers Fellowship was founded in 1955 by Arthur Ford, psychic spiritual medium and clairvoyant. He was an ordained minister of the Disciples of Christ. My first visit to Spiritual Frontiers was the fourth annual retreat. They normally had over two hundred in attendance each year. People from all walks of life and ministers from many different denominations attended. Bishop Tom Pike of the Episcopal Church was listed as a speaker at the first retreat. Allen Spraggett, a Methodist minister from Toronto, Ontario, Canada, was also a speaker and offered many books he had authored in the metaphysical field, including one on the life of Kathryn Kuhlman. He had a nation-wide radio program, called "The Unexplained." Typical lecture topics included the following: "The Light of Love," "Healing and Wholeness," "Mind, Intuition and the Greatest Gift," "Affirmative Living."

Carleton College, Northfield, Minnesota – Watson Hall

As I arrived on the Carleton College campus for the first time, I sensed excitement and anticipation of what I was about to experience in my life. Registration took place in Watson Hall, a seven-story dormitory building. Leone and I were assigned a room on the sixth floor. We went over the schedule of lectures, classes and workshops, from which we could choose. Jack Young was listed as a medium from Colorado. I chose his workshop for the first night. There were some thirty-five in attendance. He picked out eight or ten people and told them personal things about their lives. To my surprise, he chose me from where I was sitting on the back row! I was even more surprised when he told me that I had left my cat at a friend's house. He added that my friend needed to fix the lock on her back door. He had no way of knowing that I had left Kitty with Lucille back in Cedar Rapids. Lucille was aware that she had a problem with her back door and had intended to have it repaired. During that first visit to the retreat, it was learned that I played the violin and, as a result, I was invited to play each year for the next four years. In the newsletter, "Insight," of March 1975, my participation was listed in this way: "Mrs. Gene Winn, Marion, Iowa, will begin morning meditations each day by playing her violin from the terrace … a most beautiful way to start the day!" In the retreat program (June 22-27, 1976) I was mentioned as follows: "… Gene has played with symphony orchestras in the South, has played violin with the Billy Graham Evangelistic Organization and has performed on television."

I remember so well the campus ambience, the cooing of the mourning doves, the dormitories surrounding the beautiful lake and my new special friend, Colleen Bedford, from Des Moines, Iowa. I enjoyed all of the sessions I had chosen, but the most astounding was the one-half hour I spent with a medium. It took place on Thursday afternoon on the seventh floor in Watson Hall. I had read about Edgar Cayce's ability to communicate with departed spirits, but I did not really know what to expect. Carla Gordan was the medium. With her was the minister of her church in New York. When the session began, the minister said a short prayer. Within a minute or so, Carla began speaking with a different voice and with a decided foreign accent. I asked Carla whether or not my grandfather, Papa, knew that I had an interest in the spiritual. I had no sooner expressed that question when a strong breeze touched my face, to the extent that I had to catch my breath. At the same time, both of my arms went up in the air above my head Carla said, "Your grandfather is here, and he is very pleased with this development in your life." I went out of the room as though I were floating on air! I was so elated over the experience. There was no way those ladies could have caused the breeze which took my breath away or the involuntary raising of my arms. This entire week was filled with new and wonderful experiences; however, I can easily understand the disbelief of some, because if someone had described to me what had transpired with the psychic Carla, I'm sure I would have had some doubts. Also, I made many new friends and kept in contact with them for years. I could hardly wait to get back to Waseca to tell Carol about the exciting events of the past week.

The week at Carleton, the astrology classes along with my daily meditations and listening to the tapes of Joel Goldsmith, I knew that I was finding answers to my life-long questions. In my meditations I would *know* the peace which passes all understanding (Philippians 4:7). That peace so filled my soul that, at times, I longed to stay in that state of meditation but realized that I had to continue my regular activities. I felt led to go to the Kirkwood campus to inquire about the requirements for their General Education Diploma. Somehow, I ended up in the office of the director of Community Education, Mr. Gay Dahn. Although I thought I had learned my lesson about bringing up the subject of the paranormal and metaphysical, remembering my conversations with the Methodist minister and the ophthalmologist, I found myself telling Mr. Dahn about Spiritual Frontiers and other experiences. He listened with interest and, when I had finished, he said, "How would you like to offer a course this September on extrasensory perception?" That sounded like a crazy idea to me. I didn't think I could teach a class, so I simply told him that I didn't think I could do it. As I had these thoughts on my way home, I came to the conclusion that I possibly could teach such a class and that I should give it a try. The next day I called Mr. Dahn and gave him my affirmative answer. He said my course would begin in September, thus giving me two months to get ready. I chose the course title as "Expanding Your ESP and Spiritual Awareness." The only reason for my search was to know God. From my readings and seeing first hand the motives of some who were drawn to metaphysics, I realized that some thought of this field for developing a power to serve their own ego while others had no qualms about using it as a power to defraud. My conviction was that any reason other than to know God was wrong and could be detrimental to body and soul.

The classes started on schedule in September 1972 with thirteen students in the first class. I was overwhelmed when I reviewed the class roll to see that there was a PhD in psychiatry on the list! Although I was eager to get started, at the same time I was quite apprehensive over *my* teaching a class and even frightened at the very thought of it. The first class began on a Tuesday and lasted ten weeks. I later added a second class which began on a Thursday and lasted eight weeks. I always began the first class period with registration and getting acquainted. I would then explain the meaning of extrasensory perception (ESP). I often hear people say they do not have ESP. We all have a subconscious, or soul, so we must have ESP within us and the ability to develop it. What does ESP mean? It means the ability to know beyond our five senses. The degree that we are able to make it work for us *depends upon our belief.* There is a well-known saying, "I'll believe it when I see it!" If this is your idea about ESP, you'll never see it, although you have all that is necessary within you at this very moment. So, let's change the saying to, "I'll see it when I believe it!" I am convinced that this is vital to your development. I would then give an explanation of meditation and play a brief tape on the subject by Allen Spraggett and others. Even at the close of the very first class, I felt pumped up and full of energy and no longer apprehensive over teaching the class.

By the end of 1972, we had two more well-known name bands at the ballroom. The Marion Jaycees had the Glenn Miller Orchestra, conducted by Mitch Miller, on October 10. Another big night was November 13, which was the Policemen's Ball. They had hired the Les Elgart Orchestra to perform.

Another memory from that November relates to a call I received from Kim's father, Jack, saying he would like to come to visit Kim. Remembering the problems he had caused, even in Iowa, it gave me a degree of concern; however, I had reached a level of forgiveness toward him, at the same time feeling that Kim needed to know from the beginning that she had a father. I believe this is true, no matter who or where, a person has only one set of biological parents. I felt it was important for them to see each other, so I agreed to Jack's visit. He had said that a friend of his had asked him to accompany him on a business trip from Montgomery to Des Moines and had said he would be happy to swing by the ballroom in Marion. Jack and his friend arrived and spent the day with Kim and left, just as promised.

CHAPTER 49

1973
THE BLIZZARD OF '73

JANUARY 1973 was already beginning to be a very busy year, with new friends and meaningful new experiences. As for ballroom events, we had scheduled well-known personalities, such as Dick Jergins and Russ Morgan in May and Myron Floren for the Policemen's Ball in November. Also scheduled was a dinner for Senator John Culver and Senator Joe Biden. In January of that same year, I attended a lecture at Rev. Mark Weston's church in Ankeny, Iowa, which was given by Mr. Fay Clark. Mr. Clark announced that Mr. Allen Spraggett of Toronto, would be coming there for a lecture series in April. Stretch would allow me to use open dates at the ballroom. On January 19, I wrote to Mr. Spraggett and, among other things, I said, "There are groups in Cedar Rapids that would be greatly interested in hearing you. I am wondering if you can arrange a lecture for the same week you will be in Ankeny." In my postscript to him I wrote, "I telephoned your home Wednesday, and your wife informed me of your recent surgery. My sincere wishes for a speedy recovery!" Mr. Spraggett had attended the Spiritual Frontiers Retreat the preceding year. At that time I talked with him at length. Well, it took quite a while, but I was able to book him for April 29, 1976!

Steve returned from his tour of duty in Vietnam. He obtained employment at Orkin Exterminating Company in Cedar Rapids. Carol, Ray, Tom and Suzy came in March 1973 for a family reunion with Steve. Kim, Tom and Suzy were always glad to see each other. They enjoyed playing games in the huge ballroom when I was present and scheduled activities were not taking place.

The first Sunday in March, the Cedar Rapids Gazette published a full page on the Rev. A. J. Wogen, a priest in the Episcopal Church. He was a leader in the nation-wide charismatic movement. He was very well known as a spiritual healer; i.e., an instrument through whom God seemingly performed miracles. The newspaper story was mostly about his out-of-the-body experience. Since this had recently happened to me, I felt that I just had to speak with him about it. A few days later, I went to Bezdek's Flower Shop, close to the ballroom, and who do you suppose I saw? Rev. Wogen. He was with his wife, so I hesitated to approach him. I did have the thought: If he walks away from his wife, I will speak to him. Guess what? He did just that. I introduced myself and briefly told him my story. He was very interested and wanted me to go to his office and tell him more of the details.

I kept my appointment with Rev. Wogen. I related my story to him in detail, as follows: First of all, I knew that this was a profound gift from God. Since my early childhood, I had believed and loved God. My out-of-the-body experience made me know without a shadow of doubt that I was not this body but, rather, a living soul. The day that it occurred, I took Steve to his job at seven a.m. and returned right away. Kim was still sleeping, so I thought I would get in another nap before she awakened. As soon as I lay down on the bed, I felt that I was being pulled. I tried to resist this pressure. Then, I heard a voice, which sounded like a radio announcer, saying, "Pardon, Systems. Systems, Go!" I then realized that I was having an out-of-the-body experience. I could look down and see my body lying on the bed. Almost instantly, I was in a strange bedroom, which had Victorian furniture. I noted numerous pictures on the dresser in small frames. Sunlight in the most beautiful colors I had ever seen was streaming through the window. A quick glance at the floor revealed a reddish-orange carpet. Then, I was back in my body at the ballroom. On a previous visit to the home of Mr. Emil Gerdes in Edina, Kim and I were in his living room and no other part of the house. In a subsequent visit with Mr. Gerdes, I told him about my out-of-the-body experience. When I told him about the bedroom I had seen, he exclaimed, "You're describing our bedroom in exact detail!"

Bob Tischer, one of the regular bartenders at the ballroom, was married to Connie, who was terminally ill with ovarian cancer. She was in the hospital and had been given only a few days to live. I had met Connie when I began working at the *Town House* as general hostess. I asked Rev. Wogen if he would go to the hospital and visit Connie. He said he would go. Bob visited Connie every day after he finished work at four o'clock. On the day that Rev. Wogen was there, when Bob arrived at her room, he was shocked to see her trying to retrieve something under the bed. Within a very short time she was out of the hospital and, seemingly, going about a normal life. She died in December of that year. Having no minister, Rev. Wogen officiated at her funeral. When the service concluded, I thanked him for what he had done. He said, "You are a very special person!"

Hazel Hopper called me late in March 1973. She said she had talked with her friend, Pierre, who lived in New York, about their mutual friend of many years, Flo Carrier. Flo was a metaphysical lecturer and practitioner. She had been instrumental in helping Hazel through some very difficult times in her life. She also had clients in the United States Senate as well as other notable people. Pierre had said that he had heard that she and her son, Chester, would be coming to their home in Vinton, Iowa. Actually, they lived six months out of the year in Vinton and six months at a resort in Minnesota. Pierre said that Flo was ill but that he did not know the nature of her illness.

Hazel asked me to please take her to see Flo in Vinton, even though she had had no contact with Flo for a number of years. I told Hazel I would be glad to drive her to Vinton and that I would just wait in the car, in view of the fact that Hazel did not know anything about Flo's sickness or whether she would be receptive to a stranger coming to see her. Hazel knew exactly where the old homestead was located, so, as planned, Hazel went in, and I stayed in the car. A minute or so passed, when Hazel came back out and motioned for me to come in. Flo had immediately told her, "You have a friend in the car. I need to see her!" This was the beginning of a new and meaningful but short friendship. Flo had no mobility, due to a stroke and, therefore, was bedfast. She and I bonded immediately. She was very interested in hearing some of my life experiences.

When I told Flo about my violin playing, she asked me to bring the instrument on my next visit and play for her. I did this several times, making the trips without Hazel. On one trip I thought I should take Flo a gift of some kind, so I decided to take her some owl bookends, which cost around $3.95. She refused to accept them, saying that it was her practice never to receive money or gifts in excess of $2.00. She firmly believed that God would take away her gift, if she accepted larger amounts. So, I have been the proud owner of the owl bookends all these years! Hazel and I made another trip together to see Flo the latter part of June. As we prepared to leave, Hazel told Flo, "We'll be back in July, before you and Chester return to Minnesota." Flo answered her nonchalantly, "Hazel, I will be making my transition in early July." In fact, Flo did pass away in the first week of July! I was very happy to have known her. I still have several letters I received from her during our brief friendship.

My parents came to Marion at the end of March 1973, having been driven from Montgomery by their long-time friends, Maggie Herring and Lucy Redman. My father was having a problem with his jaw. His doctor had recommended that he go to Mayo Clinic in Minnesota. It was located fairly close to Carol and Ray in Waseca. Maggie and Lucy stayed in my apartment at the ballroom with Steve and Kitty. On April 03, Mother, Daddy, Kim and I left for Waseca. The weather was cloudy and misty. We had not traveled far, when it began to snow. I continued, thinking that it would stop soon. You do not normally see snow in April, but it was not to be normal.

By the time we were close to Mason City, I realized that we were in the midst of a snow storm. In fact, it became known as the "Blizzard of '73." I was getting pretty nervous, as we continued on our way. All of a sudden, the highway was getting icy. Thank God, there were no other vehicles in sight, because my car suddenly turned around and headed in the opposite direction. Mother was sitting in front with me. When we realized we were still alive, we both began to laugh. Daddy angrily exclaimed from the back seat, "Don't do that again!" The weather continued to deteriorate, but we made it safely to Mason City. By then, I realized that we needed to check into the nearest motel.

Mother was aware of the classes I was teaching and the spiritual subjects about which I was reading. Most of all, she could see the change in my life, and she couldn't help but realize that it was for the better. She never commented about it until that night when we were snowbound in the motel. She said, "Now, Gene, I don't understand your religion, but I'm praying that God will help me understand." The next day, we continued on to Waseca. Daddy did not go to Mayo Clinic as planned, due to the snow. They decided to return home, so I drove them back to the ballroom, and Maggie and Lucy took them on to Montgomery. It was then discovered that Daddy had cancer in his jaw, probably due to his life-long pipe smoking. The operation was successful, but he could not get used to using dentures. So, he lived the next twenty years mostly eating grits and eggs and other soft foods.

On Friday, April 13, the Dave Dighton Band was playing for an anniversary dance. That morning I had asked Carla, who worked as a busgirl in the ball-room, to help me clean the apartment. We were working in my bedroom, when the picture hanging over my bed came out of the frame and fell to the floor, the frame itself staying in place on the wall. This was a favorite painting of mine. It was the famous painting by Renoir of the red-headed girl sitting in a chair. We were surprised to see what happened. I was even more surprised at my immediate statement to Carla, "This means a death." I never talked to the ballroom staff about my interest in the paranormal. There were some two hundred who attended the dance that night. On dance nights I mostly worked in the office. This allowed me to go up and check on Kim and make periodic checks on the bars to see if anything was needed.

On this particular night, I had just gone upstairs to make sure Kim was in bed and, then, I returned to the office. The band started playing, suddenly stopping. Of course, I went out to investigate. People were gathered around a man who had fallen on the dance floor. He had died instantly. I stood at the stone wall which circled a small area of the dance floor in front of my office. I prayed for his transition as his soul left this life. Of course, the dance broke up, and the guests went home.

Two nights later, on Sunday night, I was almost asleep when I was awakened by a whispering in my ear. The next moment I heard the music and normal sounds of the ballroom, completely unusual, because we never scheduled any activities for Sunday nights. This was the one time I was truly afraid during all my years at the ballroom. I called my friend, Beryl, and asked her to please come and spend the night with Kim and me.

Steve wanted to go to Montgomery and look for a job and be able to divide his time between his father and his grandparents. Following his return from Vietnam, he returned to practicing his drums. He wanted his father to help him with his technique. Daddy was recuperating from the surgery on his lower jaw. So, Steve, Kim and I left for Montgomery the first week of July. Our visits home were always filled with going to see Mother's friends as well as mine.

I made what was to be my last visit to my violin teacher, Mrs. Fanny Marks Seibels. Walking through her home where I had taken lessons and had spent Saturday mornings and Sunday afternoons for orchestra rehearsal brought back a flood of memories. The large living room and equally large adjoining music instruction room could be opened up and, thus, make room for orchestra rehearsals. In the living room there was a large gold-framed mirror which extended from the ceiling to the floor except for a low marble shelf on which the short legs of the mirror rested. The black baby grand piano was in one corner of the living room. I always liked her paintings very much, especially the large one of her as a little girl in which she was holding her doll.

Mrs. Seibels was from an aristocratic Alabama family. She lived in a beautiful home; however, she and her husband, Emmet, never owned a car. They would usually walk about a mile and a half to the Whitley Hotel for their evening meal. I remember that Mr. Seibels would walk ahead, and Mrs. Seibels would follow along behind him. She had never washed dishes in order to protect her hands for the violin. (This did not work for me!) She was a very principled lady. She would not participate in gossip. She would quickly say that she did not want to hear it. Another memory is that one did not dare to stand in her presence with chewing gum in her or his mouth. She would immediately tell you to remove your gum! I wholeheartedly agree with her opinion on this subject.

The traumatic memory for me was when I was fourteen years of age and ran from my home on Lawrence Street to this very living room on Perry Street to ask her to call my mother and tell her that I was married. She instantly refused. I shall never forget the concert one evening at Lanier High School. The auditorium was filled to capacity. Mrs. Seibels raised her baton for us to play. After a few notes someone in the brass section played a sour note. She then banged loudly on the music stand with her baton. She threw the baton on the floor and walked off the stage. She quickly returned … and I suppose we played pretty well after that.

I was twenty-six years of age when I played in symphony concert for Mrs. Seibels' Twenty-fifth Reunion at the Montgomery Museum of Fine Arts. The concert program listing "Personnel of the Orchestra" included Toni Tennille, as one of the seven piano accompanists. My readers will remember the famous duo, Captain and Tennille. On this last visit to see her in 1973, Mrs. Seibels looked very frail. I took a picture of her sitting in front of the gold-framed mirror and the black baby grand piano. She passed away a short time later.

Kim, Steve and I went to see Barbara Parker. The development following my going to Biloxi for the purpose of marrying Dawson was not even mentioned by either of us. She did try very hard to convince me to move to Montgomery to take care of her. I thought Steve and Kim might like to see the house on Hull Street where I was born. There was only an empty space where the house once stood. Steve took a picture of me standing in the middle of the empty lot.

My good friend at The Ranch in Montgomery, Quinn

Another visit made on that trip was for me to see my long-time friend, Quinn. She had driven my parents to Iowa. I always went to see her when I returned home to Montgomery. She became more and more interested in my spiritual journey. We also talked by telephone quite a lot. I can only remember one specific thing I said to her. She desperately wanted to stop drinking, but did not seem to be able to get over her sense of tremendous guilt. I remember telling her, "God is love. God loves us, and God forgives us. Knowing then that God forgives us, how can we not forgive ourselves?" Finally, in the

depths of despair, she said one day she went into her back yard, crying out to God to help her ... or let her die! To her amazement, there appeared two very large letters in the air: "A. A." She went back into her house and called Alcoholics Anonymous. From that day until her death in 1997, she did not touch another drop of alcohol! She also traveled all over Alabama as a spokesperson for Alcoholics Anonymous.

Steve stayed in Montgomery, as planned, and Kim and I returned to Cedar Rapids without any problems that I recall. Oh yes, I should mention that Kitty didn't mind riding in a car. So, after the experience of leaving her with Lucille that one time when I went to Carleton College, I would either take her with me or board her at the kennel near the ballroom.

My Dream Log was a tremendous help to keep track of my dreams. The night of August 07, I dreamt of seeing piles of injured and dying young men, stacked on top of each other and screaming in pain. Upon awakening, I was alarmed due to its being such a vivid and horrible dream. I had learned that, following such a vivid enactment, I should pay special attention to the details. So, I faithfully wrote out my dream. The very next day, on NBC News I listened in horror as they told the details of the uncovering by Houston, Texas police of twenty-eight boys and young men who were brutally tortured and killed in a bizarre mass murder. In recounting and writing on June 09, 2008 about my dream and the actual event of 1973, I decided to Google it on my computer and was totally surprised upon opening my home page on America Online to find that the news story was all about this terrible event on its 35th anniversary!

Senator John Culver's campaign manager had booked October 19, 1973 for a dinner in honor of Senator Joe Biden, who came to Iowa to give his support to Senator Culver's campaign. Usually, Senator Ted Kennedy would have been there for the occasion. He had been there several times during the years I worked at the ballroom. Kennedy was very supportive of Culver. They had been college roommates. The first engagement for which Kennedy was at the ballroom, the staff and Stretch and I were very excited to see him. I thought that when Senator Kennedy and his party arrived they would come through the front door, so I made sure I was stationed there for the big moment. I was beginning to wonder, "What could be keeping them? They should be here by now!" I then saw Stretch coming out of the Party Room, which was far from the front door. Several people were following him. Stretch knew that Kennedy would be coming in through the Party Room ... and he didn't even tell me! Well, he knew I didn't like it one bit.

Greeting Senator Ted Kennedy in my office at the ballroom

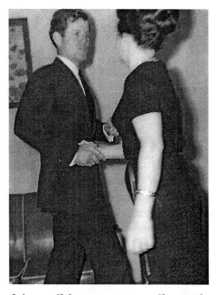

Senator Kennedy was there for the Boy Scouts and for Senator Culver. The ceremony began with Kennedy and the Boy Scouts marching around the dance floor. While this was going on, Stretch handed me a telegram for Senator Kennedy and told me to go onto the dance floor and give it to him. It didn't seem right for me to go out on the dance floor while they were marching. I didn't know what to do, but Stretch was my boss. So, I intercepted the senator and handed him the telegram. I shall always remember the startled look on his face, for he jumped in surprise when he saw me; nevertheless, he took the telegram from my hand. When the evening's activities ended, he came to my office. I had one of the staff from my outer office ready with the camera to take a picture as the senator shook hands with me. She took another one of him waving good-by to her as he left.

Steve was still in Montgomery, so Kim and I spent Christmas 1973 in Waseca with Carol, her family and Josie, Ray's mother. I'm sure that Josie and I danced, as she enjoyed dancing as much as I did. Ray was Catholic; however, he and Carol were attending the First Congregational Church. Their minister, Rev. Tom Slocum, had been told of some of my experiences. He asked if they thought I would speak at the church on March 31, 1974 for the Sunday morning Lenten worship service. I had accepted the challenge of the ESP classes, and they were turning out to be successful. But, speaking at a church worship service? How would I ever be able to do this?

CHAPTER 50

1974
ESP AND SPIRITUAL PERCEPTION

OUR next political function was on January 10, 1974. Senator Nelson Rockefeller of New York was there to support Iowa Congressman Tom Reilly. Some three hundred and fifty attended the cocktail hour and dinner. Collins Radio booked the Tex Beneke Orchestra for February 23.

Mr. Darrell Larson, a teacher at Jefferson High School in Cedar Rapids, called and asked me to speak to his psychology class on February 18, which was my 46th birthday. I was gaining more and more confidence with my adult classes but wondered if I would be less confident with high school seniors. There was no need for concern. The students were very attentive and asked me many questions concerning extrasensory perception. A few days later, I received a very nice letter from Mr. Larson, dated February 22, thanking me for taking the time to come and share some of my experiences. Twenty-seven students signed the letter! Several of them added brief comments after their signatures. One of them, Kathy, said, "Please keep up your work. Don't let anyone discourage you. You've got quite a gift!"

The Kirkwood ESP classes were taught at Washington High School and were going well. In order to maintain a class in active status, there had to be at least eight students in attendance. I usually had from ten to fifteen. Meditation was a big part of every class. However, each week I would introduce a different subject for the remainder of the class period, such as auras, dreams, reincarnation and astral projection. The Gene Winn's Dream Log referred to previously, was published early that year and was available through Spiritual Frontiers. I later received a letter from Parker Publishing Company in West Nyack, New York, asking me if I would consider writing "a fairly short book for the average layman of an inspirational nature that would show him how to live the life he always wanted to live." I did not accept their kind offer due to the fact that my soul journey was of a "spiritual" nature. That was exactly the reason why I accepted the offer to teach the ESP classes at Kirkwood.

Again came the question, "How would I be able to speak at the Lenten service at First Congregational Church in Waseca on Sunday, March 31?" It was possible because I was able to get my ego out of the way and let God speak through me. The audience was very attentive. I didn't see anyone walk out! Carol, Ray and the children sat on the front row. They gave me a bouquet of flowers! The Order of Worship included the following: " ... *We have a special* guest with us today, Ms. Gene Winn, who needs no introduction other than to say that she is Carol's mother. ... Ms. Winn has been psychic all her life. She was brought up in a strict Baptist home in Montgomery, Alabama. Although she was 'saved' at an early age, her search for God was not complete. Since then, she has intensified her search for God through mystical experience. Now living in Cedar Rapids, Iowa, she hasn't completely lost her charming Southern ways and speech."

The following is a brief excerpt from my message notes of that Sunday morning:

Being invited to come here to talk about some of my psychic experiences brings back a memory when I was five years of age, when I would go up and down my street preaching to my neighbors. Now, at last, I have my chance!

I discovered the way for me to have direct guidance from God was through meditation. I naturally had heard of prayer and meditation all my life, and I thought they were the same thing, but I soon learned from reading and, then, from experience, that prayer is talking to God, while meditation is quieting our physical bodies and listening to God. Jesus said, "When you pray, go into your inner room ... and shut the door." (Matthew 6:6 NASV). I used to think this meant to go into a closet or some other room and shut the door, but I began to understand this to mean we should shut out the world around us and completely still our physical body; then, we are ready to listen to God. I have tried to spend at least thirty minutes a day for the last six years in meditation. It is very rewarding, physically and mentally, but most of all, spiritually. Meditation is not a new black magic wrinkle for the attainment of material riches and personal power. Its objective is an appeal to the Supreme Intelligence for knowledge and guidance.

It is through your own soul or subconscious that the voice of God speaks to you. All things that are valuable for us to know will come to us, if we will open ourselves to the voice of God. It is in this way that we become developed psychically and spiritually and have the power of seeing into the very heart of things.

In finding God and truth at the center of my own being, I began to develop an awareness of myself and other people. I began to see new meanings for Bible verses, such as "Love ... God with all your heart and with all your soul and with all your mind ... and love your neighbor as yourself." (Matthew 22:37,39 NIV) " ... you have great faith! Your request is granted." (Matthew 15:28 NIV) "You shall know the truth and the truth shall make you free." (John 8:32 NASV) And, this is one of my favorites, in which I find great comfort, "If God be for us, who can be against us?" (Romans 8:31 NIV)

Looking back and comparing my life to six years ago, I used to get very depressed with both high and low periods. I didn't know what was wrong with me. While I never get depressed now, I sometimes get discouraged; then, I stop and take stock of my life and compare it to six years ago. The difference is almost unbelievable. The joy and wonder of my true being take me out of my discouragement and lift me a little higher. (Bible Translations: NASV, New American Standard Version; NIV, New International Version)

We left Waseca early the next morning, because Kim needed to be back in school. There was bad news when we returned. Brad Hopper, Hazel's son, called to tell me that his mother was in the hospital. I went to see her right away. She was talking and in good spirits. So, I thought she would probably be out of the hospital soon. However, she passed away the next day. I played the violin for her graveside service. I chose her favorite hymn, "In the Garden."

Spiritual Frontiers held a four-day seminar at the Bismarck Hotel in Chicago the latter part of May. Kim was out of school, so Beryl, Kim and I made the trip together. The Bismarck was a beautiful, old hotel. Our room was on the sixth floor. Kim enjoyed looking out of the window at the tall buildings. She had spotted a gift shop on the first floor when we were checking in. Although she was afraid of the elevator, she persuaded me to let her go down to the gift shop alone. She wanted to buy me a gift but didn't want me to go with her. She was now eleven, and it wasn't as dangerous back then as it would be today. Besides, the hotel was filled with people who were attending the seminar. She was gone about twenty minutes, when she returned to the room and presented me with a beautiful Chicago plate. I still have it on display in my dining room curio buffet. Guess what happened? On her return trip on the elevator, it got stuck! It was a long time before Kim asked for permission to go some place by herself.

As we approached the hotel we saw a Japanese restaurant. We thought it would be fun to eat there. It was a new experience for us to dine at the low table, sitting almost on the floor. As we were walking back to the hotel, we became aware that we were getting some strange looks from men on the street. This caused us to realize that two women and a child had no business being out at that hour and place at night. We very much enjoyed going to the Chicago Zoo. Kim saw animals she had never before seen. We didn't stay long due to the terrible odor. Before returning to the hotel, we drove along Lake Shore Drive on Lake Michigan.

We had come here to attend and participate in the seminar. The most memorable workshop for me was Biofeedback, where you would be connected to a machine. When the instructor attempted to turn it on, it would not function. So, he asked if a volunteer from the audience would come up and be connected to the machine while he worked on it. So, I quickly went forward. He asked me to meditate. Very quickly, he stated, "It's working. This lady is in the alpha state." It seems appropriate to state the four levels of consciousness: Beta – wide awake, 14 to 40 cycles per second, with the eyes wide open. You are awake, as you are right now. Alpha – 7 to 14 cycles per second. ESP, meditation, daydreaming, hypnosis. This is a relaxed, pleasant condition. Theta – 4 to 7 cycles per second, the borderline of sleep. Possibly a person's most creative, problemsolving range. Delta – 0 to 4 cycles, the brain waves of deep sleep or trance. Today, biofeedback is universally used and accepted in the medical field.

I attended a workshop on Kirlian photography, a method of capturing on a photographic plate an image of what is purported to be an aura of energy that emanates from the hand of the subject placed inside a biosensor box. When members of the class went forward to take their turn, they were told to try to place themselves in a meditative state. Afterwards, each one received a photographic print of his/her hand, indicating the color and the extension of the aura. Some of them were disappointed, due to seeing only an outline of their hand with no indication of an aura. This proved that they were still in the wide awake or Beta state of consciousness. The picture of my hand, however, showed that I was in the Alpha state. I have the picture on file to this day and treasure it very much.

The summer of 1974 was beginning to be very busy. In addition to my work at the ballroom and my classes at the college, I was now given an invitation to speak at the American Business Women's Association, Triangle '64. The dinner was held at the Sirloin 'n' Brew Restaurant at 6:30 p.m. on June 05. The newspaper advertisement of the event, among other things, stated, "Speaking on 'Expanding Your ESP and Spiritual Awareness' is Mrs. Gene Winn of Kirkwood Community College." After my message at the First Congregational Church in Waseca, I was now feeling more confident. After the meeting, two ladies told me they would be signing up for my new class which would begin in September.

Insight, the newsletter of the Minnesota Area Spiritual Frontiers Fellowship, came in June, announcing the seminar to be held at Carleton College later that month. As usual, this week was almost like being in another world. It made me feel as though it would be nice not to return to normal daily activities. Carol attended the last day of the retreat. She enjoyed the activities and meeting some of the leaders.

I received a letter on July 05 from David Graham, from the office of Brad Steiger at Other Dimensions, Inc. Anyone interested in the metaphysical or paranormal would recognize the name of Brad Steiger. He is the author-coauthor of 162 books with over 17 million copies in print. His titles include Valentino, Judy Garland and Tom Thorpe. He appeared on television with Ted Koppel, Peter Jennings, Tom Brokaw, David Brinkley, Mike Douglas and others. David Graham was in the process of writing a book on dreams, titled "Dreaming Your Way to Happiness and Awareness."

Mr. Emil Gerdes was the chairman of the retreat committee of Spiritual Frontiers Fellowship at Carleton College. He and his wife, Edythe, seemed to take a personal interest in my dream log and in my violin playing since we first met in 1972. He had a long and distinguished career as a sales executive and manufacturer. He was also an author, lecturer and private researcher in the field of psychic phenomena for over thirty years. I felt very fortunate to have him and his wife as my friends. They lived in Edina, Minnesota. We maintained frequent contact by telephone. He was very pleased when I received the letter from Parker Publishing Company on February 28, to which I referred earlier. He was instrumental in helping me get my dream log in the bookstore at Carleton College. Emil Gerdes had spoken to David Graham about my dream log. He invited me to come to Decorah, Iowa for lunch and an interview with him and Brad Steiger on Monday, July 08. A very positive result of our time together was David's generous inclusion of the following paragraph in his book:

In spite of the confusion in the definition and language of dreams, many have used dreams as a guide in daily living. Ms. Gene Winn, an avid amateur dream researcher, has recently developed and published a dream log for those interested in recording dreams. She recommends the daily recording of dreams. Her log has an outline that allows a quick and accurate recording when in a semi-sleep state. She recommends this daily recording immediately after being received, and if unable to waken sufficiently to record the dream in detail, to make sufficient notes to allow recall of details. Ms. Winn claims that her dreams have caused her to become a completely changed person and have allowed her to gain confidence in her work in teaching extracurricular classes on a college level. Her acceptance of dream-direction has shown her a new path of endeavor for her future. She also recommends that, if possible, friends join in small groups of three or four to study and analyze their dreams. This develops a greater understanding and a positive conclusion of the interpretations.

CHAPTER 51

ANNUAL TRIP
TO MONTGOMERY (1974)

MY employment at the ballroom with the rent-free apartment and less book-ings in the summer months all worked together to make possible visits to my parents in Alabama, my sister in California and attendance at Spiritual Frontiers in Minnesota. In August, Steve, Kim and I drove to Montgomery. Among other customary visits, I took Kim to see her Aunt Betty. Betty's sister, Ann, had recently moved from Panama City Beach, Florida, to Millbrook. If her father, Jack, were in town, I planned to take Kim for a brief visit with him. I had the conviction that it was very important for Kim to know that side of her family.

I visited my old friend, Quinn, who continued to be a spokesperson for Alcoholics Anonymous and to write newspaper articles for that organization. She was still living with her husband, Dick; however, they divorced a short time later. She and her daughter, Ginny, moved to Asheville, North Carolina. Quinn found employment and faithfully promoted A. A.

I also went to see Rebecca. I had heard that she had recently re-married. My visit was quite short, as she now had Alzheimer's. She did not have an inkling of who I was! Her husband was nice and, coincidentally, I had known him years before. From there, I went to visit her sister, Susan, and Susan's daughter, Rachel. They had a very nice condo on the east side of Montgomery. Rebecca and Susan's sister, Edith, who had caused me so much trouble years ago but who became my friend, now lived in Lumberton, North Carolina, so I didn't get to see her.

I would never fail to visit my good friend, Martha Peck, who had worked for me before I moved to Iowa. Blacks had come a long way since the Civil Rights Movement of the 1960s. Just a decade before, they worked for $10-$15 a week. Now, they were able to find employment which provided livable income. Martha had found a job in a furniture factory and eventually was able to pur-chase a two-bedroom home. She had it very nicely furnished. We enjoyed our visit that day.

As usual, the visits to Montgomery always involved going back and forth to visit my friends and Mother's friends, whom she expected us to visit as well. Daddy had built a small frame house in the back yard for his art studio. All the members of the family were delighted to receive paintings and crafts that he made especially for each of us. As mentioned previously, I treasure ten paintings he gave me over the years. He made jewelry boxes to look like books. He would paint a picture on the cover which would have a special meaning for the recipient. We also enjoyed the puzzles and walking sticks he made. I knew better than to make other plans for Sunday, as Mother eagerly looked forward to presenting us to her friends at Forest Avenue Baptist Church, where she was a member since moving to East Montgomery. I have a vivid memory of the sad look on her face, as we packed the car to leave early the next morning to return to Cedar Rapids.

On the return trip we stopped in Alabaster, near Birmingham, to visit one of my childhood best friends, Muriel—my tap dancing buddy! We had kept in touch over the years with Christmas cards. She had married Frank Russo, an Air Force master sergeant. They lived in several countries in his military career. I would have loved to accept their invitation to stay overnight, but it was necessary to get back to my job. Also, I needed to prepare for my ESP classes which would be starting in September. I would have loved to have checked on my other best friend, Stella, referred to previously. I knew that she had married Richard Richey and that they were foreign missionaries, but we had lost track of each other.

CHAPTER 52

MY EDGAR CAYCE
LIBRARY

MY library, especially the books on Edgar Cayce's life, was steadily increasing. On a Saturday, after lunch, I was reading "There is a river," by Thomas Sugrue, a Cayce biography. I glanced across the room and, to my amazement and then terror, I saw a mist forming and rising and getting larger. I thought, for sure, there was a fire downstairs in the ballroom. I called the Fire Department, and they responded right away. After a thorough inspection, they assured me that there was no fire. I soon realized that what I had seen was ectoplasm. This word is from the Greek *ektos*, "outside" plus "plasma"; i.e., something formed or molded, a term coined by Charles Richet to denote a substance or spiritual energy "exteriorized" by physical mediums. Ectoplasm is said to be associated with the formation of ghosts. This experience was the only time I have seen ectoplasm take form and, of course, not knowing what it was at the time, I naturally called the Fire Department.

On November 18, we had the Policemen's Ball with Myron Floren of the Lawrence Welk Show. As I've said before, I would go upstairs to check on Kim. On this night, after seeing that she was asleep, for some reason I went into the bedroom in which she no longer slept, due to the "horse" incident. The ballroom neon sign was just outside the windows of that room. I immediately saw that the sign was smoking and was about to ignite. Once again, I called the Fire Department. It was located nearby, thus they were able to arrive on the scene quickly. Providentially, I had checked on Kim and stepped into that room and called for help; otherwise, there could have been a disaster with the ballroom filled with people that night.

Chapter 53

1975
Sleeping In A Dead Man's Bed

THE New Year's Eve Dance was always our busiest night with the largest crowd of the year. On New Year's Day 1975, I began to notice that something was wrong with my hands. As I was counting the receipts from the night before, I had trouble picking up the coins. It became difficult for me to play the violin and shop for groceries in that I could not pick up the cans from the shelves. I made an appointment with my regular doctor. He suspected that I had carpal tunnel syndrome, which I had never heard of. He made an appointment for me to go to St. Luke's Hospital to have an electro-diagnostic test. Electrodes were placed on my hands and wrists. Small electric shocks were applied, and the speed with which nerves transmitted impulses was measured. The results of the tests showed that I had carpal tunnel syndrome in both hands and wrists. Needless to say, there was no apparent solution for me other than surgery. The condition was worse in my left wrist and hand than in the right. The surgeon decided to operate on my right wrist first, so that it could heal and I would have the use of it, before he proceeded to the left wrist. This was an out-patient procedure.

My main concern was that I had accepted an invitation to speak at the Long Branch Supper Club to the Five Star American Business Women's Association, which would hold its meeting on January 14. My subject was "Expanding Your ESP and Spiritual Awareness." Also, I needed to be able to practice my violin for the upcoming retreat of Spiritual Frontiers in July. The surgery was scheduled for January 16, thus solving the problem of the speaking engagement. The surgeon assured me that both my hands would be well, and I should be able to play my violin by the middle of April. The surgery went well; however, I do remember being very annoyed with the surgeon and his nurse, as they carried on a casual conversation while they were cutting on me!

I was perplexed over the healing aspect of my surgery. Meeting Rev. Wogen and witnessing his going to the Source of the healing power and, also, devoting one hour daily to listening to my Joel Goldsmith tapes, I came to believe that there was a principle involved in healing. This principle is that God is all power, and nothing can come from Him except His perfect will. We go to God, knowing that we are only His instruments and take no credit, regardless of the outcome. This principle worked for me on several occasions. One example was when Kim was very sick with the mumps. She came out of the bedroom crying with pain and asking me for help. I said, "Kim, don't worry. You're going to be all right." She returned to the bedroom with instant healing and without pain!

Could the carpal tunnel syndrome of my right hand have been healed and its surgery found unnecessary? Well, I hadn't really thought of anything other than the prescribed surgery on both hands. The surgeon had told me that the electro-diagnostic test revealed that my left hand was in worse condition than my right hand. A healing took place, in that I did not return to the surgeon, due to my left hand being completely well *without the surgery!* For the past thirty-eight years I have had no problem with either hand.

Emil Gerdes encouraged me to arrange a date and to invite Carla Gordan, the psychic consultant with whom I had my first reading, to come to the ballroom. She accepted the invitation and came from New York the end of May to be with us for a week. She stayed in the ballroom apartment with Kim and me. I had no trouble in booking the readings for her, because I had many friends and students who knew of my first reading with her. They were more than happy to sign up! My friend, Lucille Yeater, occasionally held meetings in her home for the Inner Peace Movement (I.P.M.). At one of her meetings I met Mr. Richard Feller. Therefore, there was no lack of interested people for readings with Carla when she came. We decided that she should use my bedroom, since it was more private than the living room. There were three or four readings a day booked for a full week. The clients were deeply pleased with the readings. I began to realize that there were three types of psychics: (1) those who desperately wanted to be psychics along with all the attention it would bring to them, (2) those who were fraudulent and were only out to scam people, (3) those who were genuine psychics, such as Carla Gordan. Richard Feller had heard about Carla and her gift as a medium. He did receive a good reading … and much more. It was love at first sight! He and Carla were married in the fall in Cedar Rapids and went to Hawaii for their honeymoon. Another couple who had come for a reading was Audrey and Vern. This was another case of love at first sight!

I looked forward to my classes since, by now, I felt relaxed and comfortable in my role as a teacher. Another benefit for me was that I made many new friends. This semester, Betty Harshman signed up for the class. She worked for the City of Cedar Rapids as Community Service Coordinator for the Department of Planning and Redevelopment. She had many psychic experiences and believed that the classes were helping her to better understand them. The next semester, starting in January 1975, her husband, John, enrolled in the class. I would take my ball to class in order that the students might see whether or not they had the ability for crystal ball gazing. So far, none of them, not even I, displayed this gift. John was to be the first! When he took his turn with the ball, at first it became misty but quickly revealed a banquet table with a white tablecloth and all the decorations for a banquet dinner. I had my interpretation of what it meant. Telling Jessie Nagle what he had seen but without telling her what I thought it meant, I was quite surprised to hear her say that she believed it was an omen of his impending death. This was exactly my interpretation!

Betty invited me to dinner for my first visit to their home. I was very impressed with the waterfall located in the foyer. In their bedroom there was a large ball hanging in the middle of the room. When it was turned on, it would project beautiful colors all around the room. Although I admired the beauty of their home, it was marred by my feeling of a presence there that was not at all pleasant. As a matter of fact, I felt as if somebody or some spirit was on the verge of grabbing me. John passed away within a month after looking into the crystal ball. On a Sunday evening at the dinner hour, Betty called me with the awful news that John had fallen in their kitchen, and she couldn't get him to respond. For some unknown reason to me, she had called me before calling the paramedics.

I left Kim next door and went to St. Luke's Hospital. John never regained consciousness and passed away that night. Betty was understandably very upset and asked me to spend the night with her which, of course, I did. I already had this bad feeling about her home. You can imagine how I felt when she had me sleep in the twin bed in her bedroom, which was John's bed! Needless to say, I had a sleepless night, because I had the sensation that I was lying directly on top of John. Well, Betty asked me to stay again the following night. Over the years, Kim and I have laughed about that next night, although it wasn't amusing then. Kim went with me that night. I slept on the floor, and Kim slept in John's bed. We both slept well without any problems.

The Seventh Annual National Retreat of S.F.F. was held June 17-22. Carol and Ray invited Kim and me to Waseca a week earlier to go with them on vacation to Nisswa Lake in Minnesota. We went in two cars, Ray's mother, Josie, riding with me. We left Waseca early on 08 June and drove to St. Cloud, Minnesota, where we had lunch. While eating, we talked about playing dominoes that evening after getting settled in the cabin. During the afternoon hours I began to feel very tired. Knowing the feeling of energy and being wide awake from the diet pill, I took half a pill, which is what I normally took, because I had experienced slight heart palpitations when taking a whole pill. For my readers who may not know this, in the 1950s and 1960s the diet pill was prescribed by doctors for curbing the appetite and for losing weight. No one gave it a second thought; i.e., until the 1970s when it became known that this diet pill, which contained amphetamines, could become harmful to the body and mind, if it was abused. Most of my friends who were my age took the pill, if they were even slightly overweight. Once it was discovered that it was harmful, it could no longer be prescribed by the doctors.

So, what was I doing with diet pills? I had a few remaining from my last prescription, written about two years previously. Knowing that I had a week of violin practice and other activities at the lake before going to Carleton, I had taken two or three pills with me. Well, that half of a pill perked me up all right, and I thought I would be able to go for a game of dominoes that night. As soon as we got settled, everyone decided to go straight to bed, leaving me wide awake! Kim and I had cots in the kitchen. She also went right to sleep. Ray usually enjoyed a drink before dinner and had taken a bottle of vodka with him.

I thought: A little shot of vodka will help me go to sleep. Big mistake! I really thought I was dying. Almost immediately after drinking the vodka, my heart felt as if it had come loose in my chest. I began to have palpitations, and it seemed that my heart was moving from one side of my chest to the other and back again, over and over. Although I was pretty sure that I was about to make my departure from the earth, I also knew that I needed to meditate. I did so, thinking that I might not awaken. Ray came into the kitchen to start preparing breakfast. When I finally awakened, he asked, "Oh, are you still alive?" I had not planned to tell them what had happened, but I responded to his question by saying, "Yes, I'm alive, but I didn't expect to be." Then, I told all of them what had happened. Carol and Ray insisted on taking me to the hospital in Brainerd, about twenty miles from the lake. The doctor diagnosed my problem as being tachycardia, an abnormally rapid heart action, caused by the pill and the vodka together. The doctor said, "You will be fine. Just don't do that again!" After that experience, I was cured for life of diet pills and alcohol.

In spite of my near transition to the other side, I did practice my violin for the coming week at Carleton. There were only a few cabins on the lake, but rather than subject the neighbors and my family, I took my violin into the woods and practiced. We all had a very nice time, just being together, playing games by night and fishing and boating by day. Ray's mother, Josie, and I enjoyed each other's company as well as dancing together. She was a very pretty lady. She was named Miss Minnesota in her teens and was offered a screen test in Hollywood.

On the return trip Josie rode with Carol, Ray, Tom, Suzy and Kim, while I went on to Carleton College for the retreat. Feeling that I needed further practice, I took my violin and slipped into the auditorium on campus, thinking that I had it to myself, except for a lady who appeared to be resting. She was there for more than rest. The next day someone, unknown to me, handed me a sheet of paper on which my observer had sketched a silhouette of my head and shoulders. She placed the following titles and comments around the sketch, as follows: "The aura is as beautiful as the woman and her music. It speaks of harmony." – "With the song 'Let this cup pass from me,' the shades of blue darkened. The song must move her greatly." - There is a band around the head, which she titled, "clear light." Beyond that band, there was a wider one, which she called, "blue—beautiful and radiant blue." "Much luminous blue." A beam of light is coming down and enclosing the figure called "infilling, white light … pulsating … pink tinges in this light." There is a beam striking the face of the figure, which she identifies as "a shaft of golden light." She refers to an "arc light" which focuses on the violin. She adds here, "blue encompasses the violin." One final comment, "There is much light all around. She illuminates the stage." She wrote my name in the upper left-hand corner of the sheet. At the lower-left, she made the following notation: "As seen from my corner: Bonnie Paulley, Friday, June 25, 1976, S.F.F., Carleton College, Northfield, Minnesota." I was overwhelmed that she could see and describe all of the details emanating from my aura. It amazed me that she had this ability and willingly wrote her comments and gave them to me. Although I have observed the auras of several people, as well as the huge yellow question mark over a minister's head, referred to previously, I have never had the keen ability displayed by Ms. Paulley.

Carla Gordan had continued to be on the retreat program since 1972 to give psychic counseling. She accepted my invitation to return to Cedar Rapids with me. Colleen Grey, who led the morning meditations and was director of music for the retreat, was well known for her exceptional voice and her ability to organize singing groups. She and her husband had recently purchased a houseboat, which they kept on a Minnesota river. Carla, Kim and I gladly accepted her invitation to come to her home in Bloomington to spend a day and night on the houseboat. We thoroughly enjoyed this new experience. The next morning, I drove Carla to the home of Emil and Edythe Gerdes in Edina, so that he could take her to the Minneapolis airport for her flight home to New York.

In late August, Kim and I went to Chicago to attend a two-day S. F. F. seminar, which was held at a suburban hotel. The night before we left home, we watched a scary TV program. It was a mystery about someone's stopping at a roadside restaurant. A lady went into the restroom -- but never came out. Shortly before arriving in Chicago, we were both hungry, so we stopped at a gas station which had a small restaurant. When we went in, we thought the place seemed unfriendly. It reminded us of the show we had seen on TV. Kim and I remember that we were apprehensive about going to the restroom. We did go, then ate our meal quickly and got out of there!

We had left Cedar Rapids after lunch, so by this time, it was really getting dark, and I couldn't find the hotel. In fact, I got lost and discovered that we were on the road to Indiana. By ten o'clock, I was getting very tired and needed to find the hotel quickly. Finally, I found an older motel. The older reader will remember how they looked. This one consisted of small, brick cottages in a semi-circle. If I hadn't been so tired, I would have kept going. Upon entering our unit, I opened the closet door, which was directly opposite the main door. A terrible odor came out of the closet. Believe me, I had second thoughts about spending the night there, but we finally went to bed. Although I was thoroughly exhausted, I began to read, as many people do, in order to relax and induce sleep. Suddenly, as if someone had blown it into my face, the heavy odor of tobacco smoke filled my nostrils. I guess I was more afraid of getting back on the highway at that time of night, so I simply took two sleeping pills!

We awakened early the next morning and continued our search for the hotel where the seminar was to be held. We did find the hotel; however, after all that had happened to us, I decided to attend the morning session only and leave for Cedar Rapids right after lunch. By the way, we never did find out what the closet odor was or the source of the tobacco smoke; however, I was convinced that they were both the result of some terrible event which occurred in that room at some time in the past.

Ballroom bookings were slower in the summer months, as compared with September through March of each year. This year, however, from September to December we had four big church dances booked. St. Pius Church had the name band of Russ Carlyle. The Policemen's ball scheduled Les Elgard. Our Wednesday night dances were held throughout the year. Wedding and anniversary dances were held on Fridays and Saturdays, when nothing else was previously scheduled. The job of ballroom manager was perfect for me. I was free to do other things that were important to me. Having Kim with me at the ballroom, I never had to worry about getting a babysitter. I also had ample time for my reading, meditation and ESP classes which had been held all year long for several years.

In 2008, while doing research and going through files from long ago, related to the writing of this book, out of all the classes I taught I was only able to find two registration forms of former students of mine. Both of their forms were dated September 1975. I mentioned Mary Jahncke previously. Since I saw her telephone number on the form, I decided to call her. I was delighted that she still had the same number, was in relatively good health and remembered me from so long ago. This encouraged me to call the number on the other form which had the name of Dean Barnum. I was equally surprised when he answered the phone. We had a long and pleasant conversation. I was happy to learn that after thirty-eight years he continues to be interested in related paranormal subjects.

New Year's Eve was, as customary, our largest attendance for the year at the ballroom. I can't remember ever having a mix-up with the seating of the reservations. I do remember Kim's answering the ballroom telephone, which was in our apartment, when none other than Roy Clark of Yee-Haw called from Branson, Missouri to inquire about a booking. She told him she couldn't bother me, because I was meditating. Of course, I returned his call shortly thereafter.

CHAPTER 54

1976
THE END OF THE ARMAR IN SIGHT

OCCASIONALLY, we booked meetings for various labor unions. On Thursday, January 28, I set up a meeting for Local Union 299. The meetings would usually be held in the mornings and, therefore, I would stay in my office doing book work, to answer the telephone and to provide whatever the members might need. The phone rang a good bit. One call which surprised me was from Dawson Parker. I had not heard from him since we left Biloxi back in 1969, following Hurricane Camille. It was not that I wanted or expected to hear from him. He said that he had been trying to locate me for over a year. Barbara kept telling him that I was in California. Also, she would tell him that I was in Virginia. He believed that she was giving him the runaround. After calling Directory Assistance in California, Virginia and Alabama and not finding me, he decided to call the ballroom. He was really surprised that he had finally found me. He asked me if I would consider marrying him again, now that his four children were soon to be out on their own. Of course, my answer was "No!" I didn't like to hurt anyone, but I didn't feel that it could ever work out for us.

For February 22, Collins Credit Union had booked a name band, Buddy Morrow, for their yearly dance. In spite of a near blizzard, they still had a large crowd. This was a night I would not forget. We had two regular bartenders who had been with us since 1967, Bob Tischer and Jim Greteman. I was awakened by a call from Bob at 4 a.m., telling me that Jim had passed away. Jim's girl-friend, Jan, was with him at the time. He died of a heart attack at midnight.

The ballroom was in need of extensive repairs. The owners of the building were not willing to provide the necessary funds. Stretch, as the lessee, did not feel that it was his place to make the repairs. There was a rumor going around at that time that a new Stouffer's Hotel was going to be built in downtown Cedar Rapids. Of course, this would provide a large ballroom and conference rooms. We could see the handwriting on the wall! I had mixed feelings about it. I was grateful for my job and many opportunities to pursue my spiritual goals, provide for Kim and me and be a stay-at-home mom for her. On the other hand, I was eager for new adventures. When the rumor became a reality, the owners' decision was that the *Armar Ballroom* would be razed and the property sold by the beginning of the next year. So, we continued our bookings through the New Year's Eve Ball of 1976.

This news prompted me to call Allen Spragett to ask if he had an open date for this year. I had been appointed local chairperson of S.F.F. Realizing that I would not have the ballroom available for my pursuits after the end of the year, I had to get busy. Mr. Spragett responded by giving me the date of April 29. His lecture topic was "The Slumbering Seer, America's New Edgar Cayce" (Ross Peterson), with question and answer period following. I had 8½" x 11" posters printed to advertise the lecture. I took them to businesses which would allow me to display them. I placed a 5" column in the Cedar Rapids Gazette. We had TV coverage by KCRG. I had taken a picture of Allen and the TV host, I've forgotten his name, but I recognized him from the picture. Allen is standing in front of my piano, while the host is seated and writing, probably taking notes from the interview.

Allen's fee, in addition to our admission charge, seems unbelievable by today's standards. I have the cancelled checks for which I paid him $271.00 for the evening. He had flown from Canada for that one occasion! He was the author of ten books, a parish minister for eight years and was also psychic. On our way to the airport, he told me that I would be moving to California and that I would have a successful career with much money coming my way!

Another well-known psychic, whom I had met at S.F.F., was John Scudder of Homewood, Illinois. I have a letter from his agent, Jim Hurska, confirming the date for which I had reserved the meeting room at the *Town House* for a week in the month of May. In the evenings following the workshops that week, a few of us would go to the home of Betty Harshman. I have tried to locate Scudder today on the Internet, but all I have found is the following: "John Scudder of Homewood, Illinois has been witnessed lighting up 300-volt fluorescent tubes, simply by holding them in his bare hands." He did, indeed, light up a 300-volt tube, because we saw him do it in Betty's home in Cedar Rapids, and we learned how to do it ourselves.

I had a very full upcoming schedule, including practicing my violin for the June 22-27 retreat at Carleton College. I was in eager anticipation of the retreat, when I would be seeing old friends and making new ones. There were several phenomena that I experienced at these spiritual retreats. I had requested a private session with H. Donald Davis, who served on the board of the Chicago chapter of S.F.F., was co-chairman of the study group committee and was president of the healing group at Pyramid of Light Church, of which Rev. John Scudder was the pastor. Mr. Davis was leaving after lunch to return to Chicago, but he was available to see me before lunch. I felt that our conversation was very informative. Afterwards, Leone and I went to lunch at Goodhue Hall. The seating consisted of long tables with ten people to a table. Leone sat across from me and was deeply involved in a conversation with the person next to her. I was seated at the end of the table with no one on my right side. I was sitting there thinking about the conversation I had just had with Mr. Davis. All of a sudden, as though someone had pushed me, I was almost knocked out of my chair. I even had to grab the table to keep from falling. This startling experience caused me to begin to understand more thoroughly the knowledge that the whole spectrum of human belief, as to who we are, where we come from and where our journey will take us, is what all souls will eventually experience.

After lunch, having some free time, Leone and I went to Northfield to the First National Bank to learn more about the infamous Jesse James robberies. After the evening program at the Music Hall Auditorium, at which I played my violin, sessions were held for anyone interested in further discussion of various subjects. On the last night of the retreat, Leone and I decided to go to medium Jack Young's session. We wanted to speak to him privately, as did several others. As we waited for our turn, a young lady sitting across from us suddenly stood up from her chair with a look of disbelief on her face, saying that the figure of a person had appeared over my head! Well, this sort of scared me, but knowing what I had experienced at the lunch table that same day, I surely had no doubt as to what she said she was seeing.

As usual, I hated to see the retreat come to an end. This was my fifth consecutive year at S.F.F. I'm sure Kim would have liked another week at Carol and Ray's. Upon arriving at their home prior to going on to the retreat, we were surprised and delighted to see a huge sign in their yard, welcoming Kim for her week's visit. After a short time with my family, Kim and I were on our way back to Cedar Rapids. She was now thirteen and had finally grown out of the habit of asking, "Are we there yet?"

The months of July and August were very slow with only Wednesday night dance bookings; therefore, Stretch was willing to give me time off for the trip to California. I had to start practicing for the marriage of Helen's daughter, Peggy, on July 31, at a Presbyterian church in Newport Beach, California. She liked Hawaiian music, so I decided to play The Hawaiian Love Song. Steve was in Alabama, thus I made the decision that Kim and I would fly out for the occasion. Kitty, our cat, was going on her first plane trip. I did not have to pay extra to have her in cabin with us. Also, I expected no problems with her, for she was already a seasoned automobile traveler.

My music artist friend, Will Jennings

Carol had told me previously that their friend, Will Jennings, had finally gotten a big break with his music and songwriting. Earlier this year, he was playing his last "gig" in Nashville and was planning to move back to his home town of Tyler, Texas. A member of the audience approached him with a Hollywood contract with E.M.I. (music publishing company), which meant that Will, his wife Carole and Mimsey, their cat, had moved to California. My Carol had given me Will and Carole's telephone number and suggested that I go to see them on my trip. I did call them, and they seemed pleased to hear from me and invited me to spend a night with them.

Our previous trips to California had been by car. This was to be my longest flight to date as well as Kim and Kitty's very first plane trip. We had a good flight. Also, it was nice to have a delicious meal served to us, an event which no longer occurs on domestic flights. I have a clear memory of a male flight attendant, who spoke in a very commanding voice. When he got toward the end of his regular instructions, including what to do in the event of crashing into the ocean, he said that anyone found smoking in the restroom would be asked to leave the aircraft immediately! I was a little apprehensive about Helen and Ed possibly not being at the huge LAX Airport to meet us. I had no reason to be concerned. They were waiting for us along with my mother. My father stayed in Costa Mesa so that there would be room for the rest of us..

Ed was doing very well financially in the real estate business and had purchased a nice home with four bedrooms, so there was ample room for all of us. Helen's pets, Boots and Dusty, had the run of the house, except for the room Kitty, Kim and I were using. Mother, Daddy and I met Peggy's future husband that first night at dinner. David Stapp was a nice-looking young man. He was employed with the Coca-Cola Company. We discussed the wedding plans after dinner. Helen had made arrangements for me to go to the church in nearby Newport Beach the next day. I took my violin and was able to practice The Hawaiian Wedding Song.

Mother wasn't happy about my going to Carole and Will's home for a day and a night. Helen offered to drive me to their apartment in Topanga Canyon, near Pepperdine University on the Pacific Coast Highway. They had rented a small, modest and sparsely furnished apartment. My first impression was that of seeing Will's guitar and older, light tan piano in the living room. Maybe I had a degree of insight into the success he was to have in his musical career, including both lyrics and music. I still have the two pictures I took. One was of his piano with music sheets, a small portable tape recorder and a drinking glass on top of some books. The other picture was of Will with a wide-brimmed hat on, sitting on their sofa.

Carole took me to dinner at a very nice restaurant on Pacific Coast Highway. Will stayed at home, busy with his music. As we were leaving, Carole backed into the garage, which I thought must have shaken the apartment. She didn't seem upset about it, and without even going in to tell Will what had happened, we continued on our way to the restaurant. She and I had much to talk about due to our mutual interests, meditation and metaphysics. The next morning, she took me to the Self Realization Fellowship Shrine on Sunset Boulevard in Pacific Palisades. There were ten acres of beautiful gardens and lakes, with separate gardens for Eastern and Western religions. Helen came back for me after lunch. Mother, Daddy and Kim were with her. We went for a tour of Santa Monica and Hollywood before returning to Costa Mesa.

I don't know how much my violin solo of The Hawaiian Love Song contributed to the occasion; however, it was a beautiful wedding with an attendance of around one hundred fifty. Uncle Eugene, Aunt Dorothy, Eugene, Jr. and Dorothy Ann were at the wedding. Previously, I wrote about their visit to Alabama when I was six years of age. Uncle Eugene had reserved a private room for dinner at a restaurant near his home. Uncle Nick and Aunt Catherine were there, also. After dinner, we all went to Uncle Eugene's home, on top of a hill in Mission Viejo. The wedding and our family gathering both went well.

Mother and Daddy stayed with Helen and Ed for another two weeks. Kim, Kitty and I took a Monday morning flight to Cedar Rapids. We arrived at LAX early enough for us to explore the huge facilities. As we walked along with Kitty in her carrying case, Kim saw none other than Flip Wilson with several teenagers around him. Kim immediately urged me to get his autograph for her. Flip made his debut on NBC in 1970 on a Thursday night weekly show. He was nominated for eleven Emmys and won two of them. Dean Martin, Ray Charles and Muhammad Ali were among the many guests on his show. Kim and I especially liked the character he played of Geraldine Jones. I noticed that he sometimes mentioned the name of Edgar Cayce. Remembering this gave me the courage to approach him and ask him for his autograph, telling him that anyone who was a friend of Edgar Cayce was a friend of mine. This made him laugh. I still have his autograph with the pen he used to sign it.

The ballroom activities were slow, as usual, for August. I knew that I needed to decide where I would be going when the ballroom closed and needed to prepare for my ESP classes in the fall. On August 25, I received a letter written by Barbara Parker saying that Dawson had died on August 19. Her stroke had affected her handwriting, but I was able to get the message. I later found out that he had cancer of the esophagus and passed away three or four days after that diagnosis was given.

My last semester of teaching ESP at Kirkwood College began in September. Hopefully, some of my students gained insight into their real identity as spiritual beings. I knew I would really miss the preparation needed to conduct the classes. Very soon, my years at the ballroom would be ending. Helen had liked the idea of Kim and me moving to California. After two or three months of considering the possibility of such a move and talking my son-in-law, Ray, into driving the truck with my furniture and other belongings, I made the decision to go. Steve had planned to go with Kim and me but decided to stay in Cedar Rapids, because he didn't want to leave behind his girl friend, Ruth.

The ballroom was booked with church dances, the firemen's ball and Wednesday night dances. Our New Year's Eve dance was the last event at the *Armar Ballroom* before it was razed in May 1977. So, these last months of 1976 were very busy for me with packing, work at the ballroom and gathering letters of recommendation for my job search in California. I collected some very nice letters, among them from Mabel Swanson, Unity minister; Earl Kempf, Area Supervisor of Community Education at Kirkwood College; Jim McCue, Executive Vice President of Employee Credit Union; and, of course, from Stretch Sedrel.

Steve, Kim, Kitty and I went to Waseca for Christmas. It was great just being there with our family. Ray's mother, Josie, and I had to have the stereo turned on a good bit of the time for our dancing. We always had a big turkey, on which Ray displayed his carving skills; however, we had to have two dressings, a Southern dressing (cornbread) and a Yankee dressing (bread stuffing). Ray and Josie were more Midwestern Northerners than Yankees, who prepared their dressing with bread and sage, while true Southerners put salt in our cornbread dressing and no sage and little or no sugar in it.

Ray and I finalized our plans for the move to California. I reserved a truck for January 15, 1977. Ray was to drive the truck with Carol following him in their car. I won't attempt to write Ray's account of their trip. It's one of the family stories which gets repeated over the years. I've asked him to write his version (tale of woe!), which I will include shortly.

I needed to get back to the ballroom from Waseca by December 27 to handle the reservations for the final dance on New Year's Eve. The dance proved to be bitter sweet, knowing that this was really the last dance after thirty years of operation. We had a full house with The Do's & Don'ts. I had a little over two weeks to finish packing, taking care of business details and saying good-by to my many friends.

CHAPTER 55

1977
BISHOP'S CAFETERIA

CAROL, Ray and kids arrived in Cedar Rapids on January 14. Ray picked up the truck early the next day, so that it could be loaded and ready to go the following morning. The beds were the last things to be loaded, because we needed a place to sleep that last night. The next morning, Stretch arrived with Bobby, the bus boy at the ballroom, to help with the loading. The truck was ready to go by noon on Sunday, so they left for California after lunch. My friend, Beryl Farland, had invited Kim and me to spend the night with her, so that we could get an early start on Monday morning. As we left town, I just had to stop by and say good-by to my good friend, Jessie Nagle. I was really going to miss her.

I don't remember having fears or concerns about driving across the country. After all, I had my CB (Citizen's Band) radio, which was very popular in the 70s. Neither Kim nor I can remember what her "handle" was, but mine was Madame Butterfly. I had chosen this name because I was fond of butterflies and even had a souvenir collection of them. Kim does remember that we talked to a number of truck drivers along the way. I wouldn't dare do such a thing today! We had three days of beautiful scenery—deserts, mountains and valleys. Talking on the CB radio seemed to make the trip go faster.

You, my reader, will remember that I asked my son-in-law, Ray, to relate a story about his mother and an episode from when he helped me move to California in 1977. The following comments are what he sent me:

When I married Carol in Cedar Rapids in 1967, Gene was able to become acquainted with my mother, Josie, at our wedding, and the two of them became instant friends – in no small measure because they both loved to dance and both could really rip it up out on the ballroom floor.

For many years after Carol and I were married, whenever Gene and Josie got together during Christmas or other visits, it was only a matter of time before the music was cranked up and the shimmyin' and shakin' began. One thing Carol inherited directly from her mom is a pair of dancing feet, and she always hopped in with the older girls. Boy, the three of them could boogie for hours. No slouch myself – being my mother's boy -- I would jump in and jiggle a while with style but never had their staying power.

For mothers-in-law, one couldn't ask for better friends. It was easy to see that Gene always loved Josie, whom we lost in 1985. To this day, Gene and Carol never hesitate to turn up the music and dance, but it always reminds me that someone is missing.

Maybe it's the dancing bug that has kept Gene so restless all her life. She never seemed content to stay too long in one place. Tragically, sometimes in her early years it was male brutality that drove her away, but more often it was a new opportunity or the chance to find one that put her on the road. She has moved countless times in her life, often locally but sometimes cross country. That's where I came in a few times.

Over the years, Gene has accumulated a good deal of furniture and antiques, over 40 sizable paintings, and a whopping volume of what I refer to as "stuff" – enough to pack absolutely full the largest moving trucks available for rent. She has some-times been moved professionally or by friends, but I recall personally loading up all her things and then driving long distances to unload them after moves from Iowa to California, from Florida to Alabama, from Florida to Virginia, and from Virginia to Georgia. I was 33 the first time I moved her and 64 the last time. When I was 65, she wondered if I could help with a local move in Gainesville, Georgia, but I told her my ambition had waned a little. She was coming up on 80 years old at the time but had no problem with packing and moving – with a little help from friends -- into a new home she and her new husband had found.

The most memorable move for me was the first one. Gene explains elsewhere in this book why she was so anxious to get to southern California. What I remember is her plea, "If you can drive a truck out there for me, I'll buy you a plane ticket home." After thinking about it and talking to Carol, I responded with, "If you give me the same amount of cash as a plane ticket, I'll have Carol and the kids follow me out in our car and Tommy and Suzy can see Disneyland." Gene agreed. Tommy was seven and Suzy was six years old, and we knew they'd be thrilled to meet Mickey and Donald.

As I recall, I had some help from Gene's teenaged son, my brother-in-law Steve, as we slowly loaded Gene's belongings throughout a cold winter morning in Cedar Rapids, Iowa. As I pulled away that afternoon, Tommy was excited to be riding with me in the truck, closely watching as I pressed in the clutch and pushed forward on the knob of the big gearshift stick that protruded from the truck floor. Suzy had been oddly quiet all afternoon, and I was surprised that she hadn't competed to ride with "Daddy" in the big cab instead of stretching out in the back of the big old Pontiac station wagon I had recently bought from a farmer in Minnesota.

The cab was very cold, as the temperature was around ten below zero outside, and I wondered how long it would take the engine to heat up enough to provide us with some comfort. I fiddled with the temperature setting and played with the fan as we rumbled along. After twenty minutes, it was apparent that something was wrong. Only cold air was blowing from the heater. I wasn't a great mechanic, but I could sure tell when a thermostat wasn't opening up. About this time, Carol was flashing her lights at me, so I pulled the big truck as far onto the shoulder as I could and walked with Tommy back to the warm car. Suzy had been throwing up for the last few miles and Carol couldn't help her while steering the car and trying to get my attention. I left Tommy with Carol and we headed both vehicles for Marshalltown, Iowa as quickly as possible. Once there, I found a Ford garage while Carol located medical help for Suzy. The truck repair didn't take too long, as a thermostat is easy to replace. After I met Carol at the local clinic, we learned that Suzy had strep throat and we quickly realized that she hadn't told us she was sick because she was worried that she *wouldn't get to Disneyland if she did. I don't recall where we stayed that night, but I do remember that we hadn't even gotten out of Iowa. California was looking a long way off.*

A day or two later, after driving through the Mohave Desert, we pulled into a restaurant in Barstow, California. It was supper time and I was not only hungry but completely worn out from wrestling the big rig all day. Carol went to the pay phone to call Helen, Gene's sister. Carol said we'd see them the next morning after getting some rest in Barstow. To my amazement, Carol came back to the table saying that Helen was insisting that we push on to spend the night at her house. I wasn't sure of the distance but knew we would have a pretty late arrival if we drove through, and I didn't think it was safe.

As Carol returned to the table from a second call, I could see from the look on her face that Helen had left us no choice, so I ordered a pot of coffee to brace myself for the final session with that big steering wheel. We pulled out from the restaurant in the twilight with Suzy already falling asleep, stretched out beside me along the vinyl bench seat. Shortly after I turned onto the highway heading south, I noticed around six big eighteen-wheeler rigs lined up along the right shoulder, partially obscuring a sign that said something about checking brakes. As I passed the front truck, I saw a yellow sign in the corner of my eye with the symbol of a truck on a very steep hill, and that's when the fun began.

I was rapidly picking up speed as the truck tilted down the top of a very long and very steep incline. As I was pumping the brakes and trying to downshift to slow the truck's momentum, Suzy began sliding off the seat in her sleep. I managed to hold her up on the seat with my right arm while I steered the racing truck with my left. I couldn't slow it down, so I began weaving across multiple downhill lanes around slower vehicles in front of me. I was terrified but resolute that I wouldn't hurt my child. Somehow, after what felt like a lifetime inside five or ten minutes, I careened safely to the bottom of the mountain, but it took me another two or three miles to get the truck fully under control and steer safely onto the shoulder. All the while, as I was soon to learn, Carol stayed right behind me, fully convinced that I had fallen asleep or lost my mind.

After getting lost just a few miles from our final destination, we limped up Helen's driveway around 3:00 a.m. Fool that I was, I figured that was the closing chapter in moving my beloved mother-in-law. A few days later we headed home, with me dozing in the back of the Pontiac, still worn out, and Carol driving along with the kids chattering happily about Mickey, Donald, and Goofy.

When Kim and I arrived at Helen's in Costa Mesa, the truck with my furniture was there in the driveway. The next step was to unload and put everything in Helen and Ed's garage. Carol and Ray were going to stay a few days, because they had promised Tom and Suzy that they would take them to Disneyland. After a day of rest, much needed by all of us, off we went to Anaheim!

I enrolled Kim in school the following Monday. After two or three weeks, Kim hated the new school and missed her old friends. I began to think more and more, *why did I leave Cedar Rapids?* It seemed that I had burned my bridges behind me. I knew Helen would really be upset, if I said I wanted to go back.

After six weeks I called Stretch and told him Kim and I were very unhappy. He said he would fly out and drive us and our belongings back to Cedar Rapids. However, he was quick to let me know he was not going to do it again! I really think he wanted to go to California, because he had told me he always wanted to visit Dr. Robert Schuler's Crystal Cathedral in Garden Grove. The church was close to Costa Mesa. Helen, Ed, Kim and I had gone there several times since returning to California. I had attended a singles' meeting which was held once a week. I even took my résumé to the church. I cannot remember actually looking for a job any place else.

On February 20, Jessie had written to tell me of Mabel Swanson's death the day before. She said that Mabel had lived a good, long, full life and that we should think of it as her being active up until this time. Eighty-five is pretty old. Of course, when we reach eighty-five, we don't think of it as being old, do we? No, we didn't think of it as old for Jessie and I were not far from that age. We found that we had many things in common, such as our love for books, dancing and high-heeled shoes! We hated it when ugly, square-heeled shoes came into style in the 90s. We felt that they did nothing for a person's legs. Jessie, however, was a great swimmer, while I did not swim at all. She was an astrologer for twenty-seven years. In her letter of March 11, 1977, she wrote, "I'm going to be on TV on April 01 (no connection with April Fool's Day!). It is that new show of Marlyce Heidt, patterned after the Johnny Carson Show. She interviews three people on each show. It will be live, starting on March 21. Marlyce promised not to have any telephone calls the day I'm on." Undoubtedly, Jessie's expertise as an astrologer was the focus point of the interview. In the same letter, she asked if I had gotten a job yet. I had not told her that I was coming back to Cedar Rapids.

Stretch arrived from Cedar Rapids on March 17. Two days later, he was able to attend a service at the Crystal Cathedral. We sat in the huge balcony. He was very impressed with Dr. Schuler and the beautiful church building. On our way back from the church, we stopped at U-Haul and reserved a truck and a trailer hitch so that my car could be towed. Stretch drove the truck to Helen's, where he and Ed loaded it for the trip. We were soon on our way back to Cedar Rapids!

We left Costa Mesa, arrived in Cedar Rapids, and the truck was once again unloaded at my old apartment at the ballroom on March 24, 1977! One fleeting memory is of Kim, Kitty and I riding in the U-Haul truck with Stretch at the wheel and my concern that my car would become disconnected from the truck. Oh yes, our CB radio was packed, because Stretch would not hear of Kim and me talking with other drivers along the way.

Finding an apartment was my first priority, followed by enrolling Kim in the proper school district. Also, I needed to find employment as soon as possible. These three needs were quickly met! I located a very nice apartment in the Pheasant Run Complex, with the move-in date set for May 16. It was located on the Northwest side of Cedar Rapids; therefore, until we moved in May, I had to take Kim from the ballroom on the East side of the city to her school on the Northwest side. The Cedar Rapids Gazette ran a large ad in the Classified Section for a hostess position at *Bishop's Cafeteria*, which was located in downtown Cedar Rapids on First Avenue. *Bishop's* was a state-wide chain of restaurants with two locations in Cedar Rapids. I applied for the job, and I was hired right away. Later, I was told by the home office management that I was chosen over ninety applicants. I don't think I ever believed that little bit of information! It was a coveted job in the restaurant field. *Bishop's* was known for delicious food and great service. My specific task was to greet customers as they reached the end of the serving line. Then, I would tell the tray carrier the exact table at which she was to seat the customers. In the foyer, as one entered the cafeteria, there were two 11" x 14" framed photographs, one of the manager, Mr. Stufflebean, and one of yours truly.

Bishop's home office sent me to their Lindale Mall location in Cedar Rapids for two weeks of special hostess training by Ms. Ann Burrie. I found her to be very thorough and efficient as well as a very pretty young lady, well liked by employees and customers alike. When my training ended, I started my new position at the downtown *Bishop's* with a pretty good level of confidence. Our busiest days were Saturdays and Sundays; therefore, my two off-days were Tuesdays and Wednesdays. Any nervousness or special concerns I might have had about starting a new job disappeared quickly. I liked the management and the employees very much. I also enjoyed working with the public and making new friends. My split-shift was 10 to 2 and 5 to 9, which was perfect for me, as it allowed me to get Kim off to school in the mornings and pick her up in the afternoons. I had made friends with a lady in the apartment complex. She would take care of Kim until I was home from work. I was so pleased with my new job that it didn't bother me at all to walk out of *Bishop's* every day and see the new Stouffer's Hotel under construction. After all, the main factor in the decision of the owners of the *Armar* to close the ballroom was that the Stouffer's would be taking much of their business. The ESP classes continued at Washington High School on Tuesday evenings. I had several students and friends who were interested in The Infinite Way, so they would come to my apartment on Wednesday evenings to listen to the tapes.

Many of the tray carriers and busboys were teenagers who worked mostly on weekends. I have remembered them over the years with much fondness, as we really worked well together. As I was standing at the end of the serving line, I noticed the tray carriers and the bus boys all looking at the entrance of the cafeteria. Well, it was a little unusual to see seven or eight African young men standing in line. Two or three had marks on their faces. I later learned that they were in Cedar Rapids to attend classes at Rockwell International/Collins Radio. Over the following weeks they returned for their evening meal. Part of my duties as hostess was to speak to the diners as they were eating.

One evening, I had a conversation with several of these young men. I discovered that one of them was interested in extra sensory perception, and was even familiar with Joel Goldsmith. His name was Bright Aregs. When I told him of my class at Kirkwood, he later enrolled. He was also interested in listening to my Joel Goldsmith tapes, so I invited him to meet with the group. I introduced him to Kim and Steve. When he finished his Rockwell/Collins classes, he returned to his home in Nigeria. We stayed in touch by mail.

Rosa Sanford was a friend I knew from Unity Church. She had a large, beautifully furnished condominium in a four-story building in Cedar Woods Hills. She called and asked if I would be interested in leasing the unit above her on the third floor. I liked the idea of living on the Northeast side of the city again, and it was closer to Washington High School for my classes. Also, Steve wanted to live with us. The condo was certainly spacious. I wouldn't have to worry about his drum playing, as he had rented an office downtown on Second Avenue, where he could play at night without disturbing anyone.

I really didn't have the nerve to ask my son-in-law to come to Cedar Rapids to move me across town, so I had to call a local furniture mover. On October 03, we moved into our new home. This was also Kim's fourteenth birthday; however, she seemed happy to be arranging her own bedroom. If Kitty had had the ability to talk, she probably would have told me, "About the time I get used to my new home, you go and move again!" Steve moved in the next day. I was feeling pretty good about the fact that after forty-nine years of ups and downs in my life, I had finally signed my first year's housing lease. But, Boy! Did I ever have a big lesson to learn about the signing of a lease. If you abhor noises as I do, you know that you don't sign a lease without first checking out the habits of your neighbors under, over and on all sides of you, along with the soundproofing of the walls and ceiling. After a few mornings, I realized that the person sleeping in the room over my bedroom was getting up at five o'clock every morning, and the floor would squeak with each heavy step taken. After trying to ignore the problem for several days, I started sleeping on the living room sofa. Now I didn't feel so good about signing the lease. I complained to the apartment manager-- but to no avail. I tried to keep the year's lease, but after seven months of disrupted sleep, annoyance and irritation, I decided I had to move, lease or no lease! This time I would not be looking for a condo or an apartment. Someone at work told me about a house on 19th Street which was even closer to *Bishop's* and my ESP classes at Washington High School. I liked the house. It had living room, dining room and kitchen on the first floor, then two bedrooms and a bath on the second floor, followed by a loft bedroom above the second floor. The basement was partially finished and had a bathroom, which was just perfect for Steve.

I don't recall having signed a lease on 19th Street; however, I do remember the threat still being made by the management of Cedar Woods Hills, where I lived previously. After installing the drapes and curtains the new location began to look like a real home. I was getting that good feeling of being able to provide a nice home for my family. In addition to this comfortable place for us to live, I was able to purchase my first new car! I arranged the financing at Peoples Bank. The assistant manager at *Bishop's*, Tom Shirbine, had fallen in love with a cashier. His new wife, Jan, had just bought a '79 Ford Mustang, and it only had

20 miles on the odometer. They felt they didn't need two cars, so they sold me the Mustang.

The previous Christmas was the first one for which we had not gone to Minnesota since Carol and her family had lived there. I had not been on my new job long enough to have any days off. Kim, Steve and I were very disappointed that we were not able to go. However, we did have great news from Carol and Ray. Tommy and Suzy were quite excited when they were told by their parents that they were soon going to have either a brother or sister. They were told not to tell anyone this news as yet. But Suzy was not able to contain her excitement. The next day she went directly to the school principal and proudly announced, "My mother is going to have a baby!" April 07, 1978 marked the arrival of Benjamin Clark. He was given the middle name of Clark after my father. Mother was quite happy over their choice of this name. Although I was thankful for my job at *Bishop's*, I really didn't like the fact that I couldn't visit my family when I wanted to or needed to. Of course, now I needed to go see my new grandson, Ben. After we were settled in on 19th Street, I was able to get *one* day off. So, we went to Waseca on Monday and arrived back home on Wednesday. Ben was certainly a handsome, healthy boy! If I am sounding like a proud mother and grandmother, well, I am! As a matter of fact, I am proud of my entire family.

After Tom's birth in Sioux City, Iowa, Carol and Ray moved to Eau Claire, Wisconsin, where he taught English at the University of Wisconsin. The reader may recall that Suzy was born there. With Tom and Suzy, Carol soon found the time for more serious study, having taken piano lessons for a short time as a child. Under the guidance of a local piano legion, Harold Konrad, who had lost his sight in a childhood accident, she began studying with him. He was also known for other skills, such as muskie fishing, a winning cribbage player and, to the great distress of his neighbors, shoveling the snow off of his roof. Carol and her family moved to Waseca in 1972 so that Ray could join the faculty at the University of Minnesota, Waseca. It was there, long after receiving a college theater scholarship, that Carol became active in Community Theater. Josie, Ray's mother, and I were in the audience for her first performance as a mute in the production of The Fantastic (1973) and, a year later, for her lead role as the blind woman in Wait Until Dark.

Our two nights and one day visit quickly ended, and we were on our way back to Cedar Rapids. I must say that Kim, Steve and I were a little upset to learn that Carol and the family were going to leave Waseca in a few months, moving to Sioux Falls, South Dakota. Ray was making a career change and would be in the land satellite imagery field with the United States Geological Survey. The new job sounded great, but Sioux Falls was a long way from Cedar Rapids for us to visit from time to time. I could hardly get one extra day off from work.

CHAPTER 56

1978
HELPING HANDS

MY work at *Bishop's* was so different from the years I spent at the ballroom. Kim was now a teenager, and I had always been at home for her. Now, of course, I had to work away from home. She and Steve would quite often get into heated arguments. They would end up calling me at work, which created tension between the manager and me.

My next six months at *Bishop's* were just not the same. It soon became obvious to me that Mr. Stufflebean was not happy with me as his hostess. After talking to the home office management, I decided to give a month's notice. The general manager gave me a very good letter of recommendation. I had never left a job under these conditions. I must admit that my ego was slightly bruised and, of course, this was contrary to Infinite Way teaching. In October 1978, I applied for unemployment. With the $200 rent money from Steve and the unemployment check, I managed to make ends meet. I was very appreciative of the party given to me by the tray carriers and bus boys. One of the best things about my job at *Bishop's* was the very good relationship with them. I was deeply touched by their caring so much for me that they had a going-away party for me. The pictures I took of them at the party have meant so much to me down through the years.

I spent a lot of time searching the want ads of the Cedar Rapids Gazette. I finally found an ad which caught my eye. It was in sales, conducting parties in homes and selling dishes, pots and pans. I called and applied for the job. It seemed like the kind of job that would lend itself to my being home more with Kim and Steve. A young man came to our home to sign me up and start the training process. I was required to purchase a sales kit made up of a few dishes, pots and pans, which I have used over the years. Two or three things remain in my memory about this job experience. I learned the meaning of "planned obsolescence." The sales manager said, "Pots and pans were made so that they would not stand much wear and tear." Thus, they would soon have to be replaced. This was what he called "planned obsolescence." It was quite a shock to find out that I would be required to go to Amarillo, Texas for a two-day trip with several new recruits as a part of our training. We were given plane tickets which made it sound kind of exciting to me. My friend, Beryl Farland, took care of Kim while I was gone. So, off I went to Texas with the hope of learning to sell pots and pans. After a full day of training, the other three trainees and I were flying back to Cedar Rapids at midnight. We were the only passengers on the aircraft! Another thing I remember is that I was convinced that selling pots and pans was not my area of expertise!

It is so difficult to put into practice what you have been reading and studying when you are in the midst of your own human struggles. God is my supply, and He never leaves me. He is right there to make the crooked places straight. This deep knowing of truth seemingly slipped away from me. I was soon so mired down in self pity and doubt that I was headed straight for the dark night of my soul. This is like having months of deep depression hitting you all at once. I finally realized that I had to let go … and let God! To me, this meant to go into meditation, and God would show me the way. Go into the closet and pray is what that Bible verse means to me. When we achieve the alpha state in meditation we are where we receive our answers. No need to tell God, for He certainly knows our need. Just be still and listen! So, on a Sunday afternoon in the middle of October, I went into a long meditation.

When I came out, I knew all the steps I needed to take in order to start my own business. I had been thinking about a business I wanted to try but had no idea how to begin. Now, I had the whole plan laid out for me. My business idea was to employ part-time workers, such as high school students, housewives, etc., and place them where needed. On that Sunday afternoon, I not only had the steps I needed to take, but I had the name for my business and, later the same day, I had sketched the logo I would be using for advertising. The very next day, I went to the courthouse and took the first steps to set up "Helping Hands." I called Peoples Bank and reserved a room for the night of October 25. I placed an ad in the classified section of the Gazette making my business and services known to the public. The effort was quite successful, for fifty people showed up and applied for employment with me. A key individual in the group was Betty Peterson, age 51. She was a valuable employee, helping me to get the business started. On November 04, I received my legal trade name of Helping Hands. With the services of my attorney friend, Bill Roemerman, it became Helping Hands Corporation. He continues to have a successful law business today.

The Classified Department at the Gazette was very helpful in getting my logo formulated to fit a 3" x 3" advertisement. Two telephone lines kept me quite busy. I was thankful that Betty was there to help me when I needed to leave for business appointments. Some months before, she had her picture and a four-column interview by free-lance writer Art Hough published in the Gazette. Her ministry had been to American Indians through an organization called CHIEF (Christian Hope Indian Eskimo Fellowship, Inc.). In her mission work she traveled from California to New York. She would walk as far as she could and would then get a ride to the next town, where she would ask the police for a place to stay overnight. When she arrived in Cedar Rapids she attended Kirkwood Community College, where she received a degree in pre-social work and certificates in several other areas. Betty's walking into Peoples Bank on October 25 to me <u>was</u> Divine Intervention.

My business was progressing faster than I had imagined with more than thirty employees who consisted of housewives and high school students filling the jobs for my clients. My largest client was Stouffer's Civic Center, followed by Cedar Memorial Cemetery. Others were Kelleys, Inc., Roosevelt Hotel, The Department of Welfare and private homes. When my VISA machine was delivered and my first check arrived from Stouffer's in the amount of $1,267.09, it was becoming absolutely clear to me that without having gone into deep meditation on that Sunday afternoon, this business simply would not have happened! In and of myself, I could not have accomplished this business venture. Neither Betty nor I knew very much about bookkeeping or payroll taxes to be sent to the Internal Revenue Service; however, Betty told me that if I called SCORE (Counselors to America's Small Business), I might qualify for their services. I did so and learned that SCORE was a non-profit association dedicated to educating entrepreneurs and the formation, growth and success of small business nationwide. That call resulted in my receiving the services of SCORE counselor Les Wright, who was very helpful and encouraging.

The old house on 19th Street was beginning to feel more like home to Steve, Kim and me, that is, until a bat got inside. I discovered it in the drapes at the top of the stairs. I called the Humane Society, and someone from there got it out for us. I can't think of anything any worse unless maybe a rat or a snake! Another traumatic happening on 19th Street with a wonderful spiritual ending concerned Stretch having a heart attack and going to the hospital. His entire family was called in after the doctor had given up hope for his recovery. He and his family were like a real family to us. Kim and Stretch were especially close, for he had been like a father to her. Iz, his wife, had called to advise me of his condition. Of course, I was very upset.

This led me to call Virginia Stephenson at her home in Hawaii. She was one of Joel Goldsmith's students who carried on the healing practice of The Infinite Way after Joel's death. I had visited her at her home in California. She had moved to Hawaii shortly after my visit. I knew of cases in which God had used her as an instrument for healing. Almost as soon as the call went through and she was on the line, also without my explaining the reason for my calling her, only that I had a problem, she said, "Gene, go lie down." I hung up the phone and did as she said. In a matter of seconds, I had a feeling of total peace. This took place about 6:30 p.m. At that time Iz and her sister were sitting together in Stretch's room at the hospital. Iz turned and said to her, "You know, I think Stretch is going to be all right." He recovered and was able to go back to work and lived until 1994!

CHAPTER 57

1979
A STUDENT AT KIRKWOOD

HELPING Hands, Inc. becoming a franchise? True, I was very happy with the growth of the business as well as positive comments I was receiving from the business community. For example, one of the owners of an advertising firm, Robert Schubert, of Creswell, Munsell, Schubert & Cerbel, Inc., spoke to me about my business becoming a franchise. Also, the students from the Cedar Rapids schools who worked after school hours and on weekends found the opportunity to be a benefit to themselves as well as to the business. The following is an excerpt of a letter I received from College Community Schools in March 1979 and is proof of the support I was beginning to receive: *I want to again thank you for employing several of our students in our Work Experience Program. It is very pleasing to note that the response from employers concerning evaluations was excellent. You are to be commended for your time and effort. We feel that this is a very important part of our school curriculum because it gives students the opportunity to gain valuable work experience and be able to earn extra money while attending school. Sincerely, Robert T. Jennings, Work Study Coordinator*

The idea of my attending Kirkwood Community College to investigate the possibility of my being a student there for my first year of college was becoming a reality and not just a dream which I had over the previous ten years. I certainly needed more knowledge and expertise that I might gain by taking college business courses. On the other hand, how did I think I could run a new business and have time to go to school? A few months went by before I could summon the courage to go to Kirkwood and check it out. Well, you can imagine the elation I felt as I enrolled for my first year of college! At the same time, I was afraid I might not be able to pass the courses. I certainly never was a good student, getting through my prior schooling with a "C" average or below. Nevertheless, with all my doubts, I started night classes in September 1979 and completed my first year of college in May 1980. Among others, the courses I took that year were the following: Small Business Organization, Advertising, Essentials of Marketing, Personnel Management, Quantity Food Purchasing, Menu Planning and Food Merchandising, Principles of Selling. The first semester, my grades were my traditional "C" average; however, the second semester I rose to an "A" average! I was pretty proud of myself but, at the same time, I knew that my success had come from divine guidance. I, on my own, could not have made it. The surprising thing about my long-awaited college experience was that I really enjoyed the studies and the homework. I guess I was what is known as a late bloomer, that is, a "very" late bloomer, because I was then fifty-one years of age!

The business was progressing, and I was very grateful to have Betty working for me as well as the much-needed advice of the SCORE counselor. Perhaps I should have taken a bookkeeping course, because I had to make the payroll for my employees. I became increasingly concerned that the IRS was going to "get" me. I was doing the payroll one afternoon and hurried downstairs to check the stove and about five or six steps from the bottom, I fell the rest of the way down! My first thought was like a command to my subconscious (a method I had used since my early ballroom days, when I operated the popcorn machine for the dances), "I will not be hurt. I have to go to class!" Consequently, I had no ill effects. I got myself ready, zipped up my boots and went to class. The command to my subconscious must have had a little fear in it, because that night, sitting in class, one of my legs began to throb, and I had a hard time getting my boot off of that foot when I got home. I do know that our thoughts have an effect on the well-being of our whole person. To this day, I continue to use this positive way of thinking. The result has been a large degree of success over the years.

Les Wright suggested that I might qualify for a small business loan. My letter to Senator John Culver regarding the possibility of federal assistance brought a quick response telling me he would be sending a copy of his letter along with my letter about my business to the local HACAP (Hawkeye Area Community Action Program). HACAP was less responsive than was Senator Culver. Also, I was becoming increasingly nervous over not having insurance for my employees. The high cost of insurance contributed to my problem. The thoughts of self doubt and lack of ability to keep the business afloat sank into my subconscious being but, then, I remembered how it had all started that Sunday afternoon in October of the preceding year. I was becoming very confused. From the beginning, Helping Hands had been a successful venture. It had its origin and development through me with God leading me every step of the way. So, what was happening to my faith? Through all my confusion, trials and struggles, God was there to lift my spirit and give me strength and guidance to carry on.

CHAPTER 58

1980
MOVE TO SIOUX FALLS, SOUTH DAKOTA

BETTY had certainly led an interesting life in her mission trips across the country. What courage she must have had. She was so determined to do what she believed God had called her to do that she was willing to give up the comforts of home and travel extensively without the security of knowing where her next meal or bed would be available. She told me many of her amazing stories. She would jokingly say, "Gene, you don't have the finesse to eat out of garbage cans." I would think, "I hope she didn't have to do that!" However, I was never sure if she had actually done this. Knowing that she was on her way to New York when she stopped in Cedar Rapids was a concern to me. I didn't know what I would do if she left. Since I was going to school, my studies took up much of my time, and she was there to take care of the scheduling of my employees, answer the telephone and help me with the payroll. She did promise, however, that she would not leave me until I finished my first year at Kirkwood in June.

My small business organization instructor expressed a desire to purchase Helping Hands. Looking back, I'm not sure why I didn't accept his offer. It had been several months since my initial application to HACAP with no reply from them that I was going to receive a loan. So, my thoughts were that I should go into the food and beverage services, in which I had years of experience in almost every phase of the industry. I began to put more time and effort into my food and beverage-related classes. As a part of our final grade, we were required to attend a four-day convention of the National Restaurant Association, to be held at McCormick Place in Chicago. I had heard of this organization; however, I had no idea how many people would be in attendance. Three of my classmates (much younger than I) traveled with me in my car to attend the convention, May 24-27. We were all very excited to be there.

We had reservations at the Ritz Carlton on North Michigan Avenue. We were glad to find out that all we had to do was walk to the corner and catch a bus to McCormick Place. If you missed one, you could get another in fifteen minutes, and the bus ride was free! I had arranged for Betty to stay in my house for the four days I would be gone to take care of Kim, prepare meals for her and Steve and keep an eye on the business. The hotel was very close to Macy's, formerly Marshall Fields. My Ford Mustang stayed several floors up in the hotel parking facility, with one exception, and that was when the four of us went to dinner at The Bakery, where I dined for the first time on Beef Wellington. It continues to be my favorite beef dish! On the last day, I went down to the hotel catering office, where I talked with the manager and gave him my résumé. Little did I realize that seven years later my career would bring me back to the other side of Michigan Avenue across from the famous Chicago Water Tower.

The next morning we began our return trip to Cedar Rapids. The girls chatted excitedly about the events of the last four days, while I was mostly in deep thought over the career path I should follow in my life. The convention had me thinking that perhaps my years of experience in the food and beverage field was safer than continuing with the Helping Hands Corporation which had no insurance coverage for the employees. Remembering how it began made the decision to move in a different direction all the more difficult for me. Was I simply scared and lacking in courage and faith?

Back at Kirkwood Community College I finished my first year of college! You would have thought I had just completed my PhD to hear me talk about it. After all, my school grades had never been very good.

Betty was getting anxious to leave for New York. Without the small business loan and with no insurance, I gradually discontinued Helping Hands. My sister, Helen, had been urging me to move back to California, and I realized that I would have more opportunity in the food service field on the west coast. However, Kim and I had not been very happy with our last move to California. Steve, Kim and I had gone to Sioux Falls, South Dakota to spend last Christmas with Carol and Ray and their children. They had bought a new home, and we liked it a lot. So far, Ray had not complained too much about moving me and my belongings; however, for him to come to Cedar Rapids to move us might be a different story! Being the great son-in-law that he had proven to be, we began to make plans and preparations for the move before the beginning of school for Kim. Steve would not be moving with us, as he had rented a very nice apartment in Cedar Tower. Also, he did not want to leave his new girl friend, Barbara.

I fulfilled my Helping Hands commitments and made the decision to move to Sioux Falls. Ray must not have minded moving us. He even located a very nice duplex for us at 316 West 34th Street, not far from their home. June and July were busy months with packing and caring for business details. Also, I had to be thinking about what kind of work I would be doing following the move. Sioux Falls did not appear to be an ideal setting for my work qualifications, but I was sure that my excellent letters of reference would help me in my search. One of them was from United States Senator John Culver, dated June 02, 1980, in which, among other things, he said, "I have known Ms. Gene Winn for a number of years and have always found her to be most helpful and courteous. ... Her business experience and training, both as employee and self-employed small business operator, should be ample evidence of her qualifications for employment."

Another letter was from Donald J. Canney, Mayor of Cedar Rapids, dated June 03, 1980, in which he stated, "It gives me a great deal of pleasure to recommend Ms. Gene Winn for a position of responsibility. She has been employed as Business Manager of Armar Ballroom of Cedar Rapids for approximately the past ten years. During this time, I have had an opportunity to observe her organizational abilities in arranging and coordinating large events in conjunction with the Ballroom. These events ranged from national political promotional events to statewide municipal meetings to the local Policemen's Ball. To the best of my knowledge, she has done an outstanding job as Business Manager. I feel that she would be an asset to any firm that would employ her." During this busy time I was happy to be moving closer to Carol and Ray and the children with a sense of excitement over new beginnings. At the same time, my thoughts would turn to the question, "I wonder if I'll be able to find a suitable job." Time would tell!

I do not recall the details of the moving day, but it was on Friday, August 01. Kitty the Cat was not a bit upset, as she had been through three out-of-state moves as well as a few in Cedar Rapids. Ray was becoming a professional mover by now, which provided good treatment for my furniture. We said good-by to Steve with plans for him to spend Christmas with us in Sioux Falls.

Kim and I were very happy with the duplex Ray had found for us. It had a nicely finished bedroom and bath in the basement. Kim's provincial furniture looked very good in her bedroom. Carol and Ray's home was only a few blocks away. Tom, Suzy and Kim enjoyed Tuthill Park, located halfway between our homes. So, it was beginning to look as though the right move had been made. I already had friends there: Harriet Geigh and several others who attended Spiritual Frontiers at Carleton College.

Now, if only I could find a good job! However, there was not much to look for, taking into account my background experience. It was very clear that my funds were getting quite low. All the while, I was trying to pass my spiritual test, knowing that God was my supply. Humanly, it is very difficult not to give in to stress and worry. Did God not supply my needs in an amazing way with Helping Hands? Well, I was in for much more difficult and trying times ahead. Searching the classified section of the local newspaper, I found an advertisement for a position with Woodman's Insurance. The applicant would receive a small salary while training to take the State Insurance Examination, which was required in order to become a duly licensed life insurance agent. This certainly was a different career goal for me, and I wasn't sure I would like going door to door. I knew several insurance agents who were successful, and I certainly needed a job!

So, I applied at the Woodman office which was located very close to my duplex; nevertheless, I did not know if I would like selling and, also, I was dubious about passing the State exam. After a few weeks of hard study, I passed the exam and had my certified State of South Dakota Life Insurance Agent's License, dated December 04, 1980. You were sent out with your trainer. You weren't given any leads. You had to get them on your own. After two or three weeks, or perhaps four, I didn't dislike this kind of selling, *I hated it!!* It was by far the worst job I had ever had.

Kim was feeling the same way about her classes at Lincoln High School. It appeared that this move was a big mistake! I just didn't know what to do. Oh yes, I would meditate, but I didn't seem to get much comfort or answer to my prayers. Kim wanted to go back to her classmates at Metro High School in Cedar Rapids. While there, she had met a very nice lady who was a counselor, named Mary. Kim called her. When Mary heard about her situation, she and her husband, Bill, offered to have Kim live with them, attend school and help them with their three younger children. Bill was an executive at Coe College, a nationally recognized four-year liberal arts college, which was founded in 1851. My sister, Helen, kept encouraging me to move to California to live with her and Ed until I found employment. I was very upset about leaving Kim in Cedar Rapids and my moving to California alone; however, this seemed to be the only way open to me.

Steve and Barbara, now his fiancée, arrived the day before Christmas. I really had been looking forward to having all of the family together; however, the intense dislike of my new employment and the indecision about what to do somewhat dampened my Christmas spirit. In spite of my uneasy feeling about *"What am I going to do?"* we still had a great time together.

CHAPTER 59

1981
ANOTHER MOVE TO CALIFORNIA

I DO believe that there are no mistakes in our lives. God gives us free will and in the life choices we make, it sometimes appears to be the wrong way. So, in my meditation and inner pondering to God (in simple human terms), I believed I had made a good decision to move to Sioux Falls and, after passing a difficult State exam in order to be an agent at Woodman Insurance, I disliked the job so much I was going to have to quit. Now, what was I to do?

My answer this time didn't come as quickly as it did with Helping Hands, so I began to think more about Helen and Ed's invitation and moving in with them in Mira Loma, California. As heartbreaking as it was to leave Carol and her family in Sioux Falls and Kim and Steve in Cedar Rapids, it quickly became my choice to leave my short-lived job as an insurance agent. I'm sure my boss realized that the position was not appropriate for me. What does one do when she has to move with no money? I had a house full of furniture and a Baldwin piano. I sold the piano for five hundred dollars. With the sale of my furniture, with the exception of my roll-top desk, I had enough money to make the move. My 2012 computer monitor occupies a prominent place on the desk in my home office today. It is a top-quality piece of furniture to have been moved so many times around the country over the years and be in service today in Northeast Georgia!

I had to take Kim to Cedar Rapids to get her settled with Mary and her family. I had many mixed feelings as I drove back to Sioux Falls. I was a little nervous about driving to California with a rental trailer hitched to my car. Helen was visiting Mother and Daddy in Alabama at the time. So, I quickly ordered my AAA map and plotted my route, going by way of Montgomery to pick her up for the trip west. I cannot recall any problems encountered on the entire trip, but I do remember being concerned about leaving the trailer overnight outside a motel room and someone taking all of my earthly possessions! Kitty was a good traveler, probably thinking that my moving so much was the normal thing to do.

Ed's real estate business had declined so much that he had to sell their home in Costa Mesa. He decided to relocate to Mira Loma near Riverside. He purchased a very nice double-wide mobile home, located at Swan Lake Adult Country Estates. I had never seen such a beautiful mobile home park. All of the homes were new, each one located on a large lot with a two-car carport. The grounds were covered with all kinds of flowers and shrubbery, and pathways wound around the lake, making it an excellent location for walking. Helen and I took a daily afternoon walk, that is, until I went to work. It was on an afternoon walk when, all of a sudden, I was attacked! Whatever made one of the swans come after me, I will never know! There were many swans in the lake and around it, and I really thought they were beautiful. It never occurred to me that one of them might attack me. He chased me quite a distance with me trying to get away from him. Helen and Ed had to come to my rescue.

After a few days of getting the car and trailer unpacked, getting settled, and prior to my search for employment in the Riverside area, Helen and I decided we would visit Uncle Eugene (I was named "Gene" for him!) in Mission Viejo and Uncle Nick in Redondo Beach. This meant that we had to travel approximately three hundred miles round trip. So, we made an early start. Uncle Nick and Aunt Catherine's condo was located very close to the beach. As we traveled there I noticed an employment agency. Uncle Nick took us out to lunch. Soon afterwards, we left for Uncle Eugene and Aunt Dorothy's home.

As we drove back by the employment agency, I decided to go in and see what was involved in getting a position with them. I really did not think I would find a job immediately, nor did I care to be so far away from Helen and Ed. To my great surprise, I had an interview for the next day at the United Church of Religious Science, located on West Sixth Street in Los Angeles. That was really amazing! I had taken a correspondence course from this very church while at the ballroom in Cedar Rapids. Instead of going to Uncle Eugene's as planned, we went back to Helen's home to prepare for the next day. As interesting as the job appeared to be, I didn't think I would get it, and it would be a long way for me to drive back and forth.

At any rate, what made me think I could be an executive secretary? I had never even been a secretary of any kind. However, when the interview ended, I was offered the position. My boss was impressed that I had taken the correspondence course. I was hired on a three-month trial basis. So, with my lack of typing skills and no previous secretarial experience, I began to realize the first week on the job that I would not be able to perform my duties as required. However … I did stay for three months! I regretted very much my lack of secretarial skills.

The church was an old two-story brick building with long, wide hallways that were lined with big statues of previous ministers and church dignitaries. The sanctuary seated around two thousand. I found this to be a great place for meditation on many of my breaks, as I could feel a sense of peace and serenity. There were ten to twelve office suites in the church building, each having secretaries who were friendly and helpful to me. One of the ladies became my life-long friend, Elizabeth Joyce. Unlike me, she was a very efficient executive secretary. She made a special effort to help me that first week. When she learned of my long freeway travel to get to work, she made an offer which I accepted right away. She said, "I have a two-bedroom condo in Culver City. I have been thinking that I would like to rent the extra bedroom. The rent is $315.00, and you can move in right away. You know, Culver City is about twenty minutes from the church, a lot closer than Swan Lake." Helen didn't want me to leave her and Ed, but she understood that I needed to be closer to my work. Helen's son-in-law, David, moved Kitty and me with my belongings the next Saturday afternoon. So, Kitty had to leave Helen's cat, Boots; however, she would have Elizabeth's cat, Astrid, with which to play.

The church held seminars, and employees were allowed to attend. One of them stands out in my mind. Elizabeth and I were seated right behind the movie star, Robert Young. Another memory involves a long blue dress I purchased at a church sale. I still have that dress which belonged to the Bionic Woman, Lindsey Wagner.

My introduction to the Santa Ana winds was on my way home from work. While eating lunch one day, the girls were talking about the forecast of impending strong winds. My Mustang was getting in need of repair; e.g., the air conditioning was not working. So, I was happy that there were going to be refreshing winds on my way home. To my dismay, that was not the case! No one mentioned to me that the Santa Ana winds were HOT!

My trial basis ended, and I had to begin the search for a new job. Uncle Nick and Aunt Catherine came to Culver City to visit me and to give me a check for $1,000 which was greatly appreciated. If I didn't find employment soon, I would have to return to Swan Lake, due to not having funds to pay my rent to Elizabeth. I returned to the same agency which had sent me to the church. I feel certain that I informed them of the reason for my departure. Incidentally, the employer paid the agency a fee for the person they decided to hire. It seems that the agency should have been more careful where they were sending me, knowing of my lack of office skills.

They sent me to an interview at the Epicurean Hollywood Park Racetrack in Inglewood, California. The fee to the agency was $2,500 ... and I was hired! I was to work in their bookkeeping department. So, since moving to California four months before, I had been hired for two jobs, jobs for which I was *not* qualified! I had never been an executive secretary or a bookkeeper, but Inglewood was not far from Elizabeth's condo, and I did not want to move.

The head bookkeeper and the girls in the office were very nice and did their best to help me. The general manager was away when I was hired. After about three weeks, he returned and was very unhappy that a large fee had been paid to the employment agency for me. Therefore, I was not too perturbed to be given my walking papers. With my California experiences to date, I began to think that I perhaps should return to my prior field of food service.

If I could not find another job very soon near Culver City, I would be forced to move out of Elizabeth's condo and return to Helen and Ed's home in Mira Loma. One thing of which I was sure, I would not consider a position for which I was not experienced or qualified. Therefore, searching the classified section I found an advertisement for manager at the Far West Restaurant and at K-Mart. With my experience in food and beverage, I decided it might be safe to apply to both of them. Far West was higher class (e.g., Perkins, Red Lobster, Olive

Garden) than K-Mart, so it became very clear what my decision should be; i.e., just start at K-Mart. It had a much smaller restaurant than Far West. After accepting the job I learned that the training would be in San Bernardino, which was close to Helen and Ed in Mira Loma. Helen was glad to see me move back to be with her. Also, Helen's son-in-law, David, didn't seem to mind moving me again.

I felt that I would never forget that first day of training at K-Mart ... and I never have! As the food manager, not only must you have the ability to manage, you must know every aspect of the operation, including cooking, inventory, hiring and training. Most of the stores had a deli located in the front, which was also under the responsibility of the food service manager. I *thought* I knew what long hours and hard work were; however, after I had worked from 8 a.m. to 6 p.m. I was so exhausted I could hardly drive myself back to Mira Loma. Gradually, I got used to it. After six weeks of training, the district manager informed me that I would be going to Thousand Oaks for the rest of my training and, then, I would be going to my own store in Simi Valley, which is about fifteen miles beyond Thousand Oaks.

Helen went with me for my first visit to the new training site and to help me find a place to live. The food service manager was Shirley Whitshell. I liked her right away. She was stern and very businesslike, but at the same time was quick to give me words of encouragement and to let me know I could do the job. We became good friends. Our friendship lasted several years after I left that store. After lunch, Helen and I began to look for an apartment or a room. I found a room with kitchen and house privileges at 51 Miramar Street in Thousand Oaks. The house belonged to Toni Armellie. She was the owner-operator of Toni's Boutique & Flowers. She also welcomed Kitty to share my room. I still have a neat picture of Kitty in Toni's garden, looking as if she were posing for the picture. I was only there for a short time, but I really enjoyed my stay. One day, I told Toni about my ESP classes in Cedar Rapids. She became interested in meditation. I gave her a tape of Allen Spraggett giving instruction on steps into meditation. I was very happy to learn thirty-one years later of her appreciation for the tape. She tells me today of her happy marriage to Jack O'Brien.

CHAPTER 60

1982-85
JOBS AT K-MART, TARGET, GIRLS' HOME AND OTHERS

SHIRLEY and the district manager agreed that I was ready to begin my position as food service manager at the K-Mart in Simi Valley. I found a very nice room at 91 La Paz Court with a view of my store down the hill a few blocks away. The home was owned by Mike Anton, who lived on the premises and had two other renters. There was a large swimming pool and a room with a pool table; however, with my work schedule and responsibilities I did not take time to use these amenities. The manager, Mr. Smith, welcomed me to the store. Three years later, I would remember my first meeting with him and what he said. "Ms. Winn, we are happy to have you join our K-Mart family. If you need anything or have a problem, you have my full support." The reception I received from the employees really took away my nervousness on that first day. Shelby Treece, Gloria Everly, Terry Kehoe and Dea Peterson are a few of the names I remember. I perceived none of the hostile attitudes that I experienced on my first day at *The Town House* in Cedar Rapids. Gloria Everly was very helpful to me. We were friends for several years, until I lost contact with her. Shelby Treece, a pretty brunette, was also very supportive. We have been in contact from time to time over the years. When she left K-Mart she started her day care for babies and young children in her home in Simi Valley. She and her husband, Ed, are now retired and enjoy traveling across the country in their motor home. They have invited us to stay with them in December of this year (2013).

After a few months I began to feel competent in my work position. So, when Mr. Smith came in for his morning coffee, I said, "Mr. Smith, I was wondering if I could offer you a hot dog which is not on the menu?" "Well, Gene, that depends. What's in the hot dog?" I explained to him how I grew up in Montgomery, Alabama and believed as did many others, that there was nothing to equal Chris' hot dogs with sauerkraut and mustard. The very next day I had my version of Chris' hot dogs on the menu. The assistant manager was my best customer. He seemed to like my hot dogs as much as I liked the originals back on Dexter Avenue in Montgomery.

Simi Valley was really a nice place to live. I liked my job as well as the employees with whom I worked. There was one problem: Simi Valley was just that, a valley, and there were hills surrounding it. I had been hearing about fires in the hills which were ignited by one means or another. As I mentioned previously, I could look from my house and see the K-Mart. On this particular day I was at work and someone said, "The hills are on fire!" I went outside immediately to look at my house. It seemed to be clear of smoke and fire, but the hills above were clearly on fire. Thankfully, it was under control, and the danger passed. It was very scary. I remember thinking, "I really prefer the earthquakes to the fires."

On my days off from work, I would sometimes go to Swan Lake to visit Helen and Ed; however, on most of my off days I would go to visit my friends that I had met through the Infinite Way tape group. Marilyn Downey lived in Van Nuys. I often visited her, and we would go to tape groups which were held in homes of people interested in Joel Goldsmith's tapes. They were mostly held in the home of Doris Crawford, located up the street from actor and politician Ronald Reagan's home. Another good friend was Barbara McCommon who lived in Corona del Mar on the Pacific Coast Highway. She attended the Baptist Church with her husband. One Sunday, I played my violin in the morning service. I do believe that was the last time I played until I returned to it in 2005. Oh yes, I did play it again for my mother's 100th birthday party on 10 March 2001. She passed away on August 14 of that same year.

On my spiritual journey of a search for truth I began to hear, or be told, "when the student is ready, the teacher will appear." I have found this to be very true in my own experience. In the year 1969, when Rev. Mabel Swanson introduced me to Joel Goldsmith's Infinite Way, I immediately knew that this was what I had been looking for, in that it was beginning to answer my childhood questions about the loving and forgiving God that I knew existed. The reader may recall that I previously wrote about my 80 year-old friend, Hazel Hopper. Her reaction to my expression of love for the Infinite Way tapes was, "Gene, you're a very old soul." I had never heard that expression. She explained to me, "It means that your soul has had many experiences." I know from that date in 1969 that the answers to my early questions began to be revealed to me through my daily meditations in both the easy and hard times in my life.

By reading Joel's books and listening to his tapes I quickly learned a lot about this man. He was a monumental teacher of practical mysticism and devoted most of his life to the discovery and teaching of spiritual principles. He was born in New York City on March 10, 1892 and passed away on June 17, 1964 in London. His early life was probably like that of most youngsters of that age and time, even though, young as he was, he later confessed to feeling a certain sense of detachment and even sadness about the world into which he had been thrust by birth, a feeling not usually found in children (Remember me!). While Joel's parents were God-fearing people of Hebrew ancestry, they were not practicing Jews. Joel was never taught any of the precepts of Judaism, except that all of the children were given instruction in the Ten Commandments.

When Joel was a little past twelve, his mother told him that someday he might want to know more about the different churches and religions in the world and especially about God. If he wanted to begin, he could have the

155

opportunity to gain some of that knowledge in the Jewish temple because, traditionally, at thirteen a boy in the Jewish faith takes on the responsibilities of manhood. He is then supposed to begin deciding his future. At about twelve and a half years, therefore, he was sent to a Reform Jewish temple and given some instruction in order to be confirmed at thirteen.

Joel completed the eighth grade, but his formal schooling terminated after a few months in high school, due to an argument he had with the principal. Even those first eight years were frequently interrupted when he played hooky to slip away to matinee performances of Shakespeare at a nearby theater. Then, as always, the theater had a tremendous fascination for him. Years later, in fact, when he was conducting an Infinite Way class in Los Angeles, he found himself quoting Shakespeare accurately on the subject of defamation of character, adding proudly, "Not bad after fifty-four years!"

The very day Joel quit school, his father began to teach him all that he knew about the importing business. A few years after that, when he was sixteen, Joel was taken to Europe on a buying expedition as an assistant to his father, who was a buyer of European laces and related lines of merchandise. To this work Joel brought an innate intuitive faculty that knew exactly the right laces to buy at the right time. So his travels began, at first in connection with the business world that was to occupy him for the early part of his life. There was always a lot of illness in the Goldsmith family when he was a child. At one time Joel wanted to become a doctor and began reading medical books.

In 1915, while his father was on a business trip to England, he became very ill and was rushed to the hospital. He remained there over two months and apparently was near to death's door when Joel began talking to the father of a girl friend in New York who was a Christian Science practitioner. The Christian Scientist said to Joel, "You don't want your father to die, do you?" "Why, no," Joel replied. The man then said that he would pray for Joel's father. Joel immediately sailed for England, thinking he would be returning with his father's body. Upon arrival, and to everyone's amazement, his father was up, dressed and waiting at the dock, ready to board a ship for America. Joel was astonished and overjoyed!

The miraculous recovery of his father led Joel to begin a study of Christian Science, in which he sought answers to the questions that naturally arose in the mind of a person who had traveled the world as he had, questions that kept plaguing him with an urgency that drove him on. When the United States entered World War I, Joel, in his enthusiasm to "lick the Kaiser," volunteered for the Marine Corps. He was stationed at Parris Island, South Carolina and there underwent the rigorous training to which Marines are subjected. During this time he served as Second Reader in a Christian Science Society organized for a little group of Marines.

There were many long hours of pondering on how it was possible to follow the teaching of the Master, Jesus Christ, and go out and kill. It was then that the Bible, which was at his bedside, dropped on the floor and opened to the verse, "Neither pray I for these alone." (John 17:20) At that moment the passage was illuminated for him, and he saw the mistaken zeal in the practice of the churches that opened their doors to pray for victory while none of them was praying for the enemy. Suddenly, he knew that the only righteous or effectual prayer anyone could pray is the prayer for the enemy, a form of prayer which from that moment on he began to practice faithfully. After the war was over, Joel found that it marked the end of an era for the world as well as for his father's importing business. By this time handmade dresses had become almost obsolete and mass production of clothing had taken over. Handmade imported lace was no longer in demand, and Joel was called upon to try to hold together the family business. In this effort he failed, and the business collapsed.

In addition to business difficulties Joel became critically ill with tuberculosis and was given three months to live. Since there was no medical hope, he decided that he would seek help from a Christian Science practitioner, which he did, and in three months he made a complete recovery. When Joel was telling of this experience a few years later, a skeptic insisted that a wrong diagnosis had been made and that Joel never had this disease, because if he had, it could not have been cured. Joel agreed to submit to an X-ray examination, which showed that he had only one lung. Where the other lung should have been there was a wall of muscle. After the family business collapsed, Joel once more became a traveling man, selling different kinds of articles, most of them in some way connected with women's apparel. Before he had been touched by any kind of spiritual experience, his attitude toward selling was quite different from that of the average salesman, which is perhaps why he was so successful.

Even in those early days Joel was intuitively aware of certain spiritual principles. So, he recognized that when a salesman goes into a business house to sell, normally the buyer immediately puts up a defense, and then the salesman is supposed to break down that defense. If a salesman, however, were to go into a business house with the realization that he had a good product and that if the buyer needed it today, it was available to him. If he didn't need it, that was all right too, for the buyer would feel that the salesman was not coming there to make a sale but, rather, to be of service. Although Joel was a master salesman and very successful for a number of years, a time came when his business became less and less, diminishing to the point of no return, even with all the spiritual help that he pursued. At this time he still had no thought of anything other than a business career.

It was during that period that he got a very bad cold and was taken sick in the city of Detroit, went to a building that was filled with Christian Science practitioners, found the name of a practitioner on the board, went up to this man's office and asked him for help. The practitioner told him that it was Saturday and that he didn't take patients on Saturdays. That day, he said, he always spent in meditation and prayer. To this, Joel said, "Of course, you wouldn't turn me out looking the way I do," and he really was looking bad. He was invited in and stayed a couple of hours. The practitioner talked to him about the Bible and its truth. Long before the two hours were up, Joel was healed of his cold. Soon after leaving the office, he discovered he couldn't smoke any more. Upon eating his dinner, he was unable to have even a cocktail. The following week he couldn't play cards any more, and he realized he couldn't go to the horse races. In effect, the businessman in him died at that time.

Within thirty-six hours after his first spiritual experience, a woman buyer who was one of his clients said that if he would pray for her she would be healed. The only prayer he knew at that time was "Now I lay me down to sleep," and he couldn't see that that was going to do much healing. However, she insisted that if he would pray for her she would be healed. So, he closed his eyes, and said, "Father, You know I don't know how to pray, and I don't know anything about healing. So, tell me what I need to do." Then, it was almost as if he had heard a voice saying, "Man is not a healer." That satisfied him. He prayed no more, but the woman was healed instantly!

The next day a salesman came in and said, "Joel, I don't know what your religion is, but I do know that if you pray for me, I could get well." Joel thought to himself, "I can't argue with that." So, he said, "Let's close our eyes and pray." He simply said, "Father, here's another customer!" While his eyes were closed, and nothing was happening, the man touched him and said, "Wonderful, the pain is gone!" That became a daily experience for Joel. His only problem was that he had too few customers and too many patients. A miracle had taken place. Where had it taken place? It took place in his consciousness, not anywhere else. He was the same individual whose sole thought had been business and pleasure. All of a sudden, his whole thought was on God and healing. He was the same person, only with an experience similar to that of Moses in the wilderness, that is, a realization of true identity.

Thus, there were two men. There was Joel, a man always around somewhere in the background but making many human mistakes, errors of judgment, human discords, but fortunately only known to him from time to time. And, then, there was the other man who on that day of revelation was ordained as a spiritual healer. From that day on, Joel paid respect to the practitioner for being responsible for the complete change in his life and for all that happened to him in a spiritual way thereafter. It is true that his thirteen years of secular work prepared him for such an experience, but it was the practitioner's touch that brought about the change. It was he who changed Joel's life, he who was accustomed to using one day every week without taking a patient, without making a dollar, without attempting to use spiritual power, one day a week in every week just to renew and fulfill himself with the Spirit. And look what that practice of spending a day like that did for Joel!

It is clear to me that Joel's experience marked the beginning of his career as an independent practitioner of spiritual healing noted for his remarkable work in transforming people's lives. Again, in his own words, he said, "The world is not in need of a new religion, nor is the world in need of a new philosophy. What the world needs is healing and regeneration. The world needs people who, through devotion to God, are so filled with the Spirit that they can be instruments through which healings take place, because healing is important to everybody."

After the publication of his originative book, The Infinite Way, in 1947, Joel traveled throughout the world as a teacher and a healer. Although his message was neither organized nor advertised, students of The Infinite Way increased in numbers. Today, a worldwide student body exists which continues to practice and preserve his work. More than thirty books have been compiled from his tape-recorded lectures and class work including The Infinite Way, Practicing the Presence and The Art of Meditation. His many books are the result of thirty years of experience in practicing spiritual healing. He felt that the three books just mentioned epitomized the essence of his teachings. In a decided departure from other books on the controversial subject of meditation, world-renowned teacher and mystic Joel S. Goldsmith alternated teaching with meditation to demonstrate that physical well-being results naturally from attaining a consciousness of oneness with God.

I was missing Kim and Steve very much. Telephone service and charges for the same have certainly improved since those years. A good part of my salary went to Pacific Telephone for calls to Cedar Rapids, Iowa and, of course, to Carol and family in Sioux Falls, South Dakota. Steve was happy with his life and his girlfriend. Kim was doing well in school; however, she was having problems with depression and low self-esteem. She was a pretty and talented young lady. Photography and poetry were two of her special talents. The following poem was written by her in 1982 and reveals how she was receiving some light on her own journey through life. I include it here with her permission and trust that just as it helped me, it will do the same for you, my reader.

THE LIGHT WITHIN DARKNESS

I was walking on a chilly, dark November day
head down, staring at the cracks in wet, hard cement;
The darkness of the day camouflaged the darkness of my
heart; cold rain falling from a grey sky pierced my skin.
The houses seemed to be quietly shivering
in anticipation of the approaching winter.
A church, the haven of life, glowed with warmth, radiating
the hope of God that sustains us all; I passed unnoticed.
Then, it reached out to me and touched my soul;
The church bells began to sing a song of exceeding sweetness;
I could hear the bells; I could feel the cold;
My thought, my life, my feelings; I am alive.
J. Kim Winn, 1982

Uncle Nick passed away on March 03, 1983. Helen, Ed and I attended his military funeral at the National Veterans Cemetery in Riverside, California. Our family was shocked and saddened, as Nick appeared to be in good physical condition for a man in his 80s. He had an aneurism which erupted. I felt badly that I had not visited him and Catherine since I had moved away from Culver

City. I am very thankful that by the grace of God I had long ago forgiven him for his having sexually molested me when I was eleven years old.

On Monday night, April 11, Carol called and wanted to know if I was watching the Academy Awards. I responded, "No, I have been reading." "Well, you should turn on the TV. Will Jennings has won the Oscar for writing the song "Up where we belong" from the motion picture "An Officer and a Gentleman."

I had been so busy with my jobs since moving to California, I had not had any contact with Carole and Will. Carol and Ray had not talked to them in years and wanted to congratulate Will, so he called Will's parents in Tyler, Texas and was given Will's telephone number, and guess what? They lived in Agoura, only a few miles from Simi Valley where I lived. To my surprise, I received a call from Carole, inviting me to visit them. She and I renewed our friendship and spiritual interests. Their home was small but a lovely town home with a pool. Carole did not always want to travel with Will; however, she was not fond of staying by herself. So, I began to drive after work to Agoura to stay with her when Will was away from home. Now, Kitty had two homes. Mimzy, their cat, had the run of the house, but Kitty had to be shut up in my room; i.e., Will's room. His synthesizer occupied a large part of the room. When Carole occasionally traveled with him, she would always bring me back some little memento. When she was away with Will I would stay in the master bedroom with Kitty.

I liked Simi Valley, my job, and I had a good relationship with Mr. Smith and the employees at work. My huge room at home was very comfortable and had a great view of the valley. My off days were Thursdays and Fridays. On Friday, March 25, I had taken the L. A. Times out on the roof over the first floor and was taking a sun bath. I was so used to turning to the classified ads in search of jobs, it was the first thing I looked at that day. As I have just written, I was very happy in Simi Valley; however, all of a sudden, there was a half-page ad for the thirteen new Target stores to be opened on April 13. Food service managers were needed. You might know that I thought, "I have to check this out!" So, the following Monday I had an interview for the food service manager's position. I don't know how I did it, but I was able to get Monday off from work at K-Mart. I had to drive twenty miles to get to the location for the interview. What stands out in my memory about that interview was that the district manager asked me, "Gene, tell me a method you would use to keep food costs down?" I told him, "I use a spatula a lot!" Maybe he thought that was a good answer. I do know that every time I am in the kitchen cooking and reach for a spatula, this memory pops up in my mind.

The next day, when I arrived home from work, there was a message saying that I was to report to the new Target store in Pacoima on Wednesday, April 06, at 9:00 a.m. It was located a few blocks from Highway 118, now called the Ronald Reagan Highway. I was happy about this new development, but I surely hated to break the news to Mr. Smith, especially due to the short notice I was giving him. He quickly turned from being Mr. Nice Manager to being Mr. Angry Manager. Among the things he said to me was, "You don't know what

K-Mart is going to do to the Target stores!" The employees were very nice about my leaving them. I have a "good luck" card from them, wishing me well, which I treasure.

One week of training at the new Target store was quite exhausting and involved a lot of knowledge that I was expected to assimilate. In addition, there was all that book work to do, and you will remember that bookkeeping was not my long suit! We started each day that week at 9:00 a.m. and were usually ready to leave at 10:00 p.m. On the third day of training, I left at about 10:00 p.m., and as I drove onto the Ronald Reagan Highway my car immediately broke down. Here I was on a California freeway when my Mustang just quit running.

Yes, I was terrified, but still I was very fortunate, because it happened just after I got on the freeway. I looked back toward the ramp I had just used and saw a service station which was open. I walked back and used their phone to call Uncle Eugene. He told me how to get the car towed. I also called Gloria Everly, my employee friend at K-Mart, and asked her to please come pick me up and take me home. I remember that my car repair bill came to $175.10. I have no idea what they repaired, but it was running again!

Thirteen Target stores did open on April 13, 1983. I was very impressed with my store manager, Melissa Hilton, as well as the operations manager, Debi Burnly. Melissa allowed me to have my week's vacation early, May 27 to June 06, in order for me to make it to Kim's high school graduation on June 02. Kim wanted to come to California, and I was happy about this move. So, I made reservations for my trip to Cedar Rapids and Kim's move on July 07. It was great to see Steve as well as my friends, Jessie and Beryl. I didn't have time to go to Sioux Falls, but it didn't matter, for Carol, Suzy and Ben were coming to California for a week starting June 13. They stayed with Helen, as I didn't have room for them, and I was busy at my new job. Carol spent one night with Carole and Will Jennings. Helen, Carol, Suzy, Ben and I went to Disneyland and Ventura. Carole Jennings was with us. I have pictures of all of us together. Tom didn't make the trip to California with his mother and siblings. He had gone to Switzerland for a ten-day tour with a group of 129 students from across the country. He was chosen for the trip for selling subscriptions to the Argus Leader.

Kim arrived at LAX on July 07. As usual, when I traveled on the freeway, I would always leave with extra time in the event of an accident en route. I didn't really mind getting to the airport early, as I rather enjoyed watching people and visiting the gift shops. With Kim's arrival, this meant that Kitty and I would have another roommate. Kitty was adopted with the idea that she would be Kim's cat; however, Kim enjoyed teasing her, which Kitty found very annoying. We were going to have a problem for in my large bedroom there was just one single bed. This meant that Kim had to sleep in my large walk-in closet.

She applied for a job at Target on Monday, July 13. A call came for her the next day from the stockroom manager offering her a job. She was to start the next day. We decided to look for a larger apartment closer to work. We soon found a nice two-bedroom apartment on Hazeltine Street in Van Nuys, which was a good bit closer to Target. The apartment was available for occupancy on the first of the month. My landlord in Simi Valley was very angry when I gave him a two-week notice. Kim remembers to this day the bad language and insults from Mike on the night we moved out. The Mustang was so full that there was barely room for Kim, Kitty and me. We arrived at our destination at about midnight that night!

I really did enjoy my managerial position but found it to be more demanding than K-Mart, especially the book work. Kim was not crazy about being a stockroom clerk. She had made friends with Melissa, the store manager, who invited her to attend Buddhist meetings with her. On our days off we would sometimes go to visit Helen and Ed at Swan Lake, but, mostly, we needed to do shopping and house work, and Kim needed to attend her meetings. I would go to my Infinite Way tape groups. We also enjoyed exploring new places. That's what we were doing on the almost fatal afternoon when we decided it would be exciting to go to Malibu.

Indeed, it was exciting but in a very scary way! We had traveled a good ways up Decker Canyon, when we began to notice the elevated view, and that was the beginning of our terrifying few minutes. The brakes on my old Mustang began to fail, although we did make it out of Decker Canyon without a crash. This harrowing experience has stayed in my mind and in Kim's memory down through the years! What I had forgotten was that Kim had her tape recorder with her and had it on "record." Just a few months ago I discovered among my old tapes the one from that day in 1983. There is no question about our being scared, realizing that our brakes were on the verge of giving out completely.

On October 15, I was selected as Department Manager of the month. The following is taken from a memo from Debi Burnley, Operations Manager, to Tom Dose, Store Manager T-182: *My selection for Dept. Manager of the month is GENE WINN, Food Service Manager. My reasons certainly will indicate why: GENE has shown a significant amount of progress in areas of TIMELINESS, selection of a STRONG STAFF and MOTIVATION of her staff members. GENE has the LOWEST amount of employee accidents in the store, year-to-date, for a high risk area. Based on her good performance record, GENE spent a week training a new Food SVC Manager in the Pacoima store. Her most recent operational audit score by District (10/12) was 87.5%--OUTSTANDING PERFORMANCE!! Her most recent regional tour (9/28) was also EXCELLENT. (Refer to memo.) She is a member of the "40% CLUB" with a year-to-date profit per cent of 43%. This is OUTSTANDING for a new store. GENE'S food cost percent is running 2.4% BETTER than district avg. and 2.2% BETTER than regional avg. year-to-date. The above only highlights the positives of GENE WINN'S performance. I am very pleased to have her on my staff. She is a great asset to the store. (signed) Debi Burnley, Operations Manager T-182.*

My sister, Helen, at left; my friend, actress and neighbor, Alley Mills, center

Kim was becoming increasingly dissatisfied with her work in the stockroom, so she began looking for another job. To my surprise, she was soon able to find employment as a teacher's aide. She continued to attend the Buddhist meetings. It was at one of these meetings in Santa Monica that she met Alley Mills. Yes, the Alley Mills who played Norma in The Wonder Years, 1988-93. This show won the Emmy award for outstanding comedy series in 1988. She played many television roles, movies and plays; e.g., Dr. Quinn, Medicine Woman, NYPD Blue, Roseanne. I had the privilege of coaching Alley with her Southern accent in her role in the film on the Atlanta Child Murders in 1985. Kim has been in touch with her over the years. My new work position, beginning in 1986, curtailed my personal contacts with her. I must say that I was quite surprised when I Googled her name and saw her many credits earned over the years. I am currently attempting to reach her but, to date, I am not having success.

All of the thirteen Target stores opened on April 13, 1983 were doing well. I really liked the way the stores reduced merchandise. Each week you could purchase great bargains which would be placed in the back of the store. Gloria and Shelby from Simi Valley called me often. Gloria would even come to Target and urge me to come back to K-Mart. Her insistence or persistence finally got to me. Although I liked the employees and manager at Target, you will remember from previous comments of mine, book work was something I didn't like, and I certainly wasn't very good at it. I began to ponder the idea of going back to K-Mart. Maybe the manager, Mr. Smith, wouldn't let me return. After all, he had really urged me not to leave. And I really hated to tell the Target manager, Mr. Tom Dose. If I did go back, I would now have to travel once again on the busy Ronald Reagan Highway. I did give this change a lot of thought for a couple of months.

So, at the beginning of March 1984, I made my decision and went to see Mr. Smith to see if he would allow me to come back. Gloria had told me they were looking for a food service manager. This gave me the needed courage to ask the previously angry Mr. Smith whether or not he would hire me again. He was cordial enough and gave me the date of April 02 to report for work. Now, I had to give Mr. Tom Dose the three weeks' notice. This was even harder to do than talking to Mr. Smith. I was dreading going to his office that morning of March 09 to give him my notice. Of course, he accepted my resignation but seemed genuinely regretful that I would be leaving his store. His comment at the end of our conversation was "Gene, I worry about what's going to happen to you!" This made me worry; i.e., what did he mean by that? Was it that I changed jobs too much? Or, maybe he had some intuitive feeling that something bad would happen to me?

Carole Jennings called to ask if I would spend the next two weeks in their town home and stay with Mimsey the cat. Carole was going to England with Will. This meant that Kim and I would have a little farther to travel back and forth to work. I had stayed there so often during the past year that it was like having a second home. Carole and I would usually eat out when I stayed with her; however, she and I did cook a big Thanksgiving dinner for Will the preceding year. Kitty didn't mind going to Carole's. Long ago, she had gotten used to moving all over the country.

Before we left for the Jennings' home, Kim received a call from Alley Mills, inviting us to a play in Santa Monica in which she had the lead role. I remember that Alley played Eva Braun, Adolf Hitler's mistress. Kim and I were delighted to go, and we even had front-row seats! I distinctly remember the thought I had: Here we are staying in the home of Will Jennings with his Oscar, and we are on our way to a play in Santa Monica, invited by the star, Alley Mills. "Kim, we have come a long way since you were born." I have come a long way spiritually which, of course, is my greatest achievement!

My apartment in Van Nuys was located close to Highway 118. As I left for my first day back at K-Mart, there was plenty of time before 8:30. I felt a little apprehensive about returning, which had to have been an intuitive feeling, as I was to find out later. It would be great to be back with Shelby and Gloria. Mr. Smith greeted me rather coolly and got even cooler as the day went by. I finally figured it out! He had let me come back out of spite. Well, I had a very good job at Target and had come back to this. So, I thought I would just have to put up with it.

As had been my routine for starting the day, I listened to my Infinite Way tapes and meditated. On this particular morning, before I left for work, I listened to Joel's tape relating his experience in a snow bank in Michigan. He stated that there is no place or situation in which you may find yourself in which God will not be there always to see you through. Joel had been traveling in light snow, which became a blizzard. He ended up in a snow bank in the country with no visible signs of life. Very shortly, a snow plow appeared and freed him from the snow bank in which he was stuck. This incident was very fresh in my mind as I drove to work on the Ronald Reagan Highway (#118). As soon as I drove on to the freeway, my car stopped. Believe it or not, it was on that very same ramp that my car stopped previously. Now, I was going to be late for work, and there was no telling what Mr. Smith would do.

I got out of the car, put the hood up (as if I knew what to do!) and was sort of in shock. While I'm standing there gazing under the hood, I saw a man coming around the car. He said, "Miss, maybe I can help you." Well, my car had a split water hose. This man had water in his truck and the tools and the material with which to repair it. It was done so quickly, the man would not accept payment, and I wasn't even late for work. As I continued on my way Joel's words rang in my ears, "There is no place or situation in which you may find yourself in which God will not be there always to see you through." His experience had also become my experience. How wonderful our God is! "God is my strength and my refuge, in him will I trust."

My days at K-Mart were soon coming to an end. Mr. Smith began to use his red-headed temper on me. It had been many years since I had been subjected to that kind of treatment! I surely needed a job, but I was not going to accept verbal abuse. So, I had no other choice but to quit.

My trip to visit Mother and Daddy was already planned for June, while I was still at Target. I had known that when I went back to K-Mart I might not be able to go to Alabama, but since I had resigned I was now at liberty to make the trip and then look for employment when I returned. Anyhow, my father recently had an operation for cancer of the mouth. Neither Helen nor I could go at that time. I had received my income tax refund, and it seemed to have Helen's name on it for a plane ticket to Montgomery. I had placed my ticket on a Delta charge card. Kim would be there in the apartment to take care of Kitty. So, I called Helen and said, "Pack your bags. I'm paying for your plane ticket to go with me to Alabama!" She was very happy with this news.

Ed had been out of work for quite some time. He wanted to relocate to Victorville and go back into real estate; however, he did not have the funds to move and to renew his realtor's license. It was going to take around $5,000 to make the transition. Also, their big car was in about as bad shape as my Mustang. Well, Helen and I had an early morning flight with changes in Denver and Atlanta. We arrived at Montgomery's Dannelly Field late in the afternoon. Clyde Shirley, Daddy's nephew, had driven my parents to the airport to meet us.

Mother and Daddy were in their mid-eighties, my age now as I write these lines. They were still living in their home on South Capitol Parkway. Daddy had built a studio in the back yard where he painted and did his craft work. They never had a car, although they had several friends who had cars and were generous in helping them get about and even to make occasional trips. Daddy's cancer surgery had been successful and, incidentally, ended his long years of pipe smoking. He was fitted with dentures after the surgery, but he just couldn't get adjusted to the bottom plate. For the remainder of his life his diet was mostly grits and eggs. He had always been a sweet and even-tempered man, but we were to see a little different side of him. What we were going to witness was very uncharacteristic of him, yet at the same time, quite comical!

On all of our trips to Alabama we could be sure of two things that would take place: Daddy would always have paintings to give us along with what-nots he had made for us; Mother would have plans made for us to visit some of her friends. Therefore, we were not surprised when she announced that we should go to visit Aunt Detty, Vera, Alice, Gail and Ginger. Clyde and Mildred picked us up at 6 a.m. with their station wagon. Although we were only going to have lunch and a short visit, it was necessary to leave that early, as they lived in Albany, Georgia—a little over 200 miles from Montgomery!

We stopped in Eufaula, Alabama on the Alabama-Georgia border to have a snack. Daddy ordered grits and scrambled eggs, as usual. Our orders were served before Mother returned from the restroom. Daddy had started eating and was having trouble with his plastic fork. As Mother approached the table Daddy's fork broke in two, and he just threw the handle which he had in his hand out onto the restaurant floor. Mother quite loudly said to him, "Have you lost your mind?" We were all shocked.

We arrived in Albany about one o'clock, and we had a nice visit. Helen and I were very grateful to Clyde and Mildred for their loving care of and devotion to our mother and father. They provided us with the needed transportation while we were in Alabama. Most of our evenings we played dominoes. Of course, on Sundays we went to Highland Avenue Baptist Church which was close to my parents' home. I flew back to California alone, as Helen stayed a week longer.

My friend, Marilyn Downey, picked me up at LAX. She lived a few blocks from me in Van Nuys. It didn't take long after searching the classified section to make a call and be given a job interview for a manager's position at Dunkin' Donuts. And just where do you suppose I was to go for training? Well, no place other than Watts, noted for its gangs (The Bloods and The Crips) and the very well-known race riots of 1965, which lasted six days with thirty-four people killed, 2,032 injured and 3,952 arrested! I certainly didn't think this was a very good place for a Southern lady, but I had to have a job. Another scary thing was that it was overnight training with only two other ladies and I working there. Yes, I soon quit! The reason? I was scared, and I couldn't get the knack of turning the doughnuts over in the hot oil.

I really believed after all those years that God was my supply. However, my question to God was, "Why do I have to keep changing jobs so often?" I didn't know it then, but I was going to have three or four job changes coming up! So, back I went to the want ads. I soon spotted a Wendy's ad, applied and was hired. But I had never taken a polygraph, and that was a requirement. I would need to go to Long Beach for the test. You know, there are some memories which are so vivid that it seems as if the events happened just yesterday. Well, I had never been to Long Beach, and I got lost trying to find the address, so I was late. I knew I didn't have anything to hide, but my being nervous about taking a lie detector test and being late getting there, I'm sure my blood pressure bordered on my having a stroke! Well, I did pass it and was assigned for training in a Wendy's store in Whittier.

Before I write about my new job I want to backtrack to the end of Helen's visit in Alabama and her arrival at LAX. Ed was there to pick her up. As they were leaving the airport and driving up the ramp to the 405 Freeway, a tire came off of an eighteen- wheeler and hit their car in the middle of the windshield. What very well could have been a terrible injury or deadly accident did not happen, and they escaped without a scratch! Their insurance company was finally able to locate the business of the company which owned the eighteen-wheeler. Not long after that happened Ed received a new car and a check for five thousand dollars, which was the money they needed to relocate to Victorville and to renew his realtor's license. You know, God surely does have some scary ways to meet our needs.

In between my doughnut job in Watts and traveling to Long Beach to take the polygraph, I had moved from Van Nuys to Ontario where Peggy (Helen's daughter) and David and their three children lived. They had a nice house with four bedrooms and a pool. Peggy called and asked if I would like to move into their spare bedroom. She was only going to charge me two hundred dollars monthly. You see, she had it all planned. We would just let David think that I was not paying any rent, and then she could save the two hundred dollars I would be paying her so that she could surprise him with a paid cruise. Well, I have to say that he was a pretty good guy. He even came to Van Nuys to move my furniture. I did feel a little uncomfortable with him thinking I was not paying any rent.

Kim had moved into an apartment in Hollywood at 1769 North Orange Boulevard, which was located right around the corner from Grauman's Chinese Theater on Hollywood Boulevard. This was very convenient for Kim and me to attend the theater for The Color Purple, shortly after the film opened on December 18, 1985. Incidentally, this is one of my favorite movies.

How was my job going at Wendy's? And how long did I stay? Not long. This store was in a seemingly nice location, so I wasn't afraid, and I liked the job and believed I was doing it well. Also, the 25-mile commute on the freeway twice a day was OK; that is, until my old faithful Mustang lost its brakes. I was already on the freeway driving home when I became aware that I had a serious brake problem. This became one of those experiences in life which you never forget. I surely can't tell you how it was possible to drive from the freeway down the ramp onto Ontario Boulevard and on to Peggy's house. So, that was the end of my job at Wendy's. This new loss of employment did not send me back to the want ads to look for a new job. I walked to the businesses on Ontario Boulevard until I was hired to work in a fast-food restaurant similar to Wendy's. I was there just long enough to find something better, as well as having my brakes repaired.

Some time later I received a letter from my good friend, Jessie Nagle, back in Cedar Rapids, talking about the protection given to me that day when the Mustang's brakes went out. Among other things, she said, "Listen! Your car was conking out with no brakes, and you had no job. You drove that car on the freeway! Don't tell me that you didn't have an angel carrying you along. You could have had a terrible accident."

While I was grateful that I now had employment, I knew I had better get back to looking at the want ads in the Ontario paper. I soon spotted an ad that I thought might be interesting to pursue. It was for a counselor at the David & Margaret Home, Inc., a center for adolescent girls from their teens to twenty-five years of age. Most of these girls came from foster homes around Los Angeles, including Watts. The home was located in La Verne, about fifteen miles from Ontario. I already had my brakes repaired, but I didn't know if I could rely on my car to travel that far daily. Also, I certainly had no experience as a counselor. So, with these factors in mind I called the home and soon had an appointment for an interview with the supervisor, Mr. Charles Rich. To my surprise, following the interview, I had another job, starting in one week. I would have to leave Kitty in Peggy's care, as I would have to work three days and nights and then have the next three days off.

There were fifteen cottages on the campus which housed eight to ten girls in each cottage along with their counselor. My duties were those of a live-in mother with all that was involved. In addition, I had to hold group therapy sessions twice a week, when they were free from school to attend. I even had to make sure they all got to the dining room on time. Also, lights out was at 10 p.m., and there was an alarm system which came on automatically, if a girl tried to leave during the night. The counselor who had the girls on weekends had to take them on outings to Disneyland, Santa Monica Beach, Knott's Betty Farm and other places. On one occasion, I had a girl go AWOL when I had my group on the beach, and I was responsible for them. I was really scared! I called the school, but they were nonchalant about it and said, "Let her go, let her go. Just bring back the rest of the girls."

Some of the girls were from gangs. In fact, that's where I first heard of the Bloods and the Creps. The one place where I didn't have any trouble was on my outings to Disneyland. Nevertheless, since I had the authority to give them demerits, from the very beginning when I heard all of those bad words coming out of their mouths, I was determined to give them demerits for bad language. It really didn't help. I even got called in by Mr. Rich who told me not to worry, that there were a lot of things they could do which were worse than using bad words. A counselor who became a good friend of mine, Betsy Tan, knew about my car situation. She had a friend, Tim Osborn, who was a car salesman at Citrus Motors Ontario, Inc. I traded my 1977 Ford Mustang for a 1986 Ford Escort. With all of the stress associated with my work, I felt that I was needed in my position with those needy girls and, also, I was now driving a new, dependable vehicle.

I was having regular contact with Kim, going to Hollywood to visit her, to go shopping and to see a movie. One day, around the first of May 1986, after being at David & Margaret for nine months, I received a shocking call from Cedar Sinai Hospital in Beverly Hills telling me that Kim had been admitted. She was having problems with depression. I immediately made up my mind that I was going to move to the Beverly Hills area. This meant, you know what, looking for another job! I was saying to myself, "I don't care what it is, as long as it is an honest job!"

I can't believe how naïve I was to think that I could just walk into an employment agency in Beverly Hills and get a job. You don't get jobs in Beverly Hills without a long list of good references and a solid work history. However, I did walk right into an agency on Beverly Boulevard, just off of Rodeo Drive, and was immediately told by Ms. Doris Romero, who owned the agency, that she had just the job for me. Well, how could that be? Maybe you're thinking, "I just don't believe that!" I didn't have an appointment, when I knocked on the agency door, true; however, Doris opened the door, as it was after her closing time of 4 p.m., and her agents were gone for the day. She invited me in and was really cordial despite the late hour.

Our initial conversation moved from one thing to another and eventually got around to philosophy and religion, which I believe made her think of two of her clients, Grady Roberts and his partner, John Kimble. Remember, I previously wrote that I would accept any job that was honest. Thankfully, by the grace of God, I knew that there was **no** room for judging others. Doris said they were nice, respectable men. "Grady is a talent agent, and John is a partner in Triad Artists, Inc., a talent and literary agency." I left her office with an interview arranged for the following Tuesday at their home at 1200 North Wetherly Drive, which is very close to Sunset Boulevard.

The rush hour freeway traffic didn't bother me, as my mind was filled with excitement. My interview with Grady went very well. I was in awe of the big home, five bedrooms and four bathrooms. I was really overwhelmed with the idea of being a housekeeper which, of course, I had never done. This was a live-in job, and my room overlooked a large pool with coconut palms in the back yard. Grady had a cat, and he did not mind my bringing Kitty along with me. Grady and John had never had a housekeeper, and they knew from my résumé that I had never worked in that position. The down side was that I would be earning quite a bit less than when I was with David & Margaret Home, but I had no rent to pay, and I would be very close to Kim.

I was even more elated on my ride back to Ontario to pack my things and move with Kitty the next day with the realization that I now had a job in Beverly Hills. Peggy surprised David with a paid-up cruise. I was glad for my part in helping to get it paid for. I was soon packed and Kitty and I were on our way to our new home. As to my new housekeeping duties, I just did as any mother would do; i.e., cleaned the bathrooms, dusted and mopped, etc. They prepared their own breakfast and were away at lunch. Occasionally, I would cook dinner for them, when they were not out with their clients.

John gave me a list of the exclusive clients of his agency: 170 men and 104 women. I recognized 45 of them. Many of them were well known to moviegoers. Ray Charles was one of them. He played and sang my kind of music. I had many of his tapes. So, it was quite a thrill when John gave me tickets to a Ray Charles performance and made reservations with front-row seats for Kim and me. The concert was in a theater on Wilshire Boulevard right there in Beverly Hills.

Another very nice surprise for me was that John called me from his office in Century City. It occupied the whole 16th floor at 10100 Santa Monica Boulevard. He said I should come to his office that afternoon at 2 o'clock. To my great astonishment he invited his employees to meet me, explaining to them that I was his and Grady's "mother." He even had ice cream and cake and coffee for everyone. Of course, they all knew that I was their housekeeper.

Although I had only been with Grady and John since May 1986, they gave me two extra days off, thus giving me four days to fly to Minnesota to visit Carol and Ray on Lake Superior. When I returned, Kim called to tell me that she was going to be admitted again to Cedar Sinai Hospital. She was depressed, couldn't eat and had lost twelve pounds. I was very grateful for the care given her by the hospital program which was made available to her. On September 03, she had started college classes. Even after she was admitted to the hospital they allowed her to attend her classes. They were impressed with her writing ability and high IQ.

I began to notice by looking at the "help wanted for housekeeper" ads that they were offering a good bit more than I was making. I certainly liked my job with John and Grady, but I knew I would have to start looking for a better-paying job!

Ed was doing very well financially since moving to Victorville and had recently purchased a very nice ranch home next to a golf course. I had Saturdays and Sundays off, so I would drive the 180 miles round trip to visit Helen and Ed. They had moved their church membership to the Presbyterian Church, located at 20700 Standing Rock Road in Apple Valley. Of course, we always attended the Sunday morning service. Helen and Ed had a certain pew they liked to sit in. They always sat directly behind Roy Rogers and Dale Evans. Dale would drive herself to church, whereas Roy would ride his motorcycle.

Before leaving for Victorville on Friday, August 29, I spotted a three-line ad in the newspaper. I very much regret that I didn't keep it for my records; however, it caught my attention enough that I decided to call before leaving for the weekend. There was no answer, but I did leave my name and number, which is something I seldom do. When I make a call, I want to talk to someone! I took with me my one good dress knowing I would be going to church. Well, when I started home Sunday afternoon and was about halfway there, I realized that I had left my one "interviewing" dress at Helen's. So, I turned around and went back for it. I'm so glad I obeyed my intuition, because I was going to need it on Tuesday morning.

When I arrived back home there was a message waiting for me. It was brief and to the point. "I have a wonderful job for you with a famous man. Please call me." Perhaps I should have been afraid to return such a strange message; however, I could hardly wait until Monday morning. Believe me, I was racking my brain to try to figure out who in the world this "famous man" might be.

CHAPTER 61

1986-1988
WALLY FINDLAY – BEVERLY HILLS

THE call was from Mr. Harvey McEntire. He was in an office on La Ciénaga Boulevard off Sunset Boulevard and not far from John and Grady's. I had no trouble in finding his office. I knocked on his door, and like Doris Romero, he was the only one there! After a brief interview, he said he would take me for an interview with Mr. Wally Findlay, who lived on Carla Ridge in Beverly Hills. He picked up his phone and called the number and arranged an interview for the next day at 11 o'clock. He then said, "You meet me back here at 10:30 in the morning, and I will go with you for the interview with Mr. Findlay." He explained to me that this was the Wally Findlay of the *Wally Findlay Galleries International, Inc.*, with art galleries in Palm Beach, Chicago, New York and Paris. The gallery in Beverly Hills on Rodeo Drive had been sold about two years previously.

Carla Ridge was almost up to the famous Mulholland Drive. My nervousness over meeting Mr. Findlay was somewhat diminished by the beautiful homes I was seeing as we drove to the interview. We arrived promptly at 11 o'clock and were greeted by a lady who introduced herself as Simone Karoff, vice president of Findlay Galleries. She escorted us to one of the large sitting rooms to meet Mr. Findlay. He turned out to be a very distinguished gentleman of eighty-three years of age. We seemed to have a good rapport right away. In fact, he said to me, "I've always tended to like Southern ladies!" It soon became apparent that I was going to be offered the job, when Ms. Karoff began explaining to me in detail that my duties and responsibilities would include the following: Mr. Findlay's personal bookkeeping, a number to call for housekeepers when needed, payroll for garden and pool maintenance personnel, contact with the masseur for service when required by Mr. Findlay, maintenance of Mr. Findlay's wardrobe, etc. Ms. Karoff said that she and Mr. Findlay would be leaving for New York on Friday and that I must move in by Saturday night. She then took me to my apartment which was at the lower end of the house. It was a large bedroom with a very small kitchen and bathroom. A sliding door led out to my patio which had a breathtaking view of Beverly Hills. The patio then became a walkway which went by the side of the garage, Mr. Findlay's room, a large living room and to the garden with a beautiful pool.

Not only was my salary a hundred dollars a week more than it was with John and Grady, but I hadn't even thought about the extras which came with the job; e.g., life insurance, medical and dental insurance at no cost to me. Also, after completing one year of employment I would be eligible to participate in their pension plan and employee stock option plan (ESOP), also at no cost to me. Ms. Karoff told me that I should come by on Thursday and pick up the keys and that I should be moved in before midnight on Saturday.

The expression "It's too good to be true!" is an understatement! I was thankful to God but maybe a little scared of this new adventure in my life. I really dreaded to give John and Grady the news, especially with only four days notice, although it turned out to be only one day's notice, as they were out very late every night. So, by Friday night without seeing them, I wrote them a letter, of which I still have a copy. I left it for them to find. The next day John was really angry. He told me "You might as well throw those books out of the window!" (my religious books). Grady, on the other hand, was very nice in understanding the situation and wished me well at my new job.

Wally Findlay

Little did I realize how much my life would change and follow the words of Allen Spragget when I took him to the Cedar Rapids airport several years previously, as the reader may remember, when he said, "You are going to move to California and come into more money than you have ever had in your life." These were my thoughts as I loaded my Ford Escort on Saturday night, September 06, 1986 to make the move from Wetherly Drive to Carla Ridge in Beverly Hills. Kim could not help me, as she was still in Cedar Sinai. Ms. Karoff had told me to move in by midnight at the latest. I beat the deadline by three hours. The first thing I did was to go into the house after disabling the ADT alarm system. I was surprised to see all of the notes with instructions Ms. Karoff placed throughout the house. I gathered up most of them to take with me to my apartment. I carefully, and I might add nervously, locked the house and set the alarm. Now, I was ready to unpack Kitty and the car.

I proceeded to unlock my apartment, which had a private entrance from the street. As soon as I opened the door, the alarm system sounded like an explosion in my ears. With all of the instructions concerning the house, nothing was said about my apartment having a separate alarm system. Doubtless the ADT people were expecting that an alarm might be set off that night, as the phone in my apartment started ringing right away. They were calling to make sure it was I who was entering, as they had been advised by Ms. Karoff that I would be moving in that night. I think I must have stayed awake most of the night, gazing out my window at the lights and sights of Beverly Hills! As for Kitty, she took it all in stride, as she had been dragged from pillar to post practically all her life.

You can imagine how I was the next day, alone and exploring my new surroundings and looking at all of the beautiful original paintings. Mr. Findlay had a Picasso in his bedroom. On a wall of one of the large living rooms was the six-paneled work of Paul Cézanne's "Aix, Les Environs d' Aix-en-Provence." I learned later that the latter was insured for twenty million dollars! I was captivated by the well-kept lawns and gardens. I think the pool was the most beautiful I had ever seen. Kim was able to leave the hospital and visit me during the two weeks I was alone prior to Mr. Findlay's return from his travels to Chicago, Palm Beach and New York on Monday, September 22.

So, I made my first call to Art Smith, the masseur, to arrange for him to give Mr. Findlay his customary massage. I also did some grocery shopping in preparation for his return. As I was putting away the groceries, the doorbell rang. It was a lady from across the street. Mr. Findlay had mentioned the day of my interview that there was an actress living nearby, but he didn't tell me her name. This lady at the door was none other than Joanne Dru, and she had come to meet *me!* She introduced herself and said, "I have been praying to God to send the right person to care for Wally." I felt privileged to become her friend, also to meet many of her acquaintances from movies and television.

Later, she gave me several of her publicity pictures, one of which was an 8 x 10 which she autographed, as follows: "To Gene, my wonderful friend. God loves you, and so do I! Much love, Joanne Dru." Some of my readers will recall that she co-starred with many well-known actors, such as John Wayne in "She wore a yellow ribbon," Burt Lancaster in "Vengeance Valley," Errol Flynn in "The Warriors," Van Johnson in "Hell on Frisco Bay," and many more. Also, "Three Ring Circus," a 1954 movie with Dean Martin, Jerry Lewis, Joanne Dru and Zsa Zsa Gabor, about which I will write in more detail later on.

Mr. Findlay arrived at LAX at noon and came home in a limousine. From the first day of getting to know him, I felt comfortable and at ease around him. He had asthma for many years and had to have his inhaler with him at all times. He told me what foods he liked, and to my delight he said, "I would like for us to have lunch tomorrow at my favorite sidewalk restaurant on Rodeo Drive!" I was to enjoy many more luncheons on Rodeo Drive as well as Hamburger Hamlet and the Polo Club.

On Mr. Findlay's next trip to his other galleries, I drove him to LAX. We arrived early so that we could have lunch in one of the lounges. I had another BIG surprise. He took out his checkbook and wrote a $500 check with MY name on it. I was to find out over the next few years that Wally was a very generous man. (Oh yes, I was now calling him "Wally," as he preferred his friends call him.) I had heard a lot about his sister, Helen, who lived in the penthouse at the gallery in Chicago. She and Wally made all the final decisions about art events and all business concerns for the galleries. They communicated by telephone on a daily basis. Wally talked about Helen very fondly. And here comes another surprise! She wanted to meet me! So, she called me to say that she had made a reservation for me to come to Chicago while Wally was there. Kim was out of the hospital and was staying with me, so I didn't have to worry about Kitty. By the way, Wally didn't care at all that I had Kitty.

So, I flew to O'Hare International Airport, first class no less! Fred, one of the employees was waiting at the airport to take me to the gallery where Helen and Wally awaited my arrival. Words escape me as I attempt to describe my feelings and knowing that I was meeting a very special lady. This quotation from a close friend of hers describes her perfectly: "She is a gracious woman who personifies what 'lady' used to mean. She is really an extraordinary person—kind, generous and all the good things. Her staff is like family to her." She and Wally took me to the Park Hyatt Hotel for dinner. After dinner, we took a taxi to the Renaissance Hotel, where they had reserved a very nice room for me. Fred arrived at 9 the next morning to take me back to the gallery. Helen and Wally gave me a tour of the entire gallery and introduced me to the employees. I was impressed with Helen's office which faced the famous Chicago Water Tower. Wally and I took an afternoon flight back to Beverly Hills. Of course, we traveled first class to LAX and then by limousine to Carla Ridge.

Wally traveled quite often to his other galleries during my first year of employment. His favorite automobile was the Rolls Royce. At one time he owned four! The two he now owned were classics from the 60s and forever needed to go to the shop for repairs. So, when he was at home, a lot of our time was spent with my driving Wally back and forth to get the cars repaired. I was really in awe of them, at first, but I got to the point where I didn't like them so much.

Wally enjoyed fixing or repairing things around the house; e.g., fixing blinds, simple plumbing jobs and other odds and ends. I became his assistant on such occasions. We had many long talks. He would recount his childhood days and his early years in the galleries. I was to hear two of his stories many times over the years. As a young man he would carry paintings in the back of his truck. One day he pulled up to a rather large home that belonged to an elderly American Indian woman who had benefited from the discovery of oil on her reservation. Wanting to sell his truckload of paintings he rang the doorbell. The owner was blind; however, he didn't leave. Instead, he suggested to the lady that she put her hands on the surface of the paintings to judge their merit for herself. She bought thirteen paintings at one thousand dollars apiece! The other story he seemed to delight in telling was the time he had to slide down a laundry chute in Chicago. He was trying to avoid a confrontation or worse with a Chicago mobster. You see, *the laundry chute was in the apartment of the mobster's girlfriend!*

Joanne Dru walked up Carla Ridge almost every day for her exercise. She would often invite me to join her. When I didn't go with her, I would walk several times back and forth from my patio up to the walk along the back side of the house into the garden and pool area. On one of my walks I had quite a scare. As I approached the garden there were two huge buck deer there. As we saw each other, they ran up the hill, and I ran back to my apartment.

By the pool in Beverly Hills

Kim and I enjoyed the pool and the garden, although we never actually got in the pool. The garden was so serene and a very nice place to meditate. One day, Kim took my picture while standing by the pool. I thought I looked rather important! Carol and Ray had invited Kim to move to Sioux Falls to live with them. She decided that she would accept their invitation. I knew that I would really miss her, but I believed that she would be happier there.

The first week in December Carol flew out for a four-day visit. Wally had invited her! He gave her four paintings and even had them shipped by two-day freight service. I have the letter of appreciation Carol sent to Wally, dated December 10, 1986: "Dear Mr. Findlay, We are all thrilled with the paintings—freight time, by the way, was a fast 48 hours. Your kindness and generosity make us feel very fortunate. Also, I thank you for opening your home to me last week. I thoroughly enjoyed my visit, of course, but most of all consider myself rather lucky for having had the opportunity to meet you and to acquaint myself with your remarkable art collection. I appreciate your kindnesses to my mother. She is an absolute original, you know! I hope we may meet again. Sioux Falls lies nicely between L.A. and Chicago. Sincerely, Carol"

Wally went to Chicago to be with his sister, Helen, for Christmas. I drove him to the airport. As he was getting out of the car, he handed me an envelope and said, "Merry Christmas!" There was so much traffic at LAX I had to keep driving, so it was a few minutes before I could open the envelope. It was a Christmas card with a check for two hundred fifty dollars! Are my surprises from him ever going to end? On December 24, Kitty and I went to Victorville to spend Christmas. Mother and Daddy arrived the day before and were staying for two weeks with Helen and Ed. I returned the day after Christmas in time to pick up Wally at LAX.

Wally, Mother and Daddy in Beverly Hills

When I told him that Mother and Daddy were at Helen's, he said, "I would like to meet them. You call them and tell them to come and stay a couple of nights with us." Of course, they were very excited over the invitation. Helen drove them down and returned home to Victorville after greeting Wally. My father felt very privileged to meet

175

Wally. Of course, I took a lot of pictures of my parents with him in the beautiful setting of his home in Beverly Hills. I took one picture of Daddy and Wally standing in front of the Cézanne painting referred to previously, "Aix, Les Environs d' Aix-en-Provence." Sometime later, Daddy made me a little jewelry box and put that picture on the cover. Today, it has its place on my desk to the right of my computer monitor.

Wally helped me set up my office in one of the bedrooms. He had returned from Chicago with Helen's instructions on bookkeeping procedures and my relationship with the Chicago office. Robert, a former frame shop employee at the Rodeo Drive gallery, helped Wally and me with the office arrangement. He would occasionally do odd jobs for Wally related to frames and paintings. Everyone seemed to know him as "Bob." He was a very friendly and personable fellow. Also, he was the person who gave me his strong opinion of Simone Karoff! I was to discover that he did not exaggerate one bit. After that, I was somewhat worried, after having been very much at ease and happy with my new situation in life.

In February, Ray came for a two-day visit to see me and to meet Wally. A clear memory of mine is of the three of us arriving at the Beverly Hills Polo Club for dinner in one of the Rolls Royce Motor Cars. Of course, the parking valets knew Wally and jumped to provide us with their services. We did our best to give Ray the deluxe tour of Beverly Hills. Ray showed an instant liking for Wally, and Wally reciprocated.

My Ford Escort, of which I had been quite proud, was running just fine, and there were no problems, except that I began thinking that it just didn't fit into my famous 90210 zip code and the two Rolls Royce Motor Cars parked in Wally's garage. So, on my way to see Helen and Ed, I stopped to see Tim at Citrus Motors in Ontario. The next thing I knew, I had a mid-size car. Wally's cars were not dependable, so we rode in my car when necessary. On May 22, 1987, I drove back to Beverly Hills in my new silver Ford Tempo.

My parents were aging, so I usually managed to go to visit them in June of every year. Wally and Helen Findlay gave me their permission to go, and my sister Helen was happy to stay with Wally and Kitty. Many times in my life I have had an inner "knowing" or "feeling" that something terrible was about to happen. This time I had no clue. On this occasion, I had taken Kitty to the house and spent the night in my office-bedroom. I was planning to leave for Alabama in two days and had taken clothes and suitcases from my apartment up to the main house in order to pack for the trip. When I spent the night in the house I would feed Kitty and then let her go out of the bedroom. She would make a circle down the hall and through the living room and then come back to my bedroom. On this morning I was busy packing my suitcases, which I had left on the other twin bed.

When I realized that she had been gone a long time, I stopped everything and started looking for her. She was lying near the Cézanné painting and was having some kind of an attack. I took her to the bedroom, and she crawled under the bed. I ran across the street to Joanne Dru's home. She had Salvador, her houseman, take Kitty and me to the veterinarian. He drove my car, and I held Kitty in my lap. She died on the way. As a matter of fact, it happened as we passed Merv Griffin's home. The vet told me she had a heart attack.

I had never realized that grieving could cause such physical pain. I vividly recall the pain, as Joanne and I stood on my patio crying, watching Salvador dig a very deep hole to bury Kitty. I have often thought that her heart attack could have been my fault. Animals are very smart. Kitty, being such a one-person cat, knew by the suitcases and the clothes on the bed that I would be leaving her again. Overall, however, I would say that she had a good eighteen years of life! Somewhere, Salvador found a large, round flagstone, which he placed several inches below ground level to protect Kitty against any animals which might dig in the grave. Then, he planted sod over it and, thus, the yard looked undisturbed.

Ed brought Helen down to Wally's the next day, and I left for Alabama. She was going to use my car for any errands that Wally might want her to run for him. Also, she took me to LAX for my flight to Montgomery. I was glad to see my parents, but there are only two things which stand out in my mind about that vacation. Helen decided she didn't want to drive my car, so she had Ed bring their car down for her, and he drove my new Ford Tempo back to Victorville. As he passed through the intersection of Third Avenue and Warwick Street in Victorville, he was hit head-on!

Ed had an injury to his right wrist and his left elbow. He was very fortunate, as the car was totaled. The other driver, Mario Javier Tarcano, was taken to Victor Valley Hospital with lacerations on top of his head. The policeman who wrote the report said that they were unable to talk to him on the scene due to his being unconscious. When the police arrived at the hospital to question him, he had disappeared. After they finally tracked him down, they learned that he had no insurance and no license but did have a juvenile record with the authorities. Of course, my car had full coverage and, consequently, my insurance company replaced it with a new, white Ford Tempo, which turned out to be a lemon.

On some of my weekend days off, I would meet my friend, Marilyn Downey, at Douglas Park on Wilshire Boulevard in Santa Monica. It seemed to be an ideal location for people interested in attending Joel Goldsmith tape group sessions. The leader, Doris Crawford, would select a tape to be played. Without socializing with the other attendees, we would quietly take our seats in the clubhouse and sit in meditation during an hour-long tape. Upon conclusion, we would sometimes discuss how we first became interested in Joel Goldsmith's Infinite Way. I had a couple of long conversations with a gentleman, Robert Mandan, of the television series SOAP, 1977-81. Other cast members you may remember are Katherine Helmond as Jessica Tate, her philandering husband, Robert Mandan as Chester, Billy Crystal as Tommy Bois (one of their three children) and Robert Guillane as Benson Dubois, the butler. Other weekends I would go to Victorville. Friday, June 12, 1987, was the date that started me thinking that I needed to call the employment agency for another job. Don't get excited! I will explain.

As I was preparing to leave to go visit my sister, a taxi drove up to the door with none other than Simone Karoff. When she and Wally hired me she advised me that I should call New York and report to her on a daily basis. I had complied with this until I mentioned to Helen Findlay about my calling Simone every day as Simone had told me. Helen called Simone immediately and told her that I was not to call her and that I was only to report to the Chicago office. So, I never called New York again. To that day, I never heard from her again, that is, until this unexpected arrival of hers took place nine months later. If Wally had been expecting her, I was wondering why he hadn't told me. So, I left for Victorville with an uneasy feeling. I returned on Sunday evening, and Simone left the next day for New York. At some time over the weekend, Bob, the shop man at the Beverly Hills Gallery, came to the house to pick up his pay check. He's the one who told me all of Simone's mean and hateful ways. He was quick to tell me all of the unkind things she had said about me. One was that I had left for the weekend looking like a streetwalker! Well, I thought I looked pretty good with my black slacks and black blouse with the white collar and cuffs. The first time I met Joanne Dru she had on slacks and blouse very similar to mine. You might say I had tried to copy Joanne. I suppose Simone returned to New York determined to contact Helen and to get her to fire me. She really did try!

Wally went to Chicago a few days later. This gave me ample time to pursue my job search. It didn't take long until I was signed up with three Beverly Hills agencies, Beverly Cross, Dorothy Wright and Beverly Hills Employment Agency. My résumé looked very good now with Wally Findlay as a reference. Also, I seemed to have two important factors which employers wanted; i.e., I was about the ideal age, and I was Scotch-Irish. So, it wasn't long before I was called to numerous interviews. I certainly did not want to leave Helen and Wally, and I never would have had any thought of leaving had it not been for Simone. I still have the list of some fifteen job interviews I went on.

After I had gone to two or three interviews and been offered positions, I began to feel less threatened by Simone, for I knew that I could find another job. I continued to go to interviews, however, because it was so much fun! Instead of admiring the beautiful homes of Beverly Hills, I was going inside, and some of the owners were famous people. I had an interview with Ed McMahon at his home on Summit Drive. As I sat in his living room waiting for him, his cat jumped on my lap and stayed there, as though she welcomed me until Mr. McMahon came in for the interview. He was very friendly and easy to talk to and even made an offer. He wanted a cook! Even though I had a few years in the food and beverage field, I didn't see myself as a cook.

My interview with Zsa Zsa Gabor was very interesting. It took place in her home on Bel Air Road in Bel Air. She needed a housekeeper, so she gave me a tour of the home. And I really must write about this, for as we walked through the house together, she suddenly said to me, "Darling, you have beautiful legs!" Of course, I thanked her and said, "I have on an Eva Gabor wig." Her sister, Eva, was famous for her TV and movie roles, also for her line of wigs. Zsa Zsa then said, "My sister has never given me a wig!" Her husband, Prince Frederic Von

Anhalt, was asleep in a bedroom down the hall. Zsa Zsa had a room with 20" x 28" posters of her movies. One poster was of the movie "Three Ring Circus," starring Joanne Dru, Dean Martin and Zsa Zsa Gabor. Although she was very friendly to me, I wasn't impressed by the way she spoke to her secretary.

The day after this interview, Joanne called me to say, "Gene, I didn't know that you were looking for another job. Zsa Zsa called me this morning to ask if I could get you to come to work for her." We were in agreement that this would not be the best thing for me to do. I told Joanne about Simone. She then said, "Gene, Wally needs you, and this is where you belong." I was feeling much more secure in my job with Wally; however, I did keep getting more and more calls from the agencies for me to go on interviews. With Wally traveling as he did, I had plenty of time which allowed me to go. Besides, I was having fun, and it was exciting having all of these different experiences. I never dreamt that I would be driving up to a big mansion with guards at the gate and that they would be expecting me, nor did I think I would be driving up to a gate at one of the movie studios and was expected for my interview with The Fonz of Happy Days; i.e. Henry Winkler.

The position to which I really gave some serious thought was when I was sent to an interview at 1900 Avenue of the Stars in Century City. That was the office of Eleanor Debus, Dean Martin's manager. I liked Ms. Debus, and she must have liked me, as I left her office with a Confidentiality and Disclosure Agreement to fill out and take to an interview with the house manager at Dean Martin's home on North Hillcrest. Dean Martin was there, but he was taking a nap. The house manager filled me in on Mr. Martin's routine when he was at home and not in Las Vegas. His two or three guys or, I suppose, his guards, would take him to his favorite places to eat, which were fast food and pizza. The housekeeper told me that it was take-out food.

Wally was gone longer than usual on his trip this time, as he had traveled to all of his galleries, including Paris, France. I was surprised and pleased when Helen called to let me know that she had made reservations for me to come to Chicago for three days. Of course, I was happy to go and, besides, this was my job! Then, I began to feel guilty due to all of the interviews I had gone to, looking for another job, even though I did not plan to accept any of them and leave Wally. My guilty feelings caused me to realize how grateful I was to Mr. Harvey McEntire for taking me to the interview which resulted in my present position. And I had never even called to thank him! Besides that, the way he had personally taken me to the interview, also the message he had left on my telephone while I was at my sister's that weekend, was not at all like the interviewing procedures of the other Beverly Hills employment agencies.

My reservation to fly to Chicago was for Friday, August 07, so I had two days to pack. The more I thought about how my interview with Wally came about, I began to think it had been rather strange. At least, it was very unusual. This led to my getting dressed up and going down to Mr. McEntire's office on La Ciénaga Boulevard to tell him how grateful I was for my job and to express my appreciation to him. Guess what? When I arrived at his office, it was empty! Now, I really thought it was strange ... and I've thought the same all these years.

My sister, Helen, was coming to stay in my apartment while I was on the trip to Chicago, so that she could feed the cat. That's right, I now had another cat. I named him Toby. Joanne had said, "Gene, you should get another cat to help you in coping with the loss of Kitty. My brother, Peter Marshall, told me to tell you to get another cat. You know, Peter just adopted a kitten he found on the street in Manhattan." I appreciated her interest and concern, but I didn't feel that I was ready for another cat. Well, I suppose she was determined that I should have another one, because she knocked on my door and was holding a carrier with a Maine coon cat in it.

My weekend visit to Chicago went very quickly. I believe Helen had me make the trip so that she could fill me in on Simone's headstrong notion that I needed to be fired. At the same time it was very clear to me that Helen was not going to let that happen. Helen, Wally and I had dinner at Helen's favorite dining place on the ninety-fifth floor of the John Hancock Center, a one-hundred story building at 875 North Michigan Avenue. This building was featured in the 1988 movie "Poltergeist III."

My camera and I had become constant companions since moving to Beverly Hills; therefore, I always had it with me. When we finished our dinner, Helen and Wally had Gallery business to discuss. This gave me ample time to add to my photo collection. I took an awesome view of the Chicago skyline with the gleaming lights of the tall buildings as darkness enveloped the city.

Helen told me an interesting story about Huldah Jaffe, an artist who lived on South Ocean Avenue in Palm Beach. Huldah had come to Chicago for a visit, and Helen wanted to have dinner with her at the John Hancock Center. Huldah was very afraid of heights and elevators; therefore, it took considerable coaxing before she agreed to go. Now, just what do you think happened? The same thing happened to my daughter, Kim, in the Bismarck Hotel in this city in 1972. You will remember that she was afraid of elevators, and her elevator got stuck. And here was Huldah, stuck in an elevator in the Hancock Building.

Sunday evening, Bob Ryan, the Gallery treasurer, joined Helen, Wally and me for dinner at the Ritz Carlton. This was the same hotel in which I stayed when I attended the convention of the National Restaurant Association in 1980. Wally and I returned to Beverly Hills the next day. My sister was at the airport to take us home. We had only been home a few days when Wally informed me of his need to go to New York. He said, "Gene, cancel my appointment with Art Smith (the masseur). I have to go to New York. I need a hair cut!" I suppose he also went to his gallery there. Surely there were good barbers in Beverly Hills.

I was busy doing some book work when Joanne called and said, "I just went for my walk up the hill. On my way back I found an injured bird lying on the road. Would you please take it to Dr. Shipp, the vet?" I told her that I would be right over. It was not very far to the veterinarian's office on Foothill Road. This was where Salvador had driven Kitty and me the sad day of her demise. There were several people in the waiting room when I got there; however, the bird was taken immediately to an examining room.

While I sat there waiting, I noticed a pretty young lady, probably in her thirties, who went to the desk and asked the receptionist if she knew of someone who could feed her cats. Without even thinking about it, I quickly went up to the desk and said to the young lady, "I love cats. I would be happy to feed them." She quickly turned to me and said, "Do you live near Cold Water Canyon?" I wasn't sure, but I knew there were lots of homes with Canyon Road addresses. Well, I said, "I live on Carla Ridge, and I work for Wally Findlay." I'm sure that when she heard the name Wally Findlay, she instantly knew that I would be a trustworthy cat sitter. We exchanged telephone numbers. She said she would call me that night.

The bird was soon ready for me to take it back to Joanne. I drove back thinking that this would be a good way for me to make some extra cash. The young lady told me her name was Robin Sherwood, and that she was an actress. Robin called me around eight o'clock that night. After giving me directions to her home, she said she would like for me to stay a few minutes and play with the cats. She informed me that her housekeeper, Carmen, would be there each morning. Then she said, "I'll pay you thirty-five dollars a day. I quickly said, "Oh, I wouldn't charge you that much." Dear reader, have you ever started saying something and in the middle of it, you suddenly realized, "You idiot, why did you say that?" Well, that describes my thoughts. I finished my sentence with, " ... , I'll charge you twenty-five dollars."

This extra job lasted as long as I lived in Beverly Hills. However, it turned out to be more than just feeding the cats. I did a little bookkeeping for her, such as paying the gardener, the housekeeper and Belle Air Security. I even received a call from Belle Air one night about midnight, asking me to meet them at Robin's home. I quickly got dressed and drove over there, which was either brave or stupid of me. Someone had attempted to break in, but we couldn't find anything missing, so we assumed that the alarm had scared them off. I liked Robin very much, also Hansel and JJ, the cats. For some years after I was no longer in Beverly Hills, I would receive cards from her. She always signed them, "Robin, JJ and Hansel." She was in films, such as "Hero at Large" (John Ritter), "Blowout" (John Travolta), "Death Wish" (Charles Bronson) and many more.

As I started to take notice and to think about some of Wally's unusual habits and mood changes, I began to have a lingering uneasiness. I was very thankful for my job, but it did concern me. In the first few months of my employment he traveled a lot, visiting Helen in Chicago and his other galleries. One thing I noticed was that he always made notes of things to do and to remember. I did not find that unusual. The rather strange thing to me was when Simone suddenly appeared in June. Wally seemed rather aloof toward me while she was there; however, he was soon back to the Wally I knew.

We continued to go to his favorite dining places, of which I was rather fond. Bob, who occasionally worked for Wally, would sometimes go with us. The next thing which really bothered me was when Bob told me that Wally had gone into my apartment snooping around while I was in Victorville with Helen and Ed. Bob said he thought Wally had the idea that I had taken something which belonged to him. But most of the time, he was his winsome, charming self. And he could be very generous. I remember Friday, October 16, when Jessica McClure was stuck in the well in Midland, Texas. Wally and I were watching TV when the story broke. He then had me go and send by Western Union one hundred dollars in his name and one hundred dollars in my name as donations.

Wally and I were invited to attend many of Joanne Dru's parties. Her husband was C. V. Wood, Jr., known to his friends as "Woody." His hobby was cooking chili, which he turned into an institution. He co-founded the International Chili Society, which sponsored over four hundred cooking contests around the world. He donated the profits to charity. He was a pioneer developer of theme parks and planned and supervised the creation of Disneyland which opened in 1954. Leaving Disney in 1956, he formed Mario Engineering, and supervised the creation of the Six Flags Adventure Park in Arlington, Texas and Pleasure Island in Boston. In 1961, Woody's firm merged with the McCulloch Corporation. In 1968, he undertook his most novel project, when Robert P. McCulloch bought the London Bridge. Under Woody's supervision, it was dismantled stone by stone and shipped to Lake Havasu City, Arizona and reassembled. It became a successful tourist attraction. I felt privileged to meet so many movie and TV personalities at their parties. Even when Wally was away, I would still be invited. One night, and I suppose my most memorable night, while attending one of their parties, I spent most of the evening chatting with Ernest Borgnine of McHale's Navy and his mother-in-law. His wife, Tova, mingled with the other guests. Oh yes, Barbara Walters and her husband, Merv Adelson (1986-92), were there. While I found him to be very friendly and personable, Barbara was rather standoffish.

Incidentally, Joanne was crazy about her white poodle. One day, as I was walking from Wally's house to my apartment, I saw the poodle running around outside of her house. I knew something was wrong, so I ran over and picked up the dog and rang the doorbell. Tova answered the door and was very grateful that I had seen the dog loose in the yard and realized that I needed to do something about it.

Joanne called me one day and said, "I want you to come over and meet my makeup artist and hairdresser." I replied, "OK, I'll be right over." Joanne introduced me to Myrl Stotz. She had driven over from her home in Hemet, California to stay with Joanne for a couple of days. We had coffee and doughnuts, while Joanne and Myrl talked about some of their movie experiences. By the way, I found their conversation fascinating. Suddenly, Myrl said to me, "Would you like for me to give you the facelift we gave in the 30s and 40s?" "Well, yes, I would really like that." With that she proceeded. I tried not to let on, but it *really* hurt, the way your hair was so tightly pulled and held with bobby pins! I excused myself as soon as I politely could do so and almost ran to my apartment to undo my facelift.

As I have written previously, my friend Jessie Nagle and I always considered October 01 as probably one of the most important dates of the year. This was the Annual Friends of the Library Book Sale sponsored by the Cedar Rapids Public Library. This became the start of my rather large collection of spiritual and metaphysical books. When I was leaving Sioux Falls, South Dakota for California I had given most of my books to my good friend Harriet Geigh. I had met her at the Spiritual Frontiers Retreat at Carleton College in Minnesota. Her home was in Sioux Falls. I kept all of my Infinite Way books and a few others which were my favorites, among which was The Psychic World of Peter Hurkos by Norma Lee Browning.

Wally and I were having lunch at the Hamburger Hamlet one day, when he nonchalantly said, "I want you to call Norma Lee when we get back home. Her phone number is in the top middle drawer of my desk. I'd like to know how she's coming along with my book." Surprise! Surprise! I didn't know anyone was writing Wally's biography.

Another surprise came when I saw the very same Norma Lee Browning as being the author of my book on Peter Hurkos. So, when we got home I made the call to Norma Lee in Palm Springs. I didn't realize until later that she was an award-winning Tribune reporter and columnist, had written more than a dozen books and had regularly interviewed such stars as Dick Van Dyke, Frank Sinatra, Richard Burton and Elizabeth Taylor. We had a long conversation about Wally's book. It seemed that the book's progress was being delayed due to none other than Simone Karoff. From what I had been told and had experienced, I said to myself, "Well, no wonder she is so adamant about stopping the book, knowing that very unpleasant facts would be written about her."

My knowledge that God was my strength and my refuge seemed to leave me temporarily in the face of bad weather. I had gone through many bad thunderstorms and a few tornados in my life. Not only the scary lightning bolts but the loud thunder really hurt my ears. So, there in my Beverly Hills apartment at 7:42 a.m. on October 01, 1987, as I was getting dressed to go over and get Wally's breakfast, my spiritual truth left me once again. Toby the cat stood staring at me, as if he were asking, "What's going on?" Everything in the room was shaking quite violently. I surely did not know what to do. What I did was to run and stand in the shower until the shaking subsided. I then finished dressing and went over to check on Wally.

He was fine and was ready for his breakfast. It seemed that the earthquake we had just experienced did not affect him the way it did me. This was the 1987 Whittier Narrows Earthquake which struck the San Gabriel Valley and surrounding communities of Southern California with a magnitude of 5.9. As I pondered my experiences with bad weather I thought, "The tornadoes can be loud and violent, but you usually get some warning about them; however, earthquakes just slip up on you."

I was getting more and more concerned about Wally's forgetfulness and repeating himself. I would talk every day with Helen in Chicago, and we would compare notes about Wally's apparently deteriorating mental faculties.

Art Smith, the masseur, had invited Wally to have Christmas dinner with him. Wally wanted to go, so that left me free to go to my sister Helen's home in Victorville. We had a nice Christmas dinner, and then I returned to Beverly Hills. When I walked through the door, Wally was waiting for me, and he was fit to be tied. He was accusing Art of stealing a painting that he saw on a wall in Art's home. Actually, it was a painting that Wally had given Art the year before as a Christmas present.

One of my New Year's resolutions was to not allow anything to interfere with my walking schedule and that was to walk at a fast pace for thirty to forty-five minutes back and forth from my apartment to the garden. Of course, when Wally was at home my exercise time would vary according to what I had to do for him. When he was away I would start early in the morning and afterwards I would just sit and gaze at the beautiful homes that I could see on the streets below. My bedroom had a sliding door onto the patio. Therefore, I had an unobstructed view of the Beverly Hills lights down the hill. Now how peaceful is that?

One night in the middle of the week I noticed a lot of lights around one of the homes and soon loud music began and continued 'way past 11 o'clock. Finally, my level of tolerance snapped, and I called the police. It wasn't much longer after the call that the music stopped! So, all of the years since then, whoever my neighbors happen to be: "After 11 p.m., don't play loud music or shoot off firecrackers. I'm calling the police!"

There were two other incidences that happened of which I am more proud. One was the fire that threatened JoAnne's home. One night as I was walking from the house to my apartment I saw flames in the shrubbery between her house and the neighboring house. Of course, I alerted them, and the fire was extinguished before any major damage was done. The other incidence concerned Wally's mail. He normally received a lot of correspondence, and there would usually be a piece or two for me. After the third day of no mail for Wally, I began to think that there was something wrong. So, I called Chicago to inform Helen. The end result was that someone had transferred Wally's mail to their address for ulterior motives. The perpetrator was soon arrested.

I became increasingly concerned about Wally's forgetfulness and his paranoia; however, he was still traveling alone to his galleries. It was on this last trip to Palm Beach, which was to be the last time he would travel by himself, that really had me worried and upset. In the past I always had his travel schedule and would know when he was to arrive back home. This night, he was to arrive about 8 p.m. I really became alarmed when at 10 p.m. I hadn't heard from him. So, I called Helen in Chicago about 11 to tell her, "Wally's not here!" He had just called her to say he had gotten on the wrong plane, thus missing his flight to LAX. This became the point of realization for Helen that Wally needed medical attention … and soon.

She began to make arrangements to come to Beverly Hills so that she and I could take him to UCLA Medical Center. Her plan was to come within a week; however, another frightening night was in store for me. Wally suddenly began talking very strangely, more or less just talking out of his head. I somehow convinced him to go to Cedar Sinai Hospital. I feel sure that they gave him medication, for they allowed him to return home. I believe that experience traumatized me to the extent that I can't really remember further details. Helen changed her plane reservation and came the following day.

The reader may remember my first meeting with Wally's sister, Helen. I wrote that words escaped me as I attempted to describe my feelings and knowing that I was meeting a very special lady. So now, over a year later, I had come to know her as one whose life really exemplified God's commandments, although she never talked to me about spiritual matters. She was a woman of much wealth and, yet, she respected all people as her equals, regardless of their status in life. I feel highly privileged to have known Helen and to have spent so much time with her.

Wally's appointment at UCLA's Department of Neurosurgery, located on Ledonte Avenue in Los Angeles, was the next day after Helen's arrival. His diagnosis was Alzheimer's disease, which Helen would only refer to as dementia. She stayed with us the rest of the week. I'm sure Wally's diagnosis was upsetting to Helen, but he wasn't told of his condition. He surely had months of knowing that something was seriously wrong with his memory, for he had always written things down and made lists. I didn't think that his memory was the problem but, rather, being the business man that he was, he was doing what was normal for him. The ride home from the hospital was rather subdued. It was getting late in the afternoon, and we had to hurry back to Carla Ridge for Wally's five o'clock nebulizer treatment. I suppose Helen thought that having our dinner in an elegant restaurant with fine cuisine that evening would lift our spirits. She said to me, "Why don't we go to the Polo Club for dinner after Wally's nebulizer?" I knew Wally was very fond of the Polo Club and always wanted to go there.

Helen suggested to me that I might like to take my two days off while she was there. I replied, "Yes, I would like to go to see Helen and Ed in Victorville, if you're sure you won't need me." "We'll be OK. I'm sure that Joanne and Salvador will help us, if we need them." I left the next morning and had a very nice visit. I returned the next day to find Wally taking his nap, and Helen talking to a lady in the living room just outside of Wally's bedroom.

My friend, Bob, had told me about Wally's mistress of about seven years and, about their palimony suit that was aired on the 60 Minute TV show. Well, this lady with whom Helen was talking was Florence Horn, Wally's former mistress. Helen had called her, thinking that a renewal of their friendship might help Wally. Florence said that, as far as she was concerned, this could never happen unless Helen could make certain that Simone Karoff would never come to California. This whole development was surprising to me, but I must say that I liked Florence right away. On the weekend Helen, Wally and I visited Florence in her town home in North Hollywood. I will have more to write about her later.

Helen called the Palm Beach Gallery and asked Gil Carter, the manager, to send Willie Brown out right away. Willie had worked in the gallery frame shop for many years. Helen felt that I could use extra help with Wally, also that Willie could talk to him about his galleries and about the Rolls Royce Motor Cars he owned. Helen needed to return to Chicago. I drove her and Wally to the airport in my car for her morning flight.

Wally and I had lunch at Hamburger Hamlet on the way home. He was in a pretty good state of mind. However, after taking a nap that afternoon, he started making plans for us to pick up Willie at the airport the next day. To my total dismay, his plan included driving to LAX in his gray Rolls Royce. That was bad enough, but he said he would be driving! He had not driven either car since I had been with him. And now, he planned to drive in all that traffic on the 405? My very clear thoughts on that day were, "What am I going to do? How am I going to get him to go in my car? This is how we're going to die!" Then, as if a voice spoke to me, I heard, *"Let go of your fear."* Like magic, Wally seemed to forget about driving his car. And, indeed, we did go in my car to get Willie.

This was Willie Brown's first visit to California. He was excited to be there, probably feeling, as I had when I moved to Carla Ridge, just in awe of all the beautiful scenery. Willie was Afro-American and had started to work in the gallery frame shop when the Palm Beach gallery opened in 1961. I served Wally and Willie breakfast every morning, and we would have our other meals out. Willie would drive and, do you know what? I really didn't mind it when Wally insisted that we take one of the Rolls. So, Willie would drive, Wally would sit in the front seat, and I got to ride in the back seat. I couldn't help but feel a little "special."

I must convey my conviction that Helen Findlay was a remarkable lady, not only for her compassion for all with whom she came into contact but for her superb managerial ability of the galleries and at the same time being very capable of the complete management of her brother's medical requirements. And she was then in her late seventies! Willie was scheduled to return to Palm Beach that weekend. Wally and I would certainly miss him; however, Helen had already arranged for his replacement, who would be Smoky Stover who worked with Willie in the frame shop in Palm Beach and would be arriving the next day. Helen's thought was that Willie and Smoky would be giving Wally someone with whom to talk shop. Smoky arrived on schedule. He had never been to California either and was quite overwhelmed by the Beverly Hills scene. Wally liked Smoky and was pleased to have him there, not only for their shop talk but to have him drive one or the other of the Rolls back and forth to the dealership service department.

I thought I loved most all of God's creatures, some of them at a distance, of course, such as wolves, bears, lions, tigers. To be honest, I don't even want to look at a snake, a rat, a spider or a bug. It came as quite a surprise to me that I didn't like Toby, the Maine coon cat that Joanne had given me. Toby didn't seem to like me either. One day I was talking to my friend, Lucille, in Cedar Rapids, telling her my tale of woe. To my amazement she said, "I would love to have Toby. You know, you could ship her to Cedar Rapids on United Airlines at very little cost." So, after waiting for a suitable temperature for the shipment of animals, I did just that. I think Lucille wanted the cat because Joanne Dru, the movie star, had given her to me. It wasn't long, however, before Lucille was calling me to complain about Toby.

Alzheimer's disease was an illness that I had hardly heard of prior to Wally's UCLA diagnosis. I didn't know it then, but I was about to start an education on the subject which lasted several years. I soon began to notice that Wally was getting more confused, especially in the evenings. Helen called to say she would be arriving the following Monday, accompanied by Bob Ryan, the secretary-treasurer of the galleries, and the attorney, Vern Squires. They needed to talk with Wally about the details of the selling of his home and relocating to Chicago. I'm sure Helen detected a bit of shock in my voice as she told me this and quickly said, "Gene, we're counting on you to make the move with him." Well, that was OK, because I didn't want to leave the Findlays, and I really liked Chicago. Also, I wouldn't have to worry any more about Simone Karoff, as she rarely went to Chicago. Bob and Vern were only there one day and returned to Chicago the next day. Helen didn't return with them, for she had much more business which needed her attention.

Helen waited until Wally was taking his afternoon nap, then she said to me, "Why don't we go and sit at the table by the pool? I would like to fill you in on our plans for the move to Chicago in June." (1988) So, I fixed two glasses of lemonade for us and grabbed my notebook and pen. Helen began by saying, "I have called the Beverly Hills Health Care office and have set up interviews in the morning for LPNs for Wally, and I would like for you to help me with two selections. I plan to have the home sold and, hopefully, make the move to Chicago by June."

Was Helen really asking me to help select the nurses? I felt flattered that she had! In no time we had chosen two nurses that we both liked. They were to cover my two days off and were to work eight to five shifts on the days that I was there. With this problem solved, Helen returned to Chicago. When Wally wanted to eat out, we all went in one of the Rolls with Smoky driving. We very much enjoyed the great food and atmosphere as well as Wally telling us the stories of his life experiences.

Actress, friend and neighbor Joanne Dru with my son Steve

My son, Steve, came to visit for a couple of weeks. With the nurses on duty, I had time to show him around Beverly Hills, Santa Monica, Malibu and other places. We also went to the Hard Rock Cafe in Beverly Hills. Steve was quite proud of the fact that Joanne Dru and Robin Sherwood, two Hollywood

actresses, invited us to their homes and served us dessert and coffee. He still has the pictures that I took of him with them, as well as some publicity pictures they autographed for him. I'm sure that he told all his friends back in Cedar Rapids and anyone else who would listen to him about his fabulous vacation in Beverly Hills.

I was very proud of the Christmas gift and card from Joanne. She inscribed the card with these words, "Your heart's desire in '88. You deserve the very best. Love you! Merry Christmas, dearest Gene, and I cherish your friend-ship! Joanne"

I surely never imagined that I would have a friend like Joanne. Not only did she introduce me to some of her friends, but she was very cordial to my family and friends. I had mentioned to her that Smoky from the Palm Beach shop would be leaving in a few days and would very much like to meet her. So, we were invited to go over and have coffee and cake by her pool. We talked about some of her movies and our mutual love for the Big Band music. The next day, which was a Saturday, Smoky had noticed an ad in the L. A. Times that Les Brown would be performing at the Hollywood Palladium. Smoky said, "I know this is your day off, but hearing you and Joanne talk so much about Big Band music, would you like to go and hear Les Brown?" My reply was, "Of course, not only to hear Les Brown, but I have always wanted to go to the famous Hollywood Palladium. I belong to the American Ballroom Association, and I was manager of the *Armar Ballroom* in Cedar Rapids, Iowa for many years! I would love to go!!" I enjoyed the evening and music very much. Les Brown tapes were on sale at the entrance. I still have mine!

Helen called to tell me that Bill Findlay would be coming from Chicago now that Smoky had returned to Palm Beach. I, of course, knew who Bill Findlay was and that he was Helen and Wally's nephew, but I had never met him. He arrived the next day. I was impressed by his good looks. And he was a redhead like Wally! I later learned that he and Wally were the only redheads in the Findlay family. Little did I know then that Bill would be there for me on several occasions in the years to come.

Although I certainly loved living in Beverly Hills, except for the earth-quakes, I was getting excited about the coming move to Chicago. I really liked Chicago from my various visits there, and it was a lot closer to my friends and family. So, I was to have quite a shock and disappointment when Helen called to tell me we were moving to Palm Beach and not Chicago. She was quick to say, "Gene, I promise you, you will not have to worry about Simone!" Although I quickly began to think it wouldn't be so bad after all, because I would be closer to Mother and Daddy, and I remember my conversation with Wally's publisher, Wally Cedar. He had described to me the Palm Beach Gallery, the really neat penthouse, Worth Avenue and the famous hotel, The Breakers. Anyway, I always wanted to live just a block away from the ocean.

Well, by now you would think that I had become used to changed plans as directed by Helen. I was quite surprised when she called and said she was sending Simone out to Carla Ridge to auction the paintings and furniture. Of course, Simone was good at this kind of business. Helen would not be coming out until two weeks before we were to make the move to Palm Beach on Wednesday, June 01. Helen also told me to ask nurse Jo Kittrell if she would be willing to relocate to Florida. Her furniture and car would be moved to Palm Beach along with Wally's and mine.

Simone arrived at Carla Ridge on Wednesday evening, May 04, 1988. The invitations to the guests had been sent before she left New York. Thursday, she called Tim O'Brien at Hoboco Caterers for the hors d'oeuvres and bar setup. She wasn't exactly friendly to me, but Helen had told me I didn't have to worry about her; therefore, I certainly wasn't expecting the confrontation which took place between us. The guests were arriving, and I was there with Wally and Jo, the nurse. Simone walked up to me and handed me the bag she was holding and said to me, "Gene, I want you to go and put on this uniform and help the waitresses. You're not a guest in this house!" Wally was talking with one of the guests and didn't hear what she had said. I refused to put on the uniform. Simone said, "Well, you can just go to your room, and I'll find someone else!" In other words, she thought she was firing me!! So, I went to my room, although I had always thought of it as an apartment. It had a bedroom, kitchen and bathroom with a great view of Beverly Hills from my patio. I walked back to my apartment and out to the patio. There I sat with my thoughts, filled with self-pity and spiritual questionings.

As I sat there staring at my beautiful view of Beverly Hills, it offered no comfort to me. Simone had taken away my self-worth with her hateful words, but my inner voice was saying to me, "She could not have hurt you one bit. It was you! You are giving her the power to do it." Well, I guess I did know that intellectually, but I had a long way to go before letting go of hurtful things that happen. Of course, I finally called Helen in Chicago to tell her what had taken place. She said, "You will have to take my word for it. I assure you again that Simone will not have any control over you, and she will leave you alone!" Although I felt better after talking with Helen, I was still a little apprehensive. I didn't see Simone the next day as she had left in a cab to take an early flight to New York. I decided to call the Dorothy Wright and the Beverly Hills employment agencies, just in case things didn't work out. Then, I went back to packing for the move to Palm Beach.

The next weekend I went to Victorville to visit my sister Helen and her husband Ed. She was planning to go to Beverly Hills the next Sunday, May 29, to stay with me and be there when we left for Palm Beach. Joanne had suggested that perhaps Helen might like to spend a couple of nights with her, as we would be leaving Carla Ridge and staying two nights at the Crescent Hotel right around the corner from Rodeo Drive. Of course, my sister was thrilled with that invitation.

Helen Findlay had been there a few days, when she asked me if I would like to keep the furniture in my apartment. I was very pleased with that offer and quickly accepted it. I took a very nice chest of drawers and the coffee table, which is in my living room today. Out of the house, I was given gold twin beds with linens, an *armoire* and a beautiful gold-plated bathroom hand mirror. On Monday, the movers loaded the furniture and left for Palm Beach. So, we went to stay at the Crescent Hotel. While at the hotel I noticed a nearby hair salon. I thought I would like to have my hair washed and set. That would be a special treat to have my hair done in Beverly Hills. At my first glance at the mirror as the hairdresser was setting my hair, I began to have a very uneasy feeling, like "I don't think I'm going to like this!" As he turned me around to see his finished creation, I was mortified! This had to be the worst beauty salon experience in my whole life. I quickly paid my bill, almost ran back to my room and put on my Ava Gabor wig. Then, I hurried off to the dining room to join Helen, Wally and Bob Ryan.

My sister and Joanne came down to tell me goodbye the next morning. Oh, I must write about my calls to the employment agencies. The Dorothy Wright Agency called the week before and wanted me to go to Palm Springs to have an interview with none other than Frank Sinatra's wife, Barbara. It was too late for me to go, but I'm sure it would have been a very interesting experience to write about.

CHAPTER 62

1988-93
WALLY FINDLAY - PALM BEACH

ON our morning flight to Palm Beach of June 06, 1988, Helen and Wally were seated across the aisle from me. First class, of course!! I sat staring at the beautiful sky, and my mind filled with anticipation of my new adventure, mixed with a bit of sadness, leaving my sister and friends in California. However, I was very glad to be leaving the threat of earthquakes and forest fires behind me! And, of course, the thought of Simone being there was still a concern. She would most likely be OK, while Helen was in Palm Beach, but Helen would be going back to Chicago in a few days.

We arrived mid-afternoon at Palm Beach International Airport. Gil Carter, manager of the Gallery, was there to welcome us. The sky cap soon had our suitcases in the trunk of Gil's car, and we were on our way to our new home. Although I had loved the Pacific Ocean beaches, I was eager to get a glimpse of the Atlantic Ocean. Very soon, after crossing I-95 and the Intracoastal Waterway, we were on Palm Beach, riding along Ocean Boulevard and passing Mar-a-Largo, the Marjorie Meriwether Post Estate, owned by Donald Trump since 1985. Gil soon interrupted his conversation with Wally to say, "Gene, there's the Atlantic Ocean!" Palm Beach, with its beautiful mansions facing the ocean, was as impressive to me as Beverly Hills. Soon, we were turning onto Worth Avenue.

Wally Findlay Galleries, Palm Beach

At the end of the block at South County Road was the *Wally Findlay Gallery*, located at 165 Worth Avenue. It was a handsome, regency-styled building that was credited with being one of the most beautiful galleries in the world!

Wally's new home was the third-floor penthouse with a beautiful patio which extended to the corner of South County Road. We had arrived before the five o'clock closing time; therefore, I was introduced to some of the employees: Gil's wife, Doris, Charlie Rogers, Dick Norton and Louise Deese. Louise had been the bookkeeper since the Gallery opened in 1961. I had already met the two frame shop employees, Willie Brown and Smoky Stover. You will recall that Helen sent them to California to help me with Wally. And guess who else was there to greet us? That's right, Simone Karoff! Well, it looked like her, but she greeted me like a long-lost friend. Quite different than the last time I saw her in Beverly Hills! She had leased a cottage for me at 225 Chilean Avenue, just two blocks from the Gallery. She had also instructed Charlie Rogers, salesman at the Gallery, to take me to Publix Supermarket to get a supply of groceries. Whatever Helen said to her seemed to be working! Our furniture arrived two days later. I remember getting very nervous about my best violin (one of three), and I was wondering why on earth I had not brought it with me on the plane; however, it arrived in good condition.

Wally decided he wanted to take Helen for a ride in his gray Rolls, and he wanted me to drive. He and Helen would sit in the back seat. I drove them around the island without car trouble and was heading back to the Gallery, when Wally said, "Gene, drive down Ocean Boulevard to the bridge past Mar-a-Largo, and go to the Rolls Royce dealership in West Palm Beach. I wondered to myself, does he want to buy a new Rolls or just locate a shop for repairs for the two he already owns? We never did find the dealership. He had forgotten where it was located. Consequently, I drove us into a very bad neighborhood. Just imagine, yours truly driving a Rolls Royce Classic with very distinguished-looking Wally and Helen in the back seat, especially in this drug-infested area of West Palm Beach! Immediately, I realized the necessity of making a quick retreat and finding my way back to Palm Beach.

Simone had already left for New York when we returned. Helen said, "Simone will be in the New York Gallery most of the time. Gil Carter is an excellent manager here, and she feels she is needed in New York. Of course, I'm sure she will be spending her weekends here. You won't have to be concerned about her, so don't worry!" Well, she has been surprisingly different than that "Simone" of Beverly Hills. My reply to Helen was, "She sure seems to have changed." I said to myself, "I just hope she stays that way."

"By the way, Helen, did I hear you tell Wally that you are going back to Chicago tomorrow?" "Yes, I was just going to tell you about it, and I've made an appointment for Wally with Dr. Wacks for next Tuesday, and I have his UCLA medical chart for you to take with you. His office is at 1411 North Flagler Drive. Oh, another thing! Wally would like to have dinner at the Polo Restaurant. It's very close to the Gallery, directly behind Sachs Fifth Avenue in the Colony Hotel. I'll stay with Wally for his nebulizer at 5 o'clock. Why don't you go to your apartment and be back here around 7 o'clock?" That sounded great to me. I could make a few calls and get dressed for dinner. My cottage was a bit small and somewhat crowded with my furniture; however, I really liked it. The palm trees surrounding it made me think I was living in the tropics now, especially when the wild parrots began their loud squawking in the early morning. On my very first morning, you can imagine how startled I was to be awakened by them.

We enjoyed a very nice dinner at the Colony Hotel. You must remember that I'd dined in some of the most elegant hotels, clubs and restaurants in Beverly Hills. So, I was beginning to feel right at home! Wally Cedar, the publicist for the Gallery, had described the penthouse over the Gallery while we were still in Beverly Hills. He said, "You're going to love Palm Beach, especially the Gallery with its ten rooms displaying the paintings and with the beautiful winding staircase to the second floor. The third floor is Wally's penthouse with a very large bedroom at each end with walk-in closets, a sitting room and another bedroom in the middle. The four rooms all have sliding doors opening onto the patio. The patio itself has a sizable bar." Just think, I would soon have the pleasure of attending the catered parties which would be held on the patio.

I had believed that I knew a good bit about art. You, the reader, may remember that I was once married to Mark, a very talented artist, Carol and Steve's father. He was very proficient in using the air brush, still life oil paintings and portraits as well as water colors. Through him, I had gained a little knowledge about the art field. My grandson, Tom, became a very talented artist. Oh yes, during this same period of time my father was still painting in his late eighties! Now, I was to have the wonderful experience of viewing French Impressionist and Post-Impressionist paintings, comprised of works by Claude Monet, Alfred Sisley, Camille Pissarro, Pierre-Auguste Renoir, Maurice Vlaminck, Louis Valtat, Louis Fabien, Raymond Quincy, Pierre Bettar, Gustavo Novoa, John Bentham-Dinsdale, to mention a few. An American still life artist was Gregory Hull. The most costly contemporary Impressionist artist was Nicola Simbari. I have treasured an autographed catalog from Simbari's exhibition of his paintings in the Gallery in November 1988. I got to know quite well Sam Barber, American Impressionist from Hyannis Port in 1991. He invited Wally and me to come for a visit. I was also privileged to meet and know the French portrait artist, well-known in Palm Beach, Vidal-Quadras and his wife, Marie Charlotte. On several occasions I had the privilege of going with Wally and Helen to their Palm Beach home.

Helen had called the interim nurses' employment agency to fill the forty hours weekly to cover the extra shifts needed for Jo's days off on Saturdays and Sundays and my days off on Thursdays and Fridays. I worked the 8 a.m. to 8 p.m. shift, and Jo the 8 p.m. to 8 a.m. shift. It had been many years since I could walk to work. Actually, it was years ago at the *Armar Ballroom* in Iowa that I just had to get up every morning, and I was literally at work. I still needed my car in Palm Beach, because I had to take Wally to his medical appointments, do the shopping and take him for his morning and afternoon rides.

I really hate to confess what I'm about to say. However, my meditation and quiet time were receiving less priority than previously. I realized that this could be harmful to my spiritual journey. My guilty conscience would say, "After all, you are working 60 hours a week, you appear to be going to school in order to be educated in art and in Wally's medical condition, not to mention stressful working conditions with him and Simone and ... you are 60 years old! Simone will be in Palm Beach almost every weekend, and you don't know how she's going to treat you." I was soon able to recover from these negative thoughts and to realize how fortunate and thankful I was to have been led to the interview in Beverly Hills which resulted in my position with Wally Findlay. Furthermore, I had come to love Helen as, indeed, she treated me as though I were a close member of their family.

Simone, Wally and I in his penthouse sitting room

Wally's bedroom had a large walk-in closet, where he would exercise and use his treadmill, except the mornings when he was depressed. His bedroom was quite large with his king-size bed, desk, television, table for his nebulizer and a large buffet which housed his very expensive collection of Dorothy Doughty birds. Jo and Elsie, the nurses, and I were advised not to open and touch the collection.

After Helen left for Chicago, Wally and I started taking a morning and afternoon drive around Palm Beach Island. I soon realized that this was one of my most reliable behavioral techniques for helping to control Wally's depression. Wally's two Rolls were kept in a garage in the Sachs Fifth Avenue Building, and that's where I wanted them to stay! For the most part, he was content to ride in my Ford, even though I now knew that I had a lemon. I was very unhappy with it and had thoughts of trading it for a new one.

I had no trouble finding Dr. Wacks' office on Flagler Drive that Tuesday morning. We walked into a rather crowded waiting room; nevertheless, after I had filled out the medical information, we were called in to have Wally's weight and blood pressure checked and were directed to go into the examining room for our first meeting with the doctor. I could tell that Wally liked him right away, and so did I. Dr. Wacks said, "Mr. Findlay, I have been in your gallery on Worth Avenue many times, and I always wanted to meet you personally. This is a real pleasure for me!" I gave the doctor the medical charts from UCLA Medical Center. He decided not to change Wally's medication for the time being. As soon as the doctor ended the examination, Wally and I went to The Breakers Hotel for lunch. This became one of our favorite eating places.

I want to mention another benefit I enjoyed while working for Wally. It was the Gallery WATS line (toll free), which I had permission to use for business and for personal needs, such as calling my parents in Alabama. I called Helen in Chicago about Wally's visit to the doctor. As we were about ready to hang up she said, "Simone is planning to come down on Friday night and stay for the weekend, but I am sure she will spend most of her time fussing over Wally and going out to eat with you and him. As I told you several times, you don't have to be concerned." I thought to myself, "I'll feel much better when this weekend is over."

There was a letter from Florence Horn (Wally's ex-mistress) waiting for me when I arrived home from work with the sad and shocking news that Wally's publicist, Wally Cedar, had died. When I met him in Beverly Hills he appeared to be in good health. You may remember his talking to me about Wally's penthouse in Palm Beach. Florence wrote, "I hope your life is as pleasant as it can be under the circumstances, and you are holding your own." This was the first of many letters I was to receive from Florence. She enclosed a copy of Wally Cedar's eulogy, dated August 06, 1988. I have found real meaning in its words, and perhaps you will, also.

My Dear Friends,

I am so pleased that you were able to be here today because I have several things that I want to explain:

Death is nothing at all ... I have only slipped away into the next room.

I am I, and you are you ... whatever we were to each other, that we are still.

Call me by my old familiar name – just Wally.

Speak to me in the easy way which you always used.

Put no difference into your tone ... wear no forced air of solemnity or sorrow.

Laugh as we always laughed at the little jokes we enjoyed together.

Play, smile, think of me, pray for me.

Let my name be ever the household word that it always was. Let it be spoken without effect, without the ghost of a shadow on it.

Life means all that it ever meant. It is the same as it ever was ... there is absolutely unbroken continuity.

What is this death but a negligible accident? Why should I be out of mind because I am out of sight?

I am but waiting for you, for an interval,
somewhere very near … just around the corner …
and All is well.

Much, much love,
W. xxxx
Wally Cedar

(On Saturday, August 06, 1988, at St. Victor's Catholic Church in Los Angeles, the above letter was read as part of Wally's eulogy. Selected by Erin Butler from the writings of Henry Scott Holland, 1847-1918, Professor of Divinity at Oxford College, it was adapted as a letter from Wally and read to the congregation by Jeffrey Butler.)

On duty at the Gallery

By now, I suppose I should not be surprised about changes in my work schedule. When I arrived at the Gallery on Tuesday morning, September 27, Wally had finished his breakfast and was talking to Helen in Chicago. As soon as he saw me, he handed me the phone and said, "Helen wants to talk to you." I took the phone and said "Good morning, Helen." "Good morning, Gene. I'm sorry to give you such short notice, but I have made reservations for tomorrow morning for you and Wally on Delta Airlines to go to the New York Gallery. President François Mitterrand of France is flying to New York, and this Thursday, the 29th, he will be visiting the Gallery at 11 a.m. I have also made a reservation for Willie. He will help you with the luggage and with Wally's nebulizer." Well, …. I was quite excited or stunned to hear this news. I had gotten used to the Beverly Hills and Palm Beach way of life, but I never thought that I would be meeting a top dignitary, such as the president of France, François Mitterrand.

We had a pleasant flight the next day. First Class, of course! Michael Brown, the New York manager, was at the airport to take us to the Gallery. It was located at 17 57th Street. The building was five stories high, and Wally's apartment was on the top floor. Reservations had been made for Willie and me at the Blackstone Hotel, which was very close to the Gallery. Simone seemed happy to see us, even me! She suggested to Michael that I might like a tour of the Gallery, and then he should take us to the hotel so that Willie and I could get checked into our rooms. As we were going out the door of the Gallery,

I noticed a lot of people and some strange activity going on in front of the IBM headquarters across the street. Michael noticed my puzzled expression and quickly explained, "That's a film crew. Al Pacino is currently working on his new movie "Sea of Love." Interesting, I thought, but after all, I had just moved from Beverly Hills!

Simone had told Willie and me to be back at the Gallery at 9:30 the next morning. I called Willie's room to tell him what time to expect me in the lobby, and we would walk to the Gallery together. Now, I've walked the streets in big cities before, such as L.A., Atlanta, Chicago and Minneapolis, but I had never seen such crowds of people walking so fast and seemingly knowing just where they were going. To tell you the truth, as we walked to the Gallery I began to feel like a hillbilly, with all the crowds and the tall buildings which kept my gaze upward. So, I was very startled when a young man, as he passed by me, turned and said, "Ma'am, your purse is open." I quickly checked to see if he had picked my purse and then told me about it, but no, he was a Good Samaritan.

Part of the entourage of French President François Mitterrand with Wally Findlay and Simone Karoff

During his two-day visit to New York President Mitterrand took time out from a round of official business to view the still life paintings of French artist Jean-Claude Chauray at the *Wally Findlay Galleries,* one of the oldest and most famous in America. I must mention that prior to the arrival at the Gallery by the president and his entourage, all Gallery employees were sent home, that is, with the exception of yours truly. I sat across the room by the windows while the picture taking took place. After the private viewing of the Chauray paintings, all of the visitors, again including yours truly, went to the nearby prestigious French restaurant *L'Atelier de Joel Iobuchon.* President Mitterrand and his party left New York to meet with President Ronald Reagan in Washington.

The Palm Beach Daily News covered the event in its Sunday edition of October 02, 1988, as follows:

MITTERRAND VISITS FINDLAY GALLERIES IN NEW YORK CITY - Eastside, Westside, uptown, downtown. In whatever direction you turned noontime on New York's 57th Street it was a sight to behold.

At the corner of Madison Avenue Al Pacino drew a crowd of hundreds as he emoted for a film crew in front of the IBM headquarters. He is currently working on his new movie Sea of Love night and day all over the city. Meanwhile, a battalion of secret service men and women were busy securing the north side of the street in anticipation of French President François Mitterrand's visit to the Wally Findlay Galleries.

Mr. Mitterrand was in New York on an official two-day visit before going on to Washington for a state dinner at The White House. In between meetings it had been arranged for the president to have a private showing of an exhibition of paintings by Jean-Claude Chauray currently on view at Findlay. Chauray, a French artist, is well-known in art circles for his still life compositions—mostly apples and other fruits painted in a super realistic style. The president reportedly has a Chauray in his Paris office.

"What's going on here?" the driver of a Federal Express truck parked in front of the gallery hawked. "Across the street, see him, that's Al Pacino. And somebody said Mitterrand is about to arrive any minute." Moments later the truck driver was told to move on, he was blocking entrance to the gallery. More interested in Pacino's antics, he was determined to stand his ground. It took a bellowing loud speaker for him to get the message. But, in a city where crowds of hundreds can form in a matter of seconds, the air of something big happening could not be abated.

The sirens, when they came could be heard blocks away, coming from the United Nations. Police Cars first, then station wagons and mini buses, all flashing red lights, then the limousines, followed by more mini buses (somehow oddly ominous-looking) and, bringing up the rear, a New York City paramedic van.

President Mitterrand stepped from the number one limousine, a French flag indicating it was his official car. In a flash he was flanked by a sea of men and women, all members of his official party, French Secret Service and the FBI as he made his way into the gallery.

Waiting to greet him were Wally Findlay, who flew to New York from Palm Beach for the occasion, Simone Karoff, executive vice president of the galleries, the artist and Mrs. Chauray. Although charged, understandably, the atmosphere was high spirited, warm and gracious. Wally Findlay has had a gallery in Paris on Avenue Matignon since 1971.

The official party numbered about 40 dignitaries, among them the French Ambassador to the United Nations Pierre Louis Blanc, and the Minister of Foreign Affairs, Roland Dumas. A tour of the exhibition followed with Chauray charmingly escorting the president from one painting to another.

Mr. Mitterrand's visit to the gallery was a tribute to Chauray, one official explained, but she also noted it is recognized that Findlay's contributions to French artists are many. "The French Government awarded him the Legion du Merite a few years back for these very contributions." she said.

After checking his wrist watch, a nod from the president indicated it was time to leave, the visit was over. Gone were the secret service, the diplomats, the walkie-talkies. Out on the street sirens began to churn again. Lights flashed. Traffic was halted. And the procession moved away on its way to a Washington-bound Concorde.

I must mention one further detail about my visit to New York. The next day I decided to go to a drug store around the corner from the Gallery. I do not remember what my purchase was; however, I shall never forget the embarrassment I felt as I paid the cashier and made my way to the door. All of a sudden, you guessed it, a loud alarm sounded. Startled, I looked around, only to see all the people at the registers staring at me. The cashier had neglected to desensitize the alarm button on my purchase. She apologized to me. I had done nothing wrong, but I felt sort of guilty of something as I made my way back to the Gallery.

There were many inquiries about the New York trip from the Palm Beach Gallery employees when we returned. Wally and I immediately went back to our morning and afternoon rides around the island. Our lunch would usually be soup and sandwich at the Gallery, but once or twice a week we would go to the beachfront restaurant at The Breakers, which I very much enjoyed. For dinner, depending on Wally's state of mind, of course, we could be seen walking to many of the well-known restaurants located very close to the Gallery, such as Café L Europe, Taboo, The Colony. But if Wally did not want to wear coat and tie, we would go to Hamburger Heaven on South County Road, which really was the best place to go for a delicious hamburger!

Wally's dementia had not taken away from his mind that he was the owner and president of the Galleries; therefore, Helen had given me a list of Gallery business which would enable me to answer some of Wally's questions. He would become suspicious and believe that someone, usually within the Gallery staff, was plotting against him. Thank God, this didn't happen very often! If this did happen, and Jo was late for her shift, *after my being there with him for twelve hours*, I well remember my thoughts. This is like being on the ocean in a boat without a paddle!

The weekends would be a little less stressful, as Simone would come down from New York. Yes, I did say Simone would be there, and I would be less stressed! Well, I was at the same time mindful that she could become that "Beverly Hills Simone." Whatever Helen Findlay did, it was still working, that is, as far as I was concerned, but there would be times when her temper would explode, mostly when whatever poor souls in the Gallery might have done to displease her. At times, her tantrums would be aimed at outsiders. On one occasion, on a Saturday afternoon, Wally was very depressed. Simone decided that Dr. Wacks could help Wally, so she called him at his home and demanded that he come to the penthouse to see Wally. Dr. Wacks was not used to being told what to do. He hung up in the middle of her demands. He did call her back and told her to get Wally to the Emergency Room. Since there was nothing physically wrong with him, and after a long wait for him to be seen, we went back to the Gallery.

Now that I was living in Florida, I could visit my parents in Alabama more frequently. It was 640 miles one way. I would drive there one day, stay over the next day and return to Palm Beach the next day. I arranged to have an extra day and with my two regular days off, this gave me time to make the trip. I didn't get to go home for Christmas, because Helen wanted me to be with Wally.

The Gallery staff received a honey-baked ham for Christmas along with a generous check. In addition to my check, I received a Christmas card from Helen with a check for $500.00! And this was my first Christmas at the Palm Beach Gallery!! Simone sent some of her Palm Beach friends honey-baked hams, also. In return, she would receive very nice gifts from those people. She really didn't like them, so believe it or not, she gave me several of those gifts. I now have a beautiful water pitcher in my bathroom which she gave me 25 years ago. Estee Lauder, whose home was not far from the Gallery, and was one of her friends, would send Simone a very large collection of her name-brand makeup, but I would be the one who would end up with the gift. That was great, because I had been using Estee Lauder makeup for years!

You may think I am making up the following, or at least exaggerating, but I have the proof! I still have the Christmas dinner menu that Simone had very neatly written out on a 4 x 6 card with gold trim around the edges, as follows:

Christmas Dinner
Sunday, December 25, 1988
Mollisol Caviar
a la '21' Club
Celery Olives

Roast Vermont Turkey
Mushroom Sausage Dressing
Giblet Gravy
Cranberry Sauce in Orange Cups
Louisiana Candied Yams
New England Mashed Potatoes
String Beans Almondine

Baked Virginia Ham
Southern Biscuits

Holiday Pumpkin Pie
Whipped Cream Garni
Espresso Coffee
Blanc de Blancs After dinner
Wine chocolates

The dinner table was set up on the second floor Gallery display room. The meal was catered by Palm Beach Catering. Wally, Simone and I were served by uniformed waiters. I said I had the proof, and I do! I have a picture of the dinner table. Also, Simone took a picture of Wally and me seated at the table.

I received a letter and a Christmas card from Florence Horn. She was Wally's ex-mistress in Beverly Hills. She had called earlier in the week and talked to Wally when she knew Simone was in New York. In her letter she wanted to know if Wally and I could come out and spend a couple of weeks in Palm Springs. She said, "If you think it possible, I'll ask Helen." Her next paragraph sort of put me back on guard. She wrote, "Whatever you do, don't let that witch get the best of you! I know Helen won't stand for it either. It's hard to believe such people exist, but I know her like a book after eight or nine years of her tricks. So, just hang in there!"

My daughter, Kim

It seemed as though my daughters needed to get away from their harsh winters: Carol in Sioux Falls, South Dakota and Kim in Saint Cloud, Minnesota. My cottage on Chilean Avenue was quite small; however, with them visiting me separately and sleeping on the couch, it worked just fine. Carol was the first to do this. She had felt very fortunate to have met Wally in Beverly Hills and to have been a guest in his home, and apparently he took a liking to her. After all, he gave her three paintings! Wally and I went to the airport to pick her up. She went to the Gallery with me the next morning. She really enjoyed looking at the paintings and meeting the staff. Around noon, I asked Wally, "Do you want me to fix lunch?" He replied, "Why don't we just go to The Breakers?" I knew Carol would love the opportunity to dine in such opulence! After lunch, we drove around the island with Wally and me serving as Carol's tour guides, pointing out famous places, such as the Kennedy Compound, the Flagler Museum and Mar-a-Largo, to name a few.

Around 10 that night, my usual bedtime, neither Carol nor I were a bit sleepy. Carol said she was looking forward to going window shopping down Worth Avenue. Now, I do not know of any city in which two unescorted females could be safe walking down a city street that late at night, except Palm Beach. So, I said, "Why don't we go now?" She agreed, of course. So, we started at Saks Fifth Avenue and went all the way down that side of the street to Coconut Row and back to South County Road on the other side. By then, we were tired and ready to go to bed, and we were only two short blocks from home.

Carol had never been to Key West, and I wanted to show her where Mother, my sister Helen and I had stayed some fifty years previously when we visited Uncle Nick. So, I called Helen Findlay in Chicago for permission to take an extra day along with my normal two days off, in view of the fact that it was a trip of one hundred fifty miles each way. I had not made a motel reservation, so I decided to try to find a room in the lower keys, close to Key West. Well, I got the last room available at Sunset Villas on Conch Key. It had a kitchenette facing the water on the south. I still have the picture I took of Carol, in which she is laughing hysterically as I snapped the picture, because, suddenly, a rush of wind opened my blouse, nearly ripping it off and leaving it hanging from each of my arms. Enough said about that!

The next day we visited the Hemmingway House and the southernmost beach in the United States. I tried to find the house that Mother, Helen and I had stayed in so long ago, but I couldn't find it. We drove by the famous Sloppy Joe's Bar at the corner of Duval and Greene Streets. We didn't go in. It was founded on December 05, 1933. Although Carol had greatly enjoyed her stay with me, she was ready to go back home to Ray, Tom, Suzy and Ben in cold South Dakota.

On my days off I would often go shopping for spiritual books. I discovered a great bookstore on South Dixie Highway, The Rainbow Bridge. While I was looking for a Joel Goldsmith book, a lady asked the manager if he had a book by Paul Twitchell called "In my soul I am free." Well, that got my attention, for I had been looking for that same book. I was glad to hear him say that the book was sold out, but that he had ordered a new supply of them and should have them in shortly. Also, this became my introduction to that customer, Jane Keen. We became close friends. Her husband was a well-known Palm Beach dermatologist.

Wally's 86th birthday was February 26, 1989. Therefore, my next stop was Burdine's Department Store to look for a new dress. Also, I could certainly use a new pair of shoes, high-heeled shoes, of course. By the way, a word of warning to ladies who love to wear high heels: I never listened to advice from people who warned me that I was going to ruin my feet. And here I am, at 85 years of age, still trying to wear heels, and ... my feet are not in very good shape!

Palm Beach Catering was serving a buffet dinner on the penthouse patio in Wally's honor. Simone had sent invitations to the Gallery employees and their families. Helen Findlay, Bob Ryan and Vern Squires from Chicago would be attending. Goldie Hawkins, well-known pianist in the Palm Beach area, provided favorite melodies throughout the evening. Another guest was a friend of Simone and Wally from Paris, Princess Ghislaine de Polignac. Things went well throughout the evening, and everyone had a good time. Following is the hand-written invitation sent to the guests by Simone:

Admission by Birthday Cards Only
Mrs. Arthur Karoff

requests the pleasure of your company
at Wally Findlay's 86th Birthday

on Monday, February 27th 1989

Cocktails 5:30 o'clock

Buffet dinner 6:30 o'clock

165 Worth Avenue

Informal. Please, No Gifts

Wally's driver's license expired on his birthday. This meant it would have to be renewed. Wally had not even mentioned wanting to drive since coming to Palm Beach. We were all thankful for that, but still, I'm thinking, "This is not going to go very well. He is not going to want to give up his license, and I'm the one who has to take him to the Department of Motor Vehicles." Helen, Bob Ryan and Vern Squires returned to Chicago on Wednesday. So, I had to wait until the following Monday to take him. That left me with my two days off and the weekend to worry about it. Well, I didn't need to be concerned. Perhaps he did realize, at least on that day, that he should not be driving. He and I went to the Motor Vehicle Renewal Offices early Monday morning. With the help of a very efficient clerk, he was finally convinced that this was the proper thing for him to do. I still have the letter which was sent to him from Tallahassee from the State Department of Highway Safety and Motor Vehicles, "We have indicated on your driver record that your driver's license was voluntarily surrendered."

Wally was surprisingly willing to give up his driver's license; however, I was about to find out that he was not about to surrender his independence, that is, his walking down Worth Avenue to his barber on Coconut Row without my tagging along. Well, he didn't know it, but that was my job. The barber shop was only two blocks from the Gallery, so as soon as he would walk out the door I would jump in my car and follow him to the shop, where I could see him getting into the barber chair. I would then return to the Gallery and phone the barber who would then agree to call me when he was about through so that I could drive back down Worth Avenue. I would park the car near where Wally was walking along the sidewalk and ask him if he would like a ride back to the Gallery. He always seemed surprised to see me and would be glad to have a quick return.

Lucille Yeater lived in Cedar Rapids, as I've said before. Finally, she gave up on Toby the cat. You may recall Toby was shipped to her from Beverly Hills a year before. Apparently she and the cat couldn't get along with each other; therefore, she called to inform me that if I didn't send for her, she was going to take her to an animal shelter. I didn't want her to do that. Somehow, my plan to get her to Palm Beach worked amazingly well. I called the Cedar Rapids Gazette and placed an ad in the Want Ads Section stating that I needed a cat transported from Cedar Rapids to Palm Beach. I thought it was most likely a long shot, but to my surprise it worked very quickly.

The very first day that the ad came out I received a call from a lady in Cedar Rapids, saying that her daughter Kathleen was there for a visit and would be leaving in two days for Palm Beach. She would be happy to bring my cat. I later found out that Kathleen worked for a famous multi-millionaire attorney, Robert Montgomery. He was known for his 11.3 billion dollar settlement for Florida from Big Tobacco and his contributions to the area's cultural scene. This tobacco suit was very much in the news in the first years I was in Florida.

My son Steve and I were having dinner at Testa's, a favorite sidewalk dining place in Palm Beach. This was the time when Robert Montgomery's tobacco suit was at its peak on all the TV and radio stations. Steve was a heavy smoker; therefore, he didn't like the idea of being told when and where he could smoke. As we were enjoying our meal, I noticed a TV reporter with his microphone and a cameraman following him to interview dinner guests.

My silent prayer was "Please don't let him come to this table." Very shortly, the reporter was talking to Steve, and the interview was to be aired the next day. Of course, Steve's comments were very much in favor of Big Tobacco.

As I write this, Steve at age 61 is finally trying to give up the habit. Kathleen arrived in Palm Beach with Toby and her two cats four days later. I found a good home for Toby on Olive Street, located on the West Palm Beach side of the Intracoastal.

Helen Findlay called from Chicago to say that the lease on my apartment would be up the next month, and she thought I might like to look for a larger place, and the Gallery would still pay seven hundred dollars monthly for another rental. This was good news for me. Although there were things I liked about my Palm Beach address; e.g., being very close to work and the beach. After a year, my apartment was really getting crowded. Also, it was very close to another building, and the loud TVs and radios could become a problem, being so close to my bedroom. And, indeed, I did allow them to be a problem. One night, after not being able to sleep, I decided to put my small radio in the window so as to drown out the outside noise. That's the way I finally fell asleep. However, I was awakened around 1 a.m. by a loud knocking on my door. Who was there? It was a police officer, telling me to turn my radio off. So far, at age 85, that was the first and last time for a policeman to knock on my door and reprimand me for anything.

Helen's suggestion that I might like to look for a larger apartment took top priority on my next two days off. I was pretty sure that I would not find a suitable place on the island for seven hundred dollars. So, I started out early on Thursday morning with a Palm Beach Post want ads section in my hand. I made an appointment to see a rental in Lake Worth at 11 a.m. Lake Worth would be a good place to live due to being easily accessible. Coming from Worth Avenue, a right turn south on South Ocean Boulevard and driving seven or eight miles would put me in Lake Worth. I had noticed previously an ad for an apartment in the White House Building on Ocean Boulevard. I decided to take a look at it, since it was on my way to Lake Worth. The manager showed me the rental on the fifth floor. I was rather surprised to see a studio apartment which was just one big room! I should have known that my seven hundred dollars would not get me much on Palm Beach.

Time was approaching for my appointment with John Carvette, the owner of the condo building on Lake Side Drive. I hurried to my car and continued south on Ocean Boulevard. Soon I was in Lake Worth and crossing over the Intracoastal on the Lake Worth Bridge. Lake Side Drive was the first street after the bridge. Mr. Carvette lived at 411 Lake Side Drive next to the large condo building on the corner. So far, so good, as I looked around the neighborhood. I was very pleased to see that it was on the Intracoastal Waterway with nothing obstructing the view of the water.

Mr. Carvette was waiting for me. After filling me in on information about a possible lease, we proceeded to the 421 condo. It was on the second floor. As soon as we stepped inside the doorway, I'm thinking, "I think I'm going to like this place." I took a few steps into the living room, and I knew this was the place for me. The dining room had mirrored walls, and the two bedrooms, kitchen, living room and two bathrooms were all beautifully furnished. The master bedroom had a white, king-sized bed and a balcony. A slight disappointment was that I couldn't see the Intracoastal without going out onto the balcony; however, the house across the street looked very interesting. I later learned it had a story behind it. The house had walls around it and resembled a small castle. Mr. Roy Reed built it as a gift for his bride around the turn of the 20th century.

I signed a lease and then went to the Lake Worth Utility Company to have the power turned on. Then I drove back to Palm Beach a little overwhelmed with the moving plans and all the packing I had to do. However, I made a rather large purchase the next day for my new home. I had grown up with a piano, and I missed the Baldwin I had in Cedar Rapids. I purchased a new Baldwin piano to be delivered on my move-in date for the next Thursday, May 04, 1989. Two weeks passed, and I found myself pretty well pleased with my beautiful condo as well as meeting new friends who lived in the building. On the second floor next to me was Mary Demerick., a snowbird from Michigan. Connie lived downstairs the year around. Oh yes, I had met Doreen Mullin at the Gallery, and we became good friends. She had inherited a home on Ocean View Drive, which was only one block long. She was able to see the ocean looking east from her home and the Intracoastal looking west! When my daughter, Carol, visited me in Lake Worth, we made a day trip to Freeport, Bahamas. Doreen joined us, and we had a great time; however, I did get a little seasick.

Speaking of making new friends, I met many interesting people. Michael Pearman was a Hollywood producer in the 40s. After his film-making years, he opened a restaurant in New York City which became rather famous. He retired and moved to Palm Beach, becoming a part-time sales employee at the Gallery. He liked to kid me and would often comment on my clothes, telling me I had more clothes than Gretta Garbo. At other times he would say, "Gene, you have more clothes than Gloria Swanson."

Another thing I especially liked about my new home was the small park in front of the condo building. On my days off, early in the morning, I would walk at a very fast pace to the Lake Worth Bridge and back to the park. At that time in the morning there were very few people around, so I would sit on a bench by the water and meditate and reflect on my life in amazement, on what had transpired in just this decade of the 80s, especially the rather strange way I was led to Wally Findlay. Of course, I know it always sounds strange. The truth is that I know that "God works in strange and mysterious ways."

Yes, I was very grateful for my new position in life. But, how can I accurately describe it? Sixty hours a week of stressful decision-making in coping with Wally's illness, dealing with the unpleasantness that would come up between the nurses, mostly on weekends when Simone would appear like clockwork from the New York Gallery. Even some of the most elegant dining places I was privileged to enjoy could at times be unpleasant!

On the other hand, where could I have been in a more perfect place? Just think: two weeks of vacation with two days added to my two weekly days off several times yearly so that I could visit Mother and Daddy in Alabama, 640 miles from Palm Beach, a salary with financial benefits, plus bonuses I never imagined, being accepted in the Wally Findlay family, and I then had my beautiful condo in Lake Worth on the Intracoastal Waterway!!

My daughters, Carol and Kim

On my vacation that year (1989), I went to Castle Haven, Minnesota on Lake Superior to vacation with Carol and Ray. Kim lived in St. Cloud, Minnesota; therefore, it was not so far for Kim and her friend, Sheila, to drive. Steve could not join us because of obligations in Cedar Rapids.

For the most part, Wally didn't give me too much trouble. I had mostly figured out ways to bring him back from his bad behavior. Of course, he was forever accusing someone of stealing his wallet. It would show up where he had put it, or sometimes he would hide it, fearful that someone was going to take it. But, one evening in the early part of November, I had my worst experience to date with Wally.

It was about 7 o'clock on a Wednesday evening. Wally was "hell bent" on leaving the Gallery and, what made it worse, he did not want me to go with him. As I have described the layout of the Gallery—two floors of art and Wally occupying the third floor penthouse; well, he went to the bathroom, the telephone rang, and I went to answer it. Wally took this opportunity to slip past me and go downstairs to the second floor, where he hid from me!

I looked and looked for him a good fifteen minutes before it dawned on me to simply go down to the first floor and sit at a desk so I could see the only door that was possible for him to get out, and if he did open the door, the alarm would go off. I didn't have to wait long until he came, straight for the door and not even seeing me sitting at the desk. I let him get almost to the door when I said in a loud voice, "Wally, don't you open that door!" I suppose I scared him, because he willingly went back upstairs with me. Thank God! Jo was supposed to be there for her twelve-hour night shift at any minute. "Please, don't be late, Jo!" That fearful thought was quickly relieved, as I could hear her coming up the stairs. With happy thoughts of my two days off starting the next day, I was soon in my car driving down Ocean Boulevard to my condo in Lake Worth.

As I was preparing to go to bed the telephone rang. It was Helen Findlay. It was unusual for her to call me at home, as we talked every day at the Gallery. I picked up the phone and greeted her with a question sound in my "Hello." "Hello, Gene. I hope I'm not calling too late. This afternoon I completed the Mayo Clinic doctor's appointment for Wally, starting on Monday, November 13 and running through Friday, the 17th. I have also made plane reservations for you and Wally to come here to Chicago Friday afternoon. You two will stay in adjoining rooms at the Park Hyatt Hotel which, as you know, is next door to the Gallery.

"On Sunday, you, Wally and I will leave for Rochester, Minnesota. I have made reservations at the Kohler Hotel which is easily accessible to the medical facilities on the Skyway or Subway. I think it would be nice for you and Wally to stay here in Chicago for a couple of days before we leave for the Mayo Clinic on Sunday. Willie or Smoky will take you and Wally to the airport Friday. Again, I'm sorry for such a short notice." I replied with a rather feeble answer, "Oh, that's all right. We'll be happy to see you Friday."

I sat down hard or flopped down on my beautiful white king-sized bed. Well, there goes my plan to sleep late in the morning! It will take me all day to pack and get ready to leave Friday. I called Elsie, the nurse on duty with Wally and explained that she should pack Wally's suitcase with enough clothes for twelve days.

We had a very nice flight to Chicago on Friday. I really do like to fly (especially first class!), but there is always a little tinge of fear which can quickly accelerate to downright terror should the plane start bouncing around due to weather conditions. However, this didn't happen on this flight, and Wally was well behaved. He was always happy to see Helen.

There was a small problem at the baggage claim area with Wally stubbornly insisting that one of his bags was missing. I finally convinced him the airline would send his missing bag to the Gallery.

The Gallery staff greeted us warmly when we arrived. There were three floors of art and offices. Helen lived in the fourth floor penthouse and, as I have written previously, her office was on the second floor and had a large window which faced the back of the famous Chicago Water Tower.

Bob Ryan, Helen and Wally had a short business meeting (I wandered around the Gallery looking at paintings.) before going next door for check-in at the Park Hyatt. Soon we were checked in and ready to go to our rooms on the third floor. Helen said to us, "Why don't I go up with you and, after Wally has his nebulizer treatment, we will go down to the dining room for dinner?" Of course, we agreed. I had noticed the beautiful dining room with the grand piano. Our adjoining rooms were located at the end of the hall. The rooms were quite large. I took the room on the end of the building, because the windows allowed me to have a very good view of the city.

Now, back to our dinner: First of all, my prime rib was cooked to a perfect medium rare. The three of us had interesting dinner conversations with Wally talking about his past experiences in Chicago (Many of them I had heard many times.) The grand piano was being played by an attractive professional pianist. Things got even better when Helen said, "Oh yes, Gene, I forgot to tell you that I've hired a nurse to stay all night with Wally tonight and tomorrow night." Wally must not have heard what she said, because he didn't say anything.

Just as we were finishing our dinner a lady in a nurse's uniform came up to the table. "Miss Findlay, my name is Judy Andrews. I'm the nurse from the

Professional Nursing Agency. The desk clerk in the lobby said you were here."
"Nice to meet you, Miss Andrews. This is my brother Wally, and this is Gene
Winn. Wally, Judy is going to stay with you tonight to give you your medication, and she'll be there if you need anything." Wally looked surprised and at
first tried not to hurt Judy's feelings. "Well, Judy, I don't know why Helen felt I
needed a nurse, but I will not have a nurse in my room." Wanting to avoid any
more unpleasantness, Helen said, "I'm so sorry, Judy. I'll call the agency, and you
will receive your night's wages from them."

Without speaking the words, the storm inside my head exploded. "What is
the matter with you, Wally? You have had nurses with you very night for the
last two years." Oh well, I guess I won't get much sleep tonight.

Wally soon got over being mad at Helen. We said good night, and she went
back to the Gallery. Wally and I went to our rooms. I was now resigned to
whatever the sleepless night might bring. Well, the night appeared to be going
pretty well. Wally took his night medication, put on his pajamas and got into
bed. I was thinking that maybe he was tired from all the activities of the day
and, hopefully, he was going to sleep. I took a few minutes to sit by the window
in my room and enjoy the scenery of the tall Chicago buildings, some of them
brightly lit up. After a few minutes I didn't hear a sound coming from Wally.
I looked into his room. He appeared to be sleeping. So, I got into my bed and
fell asleep; i.e., I was asleep until the telephone rang. It was the night desk clerk
downstairs. I was still half asleep when I picked up the receiver. "Hello." "Yes,
this is the desk clerk. Mrs. Findlay, your husband is down here in the lobby. He
has nothing on except his pajama bottom." Believe me, that awakened me! I
replied, "I'm not Mrs. Findlay. He is not my husband. I'm his nurse." Wally gave
the bell boy no resistance as he was escorted back to his room. How could I try
to sleep now? Finally, I could hear him snoring. As far as I know, we both slept
the rest of the night.

As I was giving Wally his morning medications and nebulizer treatment,
Helen called to tell me she would be joining us for breakfast in the dining room
at 9 o'clock. Well, it looked like I'd have the day off, as Bob Ryan and Helen
would have Wally busy talking to him about business, more or less, to make
him feel as though he were still in control of the Galleries.

I did have the thought that I really should go back to the room and try to
get a little sleep. Who knew what might happen that night; on the other hand,
why not go down Michigan Avenue? There's a Walgreens right across the street,
and Macys is a little farther down, so the latter is what I decided to do.

Bob joined us for dinner at the Ritz Carlton on North Michigan Avenue,
which is also close to the Gallery. Helen, Bob and Wally continued talking
about Gallery business, while I sat reminiscing about the time I stayed in this
very same hotel in 1980. That year I had attended the Restaurant Association
Conference at the McCormick Place Convention Center. I had driven to
Chicago from Cedar Rapids, Iowa with three of my classmates.

Helen suddenly interrupted my reminiscing with "Gene, I think we should
go. It's getting late. You know we leave at noon for Rochester, but it's going

to be a long day. We have to change planes in Minneapolis with a one-hour layover, before we can board the flight to Rochester. You and Wally meet me in the dining room for breakfast at 7:30." We said goodnight to Helen and Bob. Wally was in a very good mood. I just hoped he would stay this way. He seemed eager to take the medications and go to bed. I got his clothes packed and ready to leave early the next morning. I quickly packed my clothes and went to bed and to sleep … but not for long. I was awakened by Wally banging things around in his room. I jumped out of bed and went into his room and said quite loudly, "Wally, what in the world are you doing? Remember, we have to leave with Helen early in the morning." Wally replied in an angry voice, "I'm looking for my wallet. It's not in this room. It's been stolen!" I started looking for it, knowing he had the habit of hiding it. He said to me, "Gene, I want you to call the police!"

So, for at least another exasperating hour, I went to my room and called the night clerk, explaining Wally's state of mind. Soon, there was a knock. I opened the door, and two tall husky paramedics came in. They were pleasant but said to Wally in a stern voice, "Mr. Findlay, it is very late. You must get in your bed and go to sleep." Well, what do you know? He did exactly what they told him to do. I'll have to say that from that night on I've had a special admiration for the Chicago Paramedics.

Our flight to Minneapolis, the hour wait there and the continuing flight to Rochester was pretty uneventful and calm, Wally and weather-wise. I had heard of this town and of Mayo Clinic, of course, but I had never been there. I was surprised to see this small city with so much activity taking place in a few tall buildings.

Our rooms in the Kohler Hotel were very nice. Helen had a room located next to the two adjoining rooms for Wally and me. Wally had his usual after-noon nebulizer treatment, while I unpacked our suitcases. I was happy to see my room was at the end of the building with windows which gave me a good view of the street below and a small lake nearby filled with geese flying in and out.

I surely dreaded my unpredictable nights with Wally; however, my days were mostly rather nice with Helen keeping Wally occupied. After dinner, we went for a brief tour of the underground shops and stores. I had never seen anything like that before. It was like a city. Anything you might need or want, I'm sure it could be found down there.

As we went back to our rooms, Helen handed me a schedule of the daily appointments for the week. As soon as Wally seemed to be settled down, I had time to go over it. I could see that we were going to be very busy!

Now you would think that we would not be late for our first appointment. Well, we made it on time to the patient waiting room; however, Helen and I must have been having a very intense conversation. We looked around and no Wally! We couldn't find him in the restroom or anywhere on the eleventh floor. Thank God, it didn't take the security police long to find him. He was walking around, looking in the underground shops. He gave them no resistance, as they escorted him back to the eleventh floor for his physical exam. For his two o'clock appointment we had Wally sit between us!

Dr. Kokman's assessment in his first interview with Wally stated, "Throughout the examination it was quite apparent that he has had significant memory loss, frequently repeating full items of history. He was also depressed, crying on three occasions during the history about suicidal ideations." The remainder of the appointments for the week went fairly well, that is, except for Wally's Wednesday appointment with Dr. Peterson for psychological testing. Wally found the doctor's questions to be quite insulting, so he just got up and walked out and refused to go back for the rest of that day.

We left Rochester Saturday morning for the return flight to Chicago, where we spent the night with Helen. The flight back to Palm Beach on Sunday morning went smoothly, at least, I can't remember any "Wally problems." I did feel fairly comforted that there was no way he could slip away from me on the plane, as he did at Mayo Clinic.

Just to be back at my beautiful condo in Lake Worth gave me a renewed sense of my ability to cope with all of the stress which came with my job. And when Christmas came I just *knew* I could, and *would*, cope with whatever!! Besides my ham and turkey which fellow employees received, my Christmas bonus from Helen and Wally was $1,050.00!! Another gift I received, which I now have in one of my curio cabinets was given to me by the Mort Kaye Studio in Palm Beach. They were the Gallery photographers. In Wally's Beverly Hills home his favorite painting was Little Miss Smith, which hung in his bedroom along with his Picasso original and a portrait of George Washington. The studio's gift to me was a small reproduction of Little Miss Smith.

Wednesday, June 20, 1990, was a pretty good day. It was the day before my two days off. I had an extra sense of well-being, as I drove along the ocean on Highway A1A on my way to work. This usually meant that something good was going to happen. Wally was finishing his breakfast when I arrived and appeared to be in a great mood, also. I greeted him with "Good morning, Wally! As soon as I give you your nebulizer treatment, we will go on our island inspection tour." You see, Wally liked for me to drive him around Palm Beach looking at the hedges which lined the properties, taking note of those which were not up to our standards. We both determined that most of them met with our approval that morning.

We then drove to the Howard Johnson at the Lake Worth Bridge for coffee and chocolate pie. It was quite busy that morning. While we waited for our order, I said to Wally, "I surely do hope I won't have to spend my days off with my car in the shop. I've had nothing but trouble with that Tempo. I'm sure it's a lemon. My daughter Carol told me I should trade it for a Honda. That's what she and Ray drive, and they are very pleased with it. Do you think we could swing by Brahman Honda on Dixie Highway in Lake Worth and check it out?" Wally answered, "Why not?" It was only a short drive to get there. After looking over the car in the showroom, I soon found that Wally and I were sitting in the office of a salesman, Mark Branco, discussing the making of a deal on a new 1990 Honda Civic. Mark's first offer on a trade for my Ford Tempo was $2,500.00. Wally, who hadn't said a word, spoke up and rather sharply said, "She will not take that!" Very quickly, the offer doubled to $5,000.00. Wally and I rode back to Palm Beach in my new Honda Civic!

My parents were in their nineties, Mother still going strong at 91. My father had a pacemaker, and he had been on a diet of grits and eggs since having an operation on his jaw for cancer three years prior. He would be 94 on March 03, 1991. My birthday is February 18, and I would be 63. Helen Findlay would give me two extra days along with my regular two days off in order to make the 640 mile-trip each way home to Montgomery. To celebrate our birthdays, we went to a nice restaurant for dinner. I'm sure I had a steak and, of course, Daddy had his grits and eggs. He never complained about his limited diet; however, he was able to enjoy ice cream and cake. I was concerned about his health, as he stayed in bed most of the time. He had stopped doing his arts and crafts. He insisted on going out for our birthday dinner. I had no thoughts that this might be my last meal with him.

Two weeks later, while Wally and I were having lunch in the penthouse dining room, I received a call on the intercom from Joan, the receptionist for the Gallery, telling me that my mother was on the telephone. With a sinking feeling, I picked up the receiver and said, "Hello." My mother replied, "Gene, your daddy has had a heart attack and is in the hospital. The doctors don't expect him to live. I've called Helen and Ed. She'll be here tomorrow." I quickly said, "I'm sure Helen Findlay will want me to leave for home immediately. So, I'll leave in the morning. Are Mildred and Clyde with you?" She said, "Yes, they're staying with me in the hospital." Clyde was Daddy's nephew. He and Mildred lived in Millbrook, just outside of Montgomery. Mother's last word to me was, "Gene, you be careful driving up here!" I called Helen in Chicago to tell her about Daddy. She did, in fact, tell me that I should go right away. The next day I drove back to Montgomery with a heavy heart. My father had always been a hard worker, and in his younger years he was a heavy drinker. He was able to turn his life around at fifty years of age. He stopped drinking and began taking art classes. His family and friends were all surprised at the beautiful landscape oil paintings he gave us.

I arrived around six o'clock and went directly to see Daddy at Jackson Hospital. Clyde had picked up my sister Helen at the airport earlier in the afternoon. Helen and Mother were in Daddy's room. I'm not sure he recognized me. He appeared to be semi-conscious. Carol had left her home in Maryland that morning. I had expected her to stop at a motel overnight, because she had a lot more travel miles than I did from Palm Beach. I was really surprised to see her walk into Daddy's room around 8:30 p.m. Mother appeared to be doing all right. She had always been a strong woman. Thank God for Mildred and Clyde. They had been looking out for Mother and Daddy for several years. I'm sure they planned to continue giving Mother their help and support.

A letter came the next day from Helen Findlay. Enclosed was a check for one thousand dollars! I divided the money between Mother, my sister Helen,

Carol and myself. Words cannot express all that Helen's words in the letter meant to me. I felt very lucky, no, *very blessed* to have been employed by such a wonderful lady. I sincerely find her letter worthy of quoting here:

WALLY FINDLAY GALLERIES, INC., Thursday, March 14, 1991

Gene, My Dear—You are very much in my thoughts. I am so deeply sorry that you and your family are faced with this great sadness.

There isn't very much which friends can do at a time like this except to send supportive thoughts, realizing that you have been blessed by having your father for so long and that when the end does come to a long, productive life it is freedom from all the physical problems which develop with time.

Wanting so much to be helpful, the only tangible thought I could come up with is to be helpful with some of the extra expenses. So, the enclosed is sent with fondest thoughts and deep sympathy for you and your family. Helen

My parents had many church friends and relatives, including a cousin that I had never met, who came to the hospital to visit. One day, I was in the waiting room talking with this new-found cousin, Bill Bazzelle, while Carol was in Daddy's room with Mother. Daddy suddenly said to Carol, "I want you to go home and bring me my walking stick." We all realized that he thought he would need his cane on his journey to heaven. Mother didn't feel that he should have it in the bed. Carol asked the nurse to explain to Mother that it would be all right to let him have it. She accepted the nurse's explanation. Occasionally, he would comment on different departed family members he could see on the ceiling of his room.

My daughter, Kim, who lives in Minneapolis, was unable to make the trip. She wrote a poem, as follows, about her grandfather from her memory of him when she and I visited over the years.

When you think of Granddaddy, think of his dancing hands.
Big and square and always moving, grasping, creating,
    expressing his world with paint and wood.
Remember, Granddaddy had Alabama hands made
    of cotton and rosewood and red earth.
See that Granddaddy's hands were like his eyes,
    full of spirit and mischief.
Be sure that Granddaddy's hands shuffled the bones
    like no other.
    When you remember Granddaddy, remember this:
    It is night, the air heavy and sweet,
A slight breeze drifts thru the porch,
    Two rocking chairs creak just a little,
    Cicadas vibrate the night rhythmically,
A match flares, pipe tobacco burns,
    And Granddaddy's hands are busy still.

213

On Wednesday, March 20, 1991, I had been there nine days. Daddy's prognosis was the same. I knew I was needed back in Palm Beach. Mother agreed that Wally needed me and that I should return to Florida. My sister was there with her, as well as Clyde and Mildred. The mention of my going back to Florida upset my sister; nevertheless, I left on Thursday, following a tearful departure which was to be my final good-by to my father. After a late start leaving Montgomery, along with stormy weather, I finally arrived home in Florida very late and very tired.

My father's last picture, Clark L. Shirley

Helen had been telling her brother where I had been and what I was doing. The next day at work he seemed to remember my parents and wanted to know how my father was doing. Around noon my sister called with an angry tone in her voice and said, "Your father is dead! Mother and I have just returned from the funeral home of Leak Memory Chapel. The service is to be at eleven o'clock tomorrow." I quickly replied, "There is no way I can be back there by eleven o'clock tomorrow. Why were the arrangements made so soon?" Helen quickly said, "It would cost a lot more to have the funeral on Sunday. At any rate, the chapel Mother wanted is already reserved for someone else." At that moment Mother took the phone away from Helen and said, "Gene, I know you want to be here for Daddy's funeral. You just said good-by to him, and I'm sure he wouldn't want you to make that long trip again so soon. Clyde, Mildred and Helen are with me, but most importantly, God is with me!" I then called Helen Findlay in Chicago to tell her. She said I should call Elsie or Doris to come to work for me the rest of my shift that day and the next day.

Saturday morning, I awakened at the usual time, even though I wasn't going to work. My first thought was of what was going to take place at 11 o'clock in Montgomery that morning. My not being able to attend the funeral added to my grief over the loss of my father. The question in my mind was, "How will I ever get through this morning?" On my patio I could see the park across the street, so I decided to take my lounge chair and find a secluded spot by the edge of the lake in order to contemplate on our lives together. It was comforting to know that, even though he had left his body, his soul was very much alive! I want to repeat the most vivid memory of spoken words to my father. I had just learned to spell "God," and I said to him, "Daddy, I know how to spell 'God'."

He said, "Well, spell it." I very proudly spelled it out, "D-o-g." He laughed, and I began to cry.

Although he was a border-line alcoholic until he was fifty years old, he never missed a day of work and always provided for the needs of our family. I don't remember his ever being abusive or ill-tempered. Although Mother would always find his liquor bottles, she would instantly pour whatever amount remained in the kitchen sink. My father frequently displayed his innate ability to express practical wisdom in homely, yet concrete, terms. For example, he would call me "Monkey" and "Silly Kate." If something was extremely funny, he would say, "That's estellary!" Down through the years I've tried to find the meaning of this word but to no avail. I think it was his own invention.

The park began to get a little crowded and noisy, so I picked up my lounge chair and went back to my condo. After having a quick lunch, I continued my contemplation and meditation in my noise-free home. I'm sure my thoughts and feelings about my father's passing were about the same as others losing their elderly and/or sick parents. You certainly grieve because they are gone, and you will not see them again in this life. Out of my past there came the vivid memory of myself as a young girl sitting on a park bench waiting for a bus and suddenly having a startling thought: *Where did I come from?* Of course, I was thinking only of my arms and legs and the rest of my body, not realizing that I was a soul. God had given me this body along with free will, and when I stepped out of line I was always forgiven.

The next day, Wally and I went on our customary Sunday ride down A1A to Fort Lauderdale. We left the Gallery early and on the way Wally said, "Let's stop at a restaurant and get a cup of coffee." I said, "OK, but why not just stop at McDonald's?" He replied, "Well, I've heard of McDonald's, but I've never been in one of them." I thought to myself, "I thought everybody in the world had been in McDonald's." Pretty soon we stopped and went into one. Wally couldn't believe the low prices of the menus on the walls. He could be very generous at times with his money, but he always liked to save when he could. I thought, "Maybe this is a mistake, bringing him in here. He may have us going to McDonald's in West Palm Beach instead of the posh restaurants that I have become accustomed to in Palm Beach."

While Wally was taking his nap on Wednesday afternoon of that same week, I called the Unity Church, located on Flagler Drive on the Intracoastal Waterway; I felt that the church would have Lorraine Sinkler's telephone number. She was the author of "The Spiritual Journey of Joel Goldsmith" and her own "Alchemy of Awareness." I knew she had retired in Palm Beach and that someone at the church might know her number. The gentleman who answered the phone said he didn't know the number, but he gave me the number of a lady named Margaret Sanders, who would probably have it. My twelve-hour shift with Wally was over at 8 p.m., so I hurried home to call Margaret at the number which was given to me. That phone call lasted two hours! She had been a student of Joel's in California. We talked about The Infinite Way and some of his students in California known by both of us. As we ended our conversation, she said, "Gene, I would like to meet you in person. When are your days off from work?" I replied, "My days off are Thursday and Friday." She said, "That's great! Could you come to my home tomorrow about 10:30 or 11? I go downstairs to the pool at 9 o'clock for an hour's swim. My address is 1515 South Flagler Drive. I'm on the 17th floor. I'll be expecting you."

Since moving to Florida I had not met anyone who knew of Joel Goldsmith. That was mostly because of my long hours at work, and my days off were busy as well. So, I was thrilled to be on the eve of meeting my new friend who had known Joel and had been in his classes. I had no problem finding the address, as I knew it must be close to the church on Flagler. At 10:25 I stepped into the elevator to go to the 17th floor. I was surprised to see life-sized statues on each side of her door. One was of Danny Thomas, and the other of Colonel Sanders. I rang the doorbell and was soon greeted by my new Infinite Way friend, Margaret. She led me into her office and then excused herself to answer the phone. I began looking around the room. The walls were filled with photographs of Colonel Sanders. "Well," I thought, "She has a statue of 'the colonel' outside her door. She must be a relative."

When she finished her telephone conversation she sat down at her desk and nonchalantly said, "Colonel Sanders was my father." Well, that was surprising, but I was still more impressed that she had been a student of Joel Goldsmith. And I was also impressed with the fantastic view of the Intracoastal Waterway and Palm Beach from her 17th floor balcony! She and I were as if we were old friends. We recognized this as a spiritual bond between us. We did not have long to talk before I had to leave for an eye appointment. As I was preparing to leave Margaret said, "I would like for you to come back for dinner this evening at 7. I am going to invite the young man at the church who gave you my telephone number and his wife to be with us." I quickly replied, "Yes, I shall be happy to be here."

I arrived for dinner at 7 o'clock. Bob Konrad and his wife were already there. They were a nice looking young couple. I immediately sensed a feeling of warmth and friendship toward them. Margaret also had a house guest named Dorothy from Hawaii. Two things stood out in my mind that evening: What do you think she will serve for dinner? Kentucky Fried Chicken, of course! I later learned that Margaret was the one who started the "Kentucky Fried Takeouts," because she hated to cook, knowing that there were a lot of women who felt the same way she did, and I was one of them!

The other thing was that Margaret insisted that Bob give me a reading. Bob is a spiritual intuitionist. My past experience since 1972 of investigating psychic phenomena had led me to the realization that for every genuine psychic there are literally a hundred fakes! I interpret a genuine psychic or a spiritual intuitionist as *"You and I have a soul. We all have a physical body and a soul. And our souls are connected with each other. The language of souls is expressed to us as feelings (when it is not destroyed by the five physical senses)."* Margaret persisted in trying to get Bob to give me a reading, although she knew that he had given up the practice. He began to think that he shouldn't be doing it, that it might interfere with his spiritual journey; nevertheless, before I left the dinner party I had an appointment with him for the next Thursday afternoon which was my next day off from work. Margaret wanted to come, also, so I invited her for lunch. Yes, I prepared lunch for Colonel Sanders' daughter. By the way, I did <u>not</u> serve her fried chicken!

When my 17 year-old cat died in California I was devastated. I was sure I did not want another cat; however, Joanne Dru brought a Maine coon cat to my door, insisting that I needed another cat. As I have written previously, that cat Toby didn't work out for me at all. I was then convinced that I would never get another one. Well, there I was, three years later, with not one but two cats! What's more, I can't even recall who talked me into taking them. They were both tabby cats. Sammy was a pretty gray male, and Mandy was a yellow female with a little white spot on her neck.

The next five days after the dinner with Margaret I worked my 12-hour shift with Wally. Then, I rushed home to do some extra cleaning and tried to decide what in the world I was going to serve Colonel Sanders' daughter for lunch. It wasn't so difficult after all. I had become used to the Palm Beach restaurants and Simone's exquisite gourmet cuisine! Anyway, Margaret did serve "take-out" Kentucky Fried chicken for the dinner in her home.

Margaret arrived promptly at 12 noon, and Bob was to be there at 2. She complimented me on my condo. She especially liked my table décor for our luncheon. Well, so did Mandy, the yellow tabby! Why would she just jump on the table, right in front of Margaret and me? I was embarrassed beyond words! Finding out later that she didn't even like cats made it worse!! My saving grace was that, while I did serve her chicken, the dish was a fancy chicken and pea pod salad in a pastry bowl along with iced coffee and a dish of black walnut ice cream with a lemon cookie!

After lunch, we sat down in the living room and continued our discussion about the Infinite Way and her personal experiences with Joel Goldsmith. She said, "Gene, there were recordings made of the classes I attended. The ones I recorded and the others that I purchased are mostly worn out." Being proud of my collection of his tapes which I had bought starting in the 1970s, I said to her, "Well, I have seventy tapes, and I will be happy to let you listen to them." To that, she replied, "Thank you so much! I would love to hear them. It's almost 2 o'clock, and Bob should be here any minute. He certainly has been a blessing to many people, but he has mixed feelings about using his gift as a spiritual intuitionist. You mentioned the other night that you had a lot of experience with the psychic." Thinking quickly, I responded, "Yes, I lived in Iowa in the 1960s and 1970s. My very first reading from a psychic was just amazing. I was at Carleton College in Northfield, Minnesota. Several others that I have had were questionable. My search for answers to my spiritual questions began at the very young age of five years, as well as the psychic experiences which have happened to me throughout my life. The Reverend Mabel Swanson was a remarkable Unity minister. She invited a small group to listen to a Goldsmith Infinite Way tape. Joel is now known as a 20th century Christian mystic." "Oh, that must be Bob at the door. Do you mind if I sit in the living room while you have your reading?" I said, "Not at all. Feel free to do so."

I told Bob, "I'm so glad Margaret talked you into coming over here this afternoon. She said you might want to hold something of mine, like a piece of jewelry. Or, how about that walking stick over by the piano? It is very special to me, as it belonged to my grandfather. My uncle had brought it to him from Africa. It is made of ebony. A few months before he passed away, he made a trip from Albany, Georgia to Montgomery, Alabama to give it to me, saying he wanted me to have it, as he would not be needing it much longer." Bob replied, "That's interesting. It will do very well." To those who read these lines and are not familiar with this form of reading, it is when one individual may obtain information from another through physical contact with a possession, such as a ring or, as in this case, my grandfather's cane. My close friend in Iowa, Jessie Nagle, was very good in the use of psychometry.

Bob began with a short meditation. I do remember the things he began saying to me had me thinking, "He is very good." I was not taping it, so I can only recall my thoughts. But believe me, I have never forgotten his words when he paused, as though he were being interrupted and said, "What's this about someone's missing a funeral?" Now, I had previously had very little contact with Bob Konrad and Margaret Sanders; therefore, I would not have discussed having missed my father's funeral. So, of course, this brought a quick response from me. I started explaining how guilty and badly I felt about not being able to drive back to Montgomery from Palm Beach for the funeral. Bob interrupted me by saying, "Your father is saying, 'Guilt is for the fishes in the sea.'" My family would immediately recognize this as something my father would say. With those few words from my father, my guilt feelings were gone! I was so thankful for Bob's healing gift in my life at that particular moment in time.

We go about making plans day by day, some good, some not so good. All the time, we think we are in control, but we are not! God, our Creator, is in charge of our lives. At times, we do things we consider to be insignificant. For instance, when I made a telephone call to the church hoping to find Lorraine Sinkler, I had no idea how important that call really was. Not only meeting my new friends, Bob Konrad and Margaret Sanders, it also led to meeting Roz Borders. Bob must have told her I had Infinite Way tapes.

As I was preparing to go shopping on one of my days off, the doorbell rang. I went to the door, and little did I know that I would be meeting a pretty young lady who was to become my lifelong friend. "Hi, Gene Winn, I'm Roz Borders. Please forgive me for not calling you first, but I was so excited to hear that you have quite a number of Joel Goldsmith's tapes and to meet someone who is an Infinite Way student." "I'm glad to meet you, Roz. Come in! Yes, I do have seventy of Joel's tapes." Roz replied, "I'm on my way to work, so I can't stay long. Maybe we could have lunch together tomorrow." I quickly said, "Yes, I would love to. I work five days a week. My off days are Thursdays and Fridays. How about the Olive Garden on Palm Beach Lakes Boulevard?" We agreed to meet at 1:30, when it would be less crowded. I ordered my usual soup and salad.

You see, I've eaten at the Olive Garden so many times, and I've never ordered anything else. Roz's husband's name is Harry, and their business is Borders Real Estate. They have two sons, Brett and Blair. Roz was going to lend me her Infinite Way tapes, and I was going to lend mine to her.

I was very happy to have met Roz. Now I would have two friends, Margaret and Roz, with whom I could meditate as well as discuss the principles of the Infinite Way. We all realized that we had arrived at this stage of conscious awareness, as Joel stated over and over in his writings, "Meditation is where we grow in our search for God." And he stressed over and over, "It is not from the man Joel but from Him." At my age of 63 at that time and thinking back over my life from the early age of five, even as I went through some very difficult times, then and in later years, there was absolutely no doubt that meditation was what was lacking in my search for God.

When I returned to work, Helen Findlay called from Chicago to give me the next scheduled visit to Mayo Clinic on April 23, 1991, which was only three days from the day of her call. Wally and I were to leave Palm Beach for Chicago and stay overnight with her. She would then accompany us the next day to Rochester, Minnesota. Wally's first appointment was set for Tuesday, April 23, at 1:00 p.m. I hung up the telephone and was somewhat excited about making another trip (I did like to travel!); however, I was more concerned about Wally's possible behavior. Well, I really had my work cut out for me.

One of the most stressful things about traveling with Wally was that he made a fuss about his suitcases, always believing that some of his bags were missing. So, I got the bright idea, I thought, "I'll just make a list of his clothes and the number of bags and give it to him to read and sign!" I was soon to discover that my "bright" idea was not bright at all but really a dumb thing for me to think that it would work. When we arrived at the airport baggage claim in Chicago, he was sure that one of his bags was missing. The paper I had him sign meant nothing at all to him and had me wonder how I could possibly think that it would work. I still have that baggage list that he signed, reminding me of my stupidity on that occasion! After fifteen or twenty minutes I was finally able to get him to leave the baggage claim area, so that we could go outside of the airport and get a taxi to the Gallery.

The next day at noon we had to come back to the airport with Helen for the flight to Mayo Clinic. The flight was scheduled to go to Minneapolis with a change there for the flight on to Rochester. We soon found out that the flight to Rochester had been cancelled, although a bus was waiting to transport passengers from the airport to the Clinic. I was so happy and relieved to have Helen with us. She could usually handle Wally's mood swings easily and quickly.

The two-day reevaluation went comparatively well with a few changes in his medications. My only problem was that I had gotten very little sleep. Wally, of course, repacked his bags, along with some things which belonged to the hotel! He insisted that we had a flight to catch the next morning. Helen realized that I had slept very little. She said, "Didn't you tell me that your daughter Kim lived in Minnesota? Do you think she could drive over and stay with Wally tonight?"

I quickly replied, "Oh, I'm sure she can!" I thought to myself, "I'm her mother, so I'll just *make* her come." Kim was able to take two days off from her job and was very pleased to make the trip. This gave her a few hours with me, and she was quite happy to receive a check from Helen for five hundred dollars!

The return trip to Chicago was very pleasant with Helen and Wally in deep conversation. I felt as free as a bird! However, this turned out to be the calm before the storm. I do not recall when the "stress-free" Wally turned into the "uncontrollable" Wally. I do remember that, as we were checking into our suite at the Park Hyatt, Wally was giving everyone in his path a hard time. That included his sister Helen. She called Bob Ryan to come to the hotel and have dinner with us in our suite, thinking that he might be able to help her calm Wally down. That did not prove successful. As a last resort, Helen thought of one of Wally's old friends and felt that Wally would certainly love to see him. She was able to reach him by telephone and invited him to come for dinner. He was the perfect solution for the situation. Wally calmed down, and they enjoyed each other's company.

I did not have dinner with the others. I suddenly began to feel very ill. Helen realized that I was not well; however, I did not tell her that I was having chest pains. She quickly called for a nurse to come to take care of Wally. Helen knew that our flight to Palm Beach was scheduled for two days later, and she realized that I would not be able to care for Wally adequately. So, she called Doris, one of Wally's nurses at home, and told her to catch a flight early the next morning, for which she would arrange reservations and tickets. Helen had called her in order that I might recuperate prior to our Palm Beach flight. I happily greeted Doris when she arrived at the Gallery. I felt much better that day without any chest pains and was ready for the trip south.

I took Doris to our suite next door at the Park Hyatt, so that she could catch a few hours of sleep before her night shift with Wally. I explained to her all that had happened to Wally. I then said, "Doris, please have Wally ready to go to the airport at 7:30 in the morning. You know our plane leaves at 9:30, and I would surely hate to miss it." I said goodnight to Doris and Wally and went to the bedroom, suddenly having a peaceful sense of being, anticipating a good night's sleep with the thought of "I'll be home tomorrow!" My alarm clock awakened me at 6 a.m. I quickly dressed and checked to see if Wally was getting dressed. You might know it! Wally would not cooperate with Doris. As soon as he saw me, he said, "I'm not going with you. I hid my wallet, and I can't find it anywhere." Well, that was a switch. He was forever accusing someone else of stealing his wallet. I said, "Wally, your wallet must be in one of your bags. It will show up sooner or later. We are going to miss our flight if we don't leave right away!" I said to Doris, "Please call for a bellhop to take our bags." Very shortly, he was at the door. Wally immediately started giving orders to the bellhop. "Don't touch my bags! I own this hotel, and I'll have you fired!" The startled bellhop quickly realized Wally's mental state and began to gather our bags. We were finally out of the suite, Doris and Wally walking behind the bellhop and me. I turned around to make sure they were coming. At that instant I realized that Wally had his hand raised and was going to hit me. I quickly said, holding out my hand with my finger pointing at him, "Wally, don't you dare hit me!" I must have startled him, for he lowered his hand and didn't say a word. We arrived at O'Hare Airport on time for our flight. Wally was not talking to me, but by the time we arrived in Palm Beach he had forgotten the whole incident.

September 13 was a beautiful, sunny day for me to drive Wally down A1A to Fort Lauderdale, which was a nice but uneventful drive. Not so on the ride back to the Gallery! I began to realize that he was getting sleepy and quiet. So, I thought I had better get him home. I decided to cross over to I-95, which was the fastest route for me to take. But I failed to check to see if Wally's seat belt was fastened. I saw it wasn't, so I yelled at him, "Wally, your seat belt is not on! Just pull the belt over your shoulder, and hook it in the buckle over here." I'm thinking, "How could I forget to check it?" Suddenly, Wally was lying straight back, as he had pulled the lever which threw him into a horizontal position. Of course, I got off of I-95 ASAP. He didn't get mad at me, and we both thought it funny afterwards.

For several months, Wally appeared to be functioning normally, for him that is. Then, on September 23, 1991, things really changed in his life. It was time for me to take him to one of his monthly appointments with Dr. G. David Raymond, gastroenterologist. In order to correctly relate the details of events in those days, I wish to quote verbatim the statement I wrote to whomever it might concern, as follows:

WALLY FINDLAY GALLERIES, INC.
165 Worth Avenue
Palm Beach FL 33480

On Duty: Gene Winn

September 23, 1991 – Monday

About 9-10 a.m. in the morning after Mr. Findlay was dressed and had eaten breakfast, he and I, Gene Winn, were ready to go to Publix Super Market for groceries when Mr. Findlay said he had an ache in his side. We went to Publix, got the groceries and, when we arrived home, Mr. Findlay still complained that he had an ache in his side. I figured maybe I should take him for a flu shot, so I called Dr. David Raymond for an appointment, which was to be at 2 p.m. today. At the appointment, Dr. Raymond poked around Wally's stomach area and examined it, saying he had an irritation which could be resolved with an antibiotic. Dr. Raymond gave us a script for an antibiotic and told me, Gene Winn, to get, also, magnesium citrate to give to Wally the next day, if he did not have

a bowel movement. (Mr. Findlay did have a small bowel move-
ment that morning.)

I got the prescription for the antibiotic from Lewis Pharmacy
and gave Wally his first dose about 3 p.m. He looked and seemed
quite tired and worn out, but nothing for me to be alarmed about.
Wally then took a nap at the usual time. I took his vitals and was
alarmed to see that his blood pressure was 188/120 (usually low
and at a safe reading right up to this time), so I took it again
thinking something might be wrong with the blood pressure
machine – but got the same high reading.

I telephoned Dr. David Raymond immediately, only to get
his answering machine. I explained the problem, asking for Dr.
Raymond to call me back. Then, I called Miss Findlay in Chicago
to inform her of the situation. She, of course, became as alarmed as
I was. Not hearing from Dr. Raymond in one-half hour, I called
again to see if he got my message; however, Dr. Tom Raymond
answered the phone, and I explained the problem to him. He
advised me to check Wally's blood pressure throughout the night
and, if it remained 188/120, I should call Dr. David Raymond
in the morning.

I felt shocked at his response. After hanging up the phone, I
called Miss Findlay again and brought her up-to-date, explaining
that I called Tom at the pharmacy again, after having talked to
him earlier in the day about Wally's infection and the prescription
for antibiotics that Dr. David Raymond had prescribed for Wally,
to tell him about my conversation with Dr. Tom Raymond and
Wally's high blood pressure reading. Tom, at Lewis Pharmacy, said
he was quite surprised that the doctor did not do more or suggest
more help for Wally than just giving that simple advice of waiting
and rechecking his vitals.

A few minutes later, I called Dr. David Raymond's office
again, hoping to get the answering service to see if Dr. David
Raymond had received my message; instead, Dr. Tom Raymond
answered the phone, so I hung up right away. The Gallery phone
rang within the next minute, and Dr. Tom Raymond was calling
back (He has the new telephone service that shows the caller's
number as the phone rings, so I was confused at first, thinking Dr.
David Raymond had gotten my message, so I started telling him
about Mr. Findlay, as though it was the first time I had spoken to
him). It was Dr. Tom Raymond, and he asked me, "Didn't we just
have this conversation? I told you, if his blood pressure was still
188/120 during the night to call Dr. Raymond in the morning,

as Dr. Raymond will not be calling you tonight." Shocked again, I called Miss Findlay and Tom the pharmacist. Tom told me to feel free to call him at home after 10:30 p.m., in case I needed meds, if Dr. David Raymond called back and prescribed any medicine for Mr. Findlay.

I continued to monitor Mr. Findlay's blood pressure until 8 p.m., which is when I am off work and leave for home. Knowing Doris Dames, the night LPN, would be working and caring for Wally gave me some relief from worrying, as Doris would know how to handle the situation. When I arrived for work the next morning at 8 o'clock, Doris informed me that Wally had been awake all night, but his blood pressure had come down almost to his normal reading. I felt relieved to hear his vitals were under control. Wally was asleep at this time, which I felt was OK, considering he had been awake all night. I awakened him about 10 a.m. to give him his breakfast. I observed that the antibiotic results may have been responsible for his health not becoming any worse, at least. I, again, gave Wally some magnesium citrate, as I was instructed to do by Dr. David Raymond. Wally went back to sleep, which I thought he needed. Upon his awakening at 2 p.m., he seemed to be in a lot of discomfort. Upon checking his blood pressure, I found it to be almost as high as the day before. Also, I thought his stomach looked rather protruding or bulging and quite hard to the touch.

I called Dr. David Raymond immediately with this information. When he called me back, it was around 3:30 p.m., and I explained the situation to him. He said, "Well, you never can tell about older people; so, can you bring him to the hospital's Emergency Room?" At this point, Wally was using his nebulizer, so I just walked over to him, took his mouth piece out of his mouth, put on his housecoat, and we went immediately to Good Samaritan Hospital's Emergency Room. With very little waiting time in the Emergency Room, we went in, and Dr. Raymond was there. He had two surgeons with him who also proceeded to examine Mr. Findlay.

(Signature) Gene Winn

Wally's personal assistant

In short order, Dr. Raymond came out to tell me that Wally had an intestinal obstruction, and that he must have Helen's permission for surgery. Of course, Helen said they should proceed immediately. Well, Wally's walking into the ER was to be the last time he would be able to walk. He stayed in the hospital for two weeks and went back to the Gallery in a wheel chair, never to walk again.

With the passing of the years, I sometimes think of the worry and stress I went through at the Good Samaritan Hospital; however, for a period of time, I was a hospital volunteer, which I enjoyed very much. It was at the time of Wally's emergency surgery that Nancy Frangella, a registered nurse, joined Wally's nursing staff. She was his RN for several years. She and I were good friends, and we have kept in touch ever since. When Wally's case ended for her, due to personal circumstances, she moved back to her home in Albany, New York. We are now both in our 80s. My good friend, Roz Borders, still lives in West Palm Beach. She is much younger than am I, that is, in her mid-60s.

Part of Wally's nursing staff

The year of 1991 was a year of sorrow for me: my father's passing and job-related stress. On the other hand, it was rewarding, as I met several life-long friends. As I write these lines in the year 2013, I continued to have frequent contact with Louise Deese, who was with the Palm Beach Gallery since its opening in 1961 (she passed away earlier this year), Roz Borders, Bob Konrad and Nancy Frangella. And, of course, Margaret Sanders, who passed away in October 2001.

I must tell the reader that I had not had a piano of my own since I left Sioux Falls, South Dakota and moved to California in 1981. My dream was to purchase another, as soon as I felt financially able to do so. I remembered the generous bonus given to me by the Gallery the preceding Christmas, which was in the amount of $1,050.00. So, I thought that with that same amount again, I could finance the Baldwin I wanted and had located in a local music store. Would you believe it? I did not get the same bonus as the previous year but, rather, a check for $2,366.00!!! Helen Findlay was a very sweet lady and generous in all her dealings. I shall be forever grateful for the memory of Helen and Wally!

February 27, 1992 was Wally's 89th birthday. Of course, Simone was planning a big celebration on the patio of the penthouse. Helen, Bob Ryan and Wally's attorney from Chicago would be attending as well as Simone's friend, Princess Ghislaine de Polignac, who was Simone's house guest for a month. Goldie Hawkins entertained at the piano for the evening. All of the Gallery employees and Wally's nurses were present.

I was the unofficial photographer for Wally. During my employment at the Gallery, I took hundreds of pictures of him. Among the pictures was one of him sitting on the penthouse patio. Simone liked it so much that she had 167 copies made and sent them to friends in the United States and France.

August 24 of that year was a date I would never forget. I experienced being in my first hurricane. According to the weather update, Palm Beach County was the predicted landfall for Hurricane Andrew. However, it actually made landfall on Elliott Key and later, Homestead. There were 65 fatalities and 25 million dollars in damages. It eventually moved through Palm Beach County. I left my Lake Worth condo and went to my son Steve's apartment in Wellington, about 15 miles to the west. It was a terrifying night! Simone had admitted Wally to the Good Samaritan Hospital for his protection from the hurricane. When I arrived at work at the Gallery, she expressed her anger due to my not being at the hospital with Wally the night before. Officially, it was my night off; therefore, I went with complete liberty to be with Steve at his home. She had not been able to contact me, but she did locate and call Nancy, Carla, Jo and Iris from his nursing staff to care for Wally at the hospital.

One month later, on Monday morning, September 14, I got up at my usual time of 6:30, in order to be at the Gallery at 8 a.m. But I could not seem to shake a foreboding feeling that something unpleasant was going to happen. As it turned out, I was to get quite a shock later that day at work. Bob Ryan called from Chicago with the sad and very shocking news that Helen had passed away. She had not let anyone know that she had lung cancer. I'm sure her many friends were deeply saddened by her death. She personified for me the meaning of the word "graciousness." I'm sure that everyone who had the privilege of knowing Helen had felt that they had lost a very special and unique friend. As for me, I was devastated! I loved her as though I were a member of her family. I was concerned about Wally, too. He talked to Helen almost daily. Somehow, it wasn't too big a problem, because of his declining memory.

January 1993 started out with a great unexpected surprise. I had just gone to bed and had turned off the light, when the phone rang. I reached over and picked it up, without getting up or turning on the light. It was Bill Findlay,

225

calling from Chicago. "Hi, Gene, I hope I'm not calling too late. I just want to tell you that my aunt Helen surely thought a lot of you. She left you in her will!" I really didn't know what to say, but I do know that I sat up and turned on the light, and I don't recall the rest of the conversation. I remembered later that he didn't even tell me the sum of money she left me. He did call the next day on a conference call with Bob Ryan. They then told me that she had left me $60,000.00 tax free!! Well, I certainly never expected to be included in Helen's will and was really amazed at her love and generosity. The realization came to me instantly that I knew that, without a doubt, I was God's child, and that He not only meets our needs, but at times He does so in abundance!

One of the most eloquent art expositions I was privileged to attend with Wally was the January 1993 annual showing of portraits by Alejo Vidal-Quadros. Also, another important exposition was that of French Post-Impressionist Jean-Claude Chauray, who flew in from Paris for the event. The guests entered the Gallery through a white, vaulted tent, complete with its own crystal chandelier, twinkling lights and orchids. What really caught my attention were the four strolling violinists. Alejo Vidal-Quadros and his wife, Marie-Charlotte were there, of course. I was honored to have visited their Palm Beach home with Helen and Wally on several occasions. They divided their time between their homes in Palm Beach and Paris.

On April 11, Easter Sunday, Simone made a reservation for a Sunday Brunch at the Governor's Club for her, Wally and me. This was a first for me. A Palm Beach photographer took our picture, and even took a shot of me standing with a life-size pink bunny rabbit, holding his Easter basket. No big deal, although later, I noticed that my hat didn't fit me anymore. I guess I had the big head!

My friend, Roz, was quite a bit younger than yours truly, but we never felt the age difference. On my off days from work we would often meet for lunch. It was at a luncheon at The Breakers one day that she said, "Gene, do you realize that you could be living in a very nice condo on the lake in the gated community of Wellesley? And the payments would be about what you're paying in rent for your condo in Lake Worth. And you would be buying this condo!" I replied, "Oh, I would love to see one of the units. The rent money from the Gallery would make the payments." Roz said, "Would you like to go see one when we finish lunch?" I said, "Certainly, I would love to!"

We were in separate cars, so I drove behind Roz to Lake Clarke Shores, which is located on the west side of I-95, about fifteen minutes from The Breakers. On this short drive, my head was whirling with thoughts and questions, such as "I'll have to buy new furniture. All I have is my desk and piano. Roz said I would need references and be approved by the Homeowners' Association. I certainly had never tried to buy a home before. Will my loan be approved?" Soon, we were approaching the gate. Roz being a realtor got us in without delay, and we quickly reached 81 Bridgewater Court. It had two beautiful bedrooms, 2½ bathrooms, living room, dining room, kitchen and a large fenced-in patio facing the lake. I loved it … instantly!

I drove back to Lake Worth thinking, "Could it be possible for me to purchase my first home?" Well, it was not a dream. On June 25, I moved in with my desk and piano. The furniture store delivered my new purchases for every room. In order to be approved by the Homeowners' Association I needed two friends to complete character reference forms. Several months had passed since Helen's death, and Simone continued to be very nice to me. She came down to Palm Beach every weekend and, generally, we had enjoyable times together, depending on Wally's mood swings. So, I asked her to fill out one of the forms. She gave me a very good reference, such as "Ms. Winn is dependable and extremely conscientious and hard-working. … She has an extensive music background, has a pleasant and friendly personality and is an excellent mother and grandmother."

My friend, Jane, and her husband, Ralph Keen, completed the other form. Dr. Keen was a well-known dermatologist in Palm Beach. Their comments included the following: "What began as social grew into a personal relationship. This is how one creates a distinct bond of friendship that spans the ensuing years. … She has wisdom that governs her responses to life's challenges. We recommend Gene for your favorable consideration."

My mother and Colonel Sander's daughter, Margaret

Mother was happy about my new home and couldn't wait to see it. I made a reservation on Delta Airlines for her to fly, instead of making a long bus trip. She was 93, but age didn't keep her from traveling! When I told Margaret Sanders that my mother was coming for a visit, she said, "You be sure to bring her to see me." My sister, Helen, had come from California to help me move. She liked Florida so much that she went back home to Victorville, California and convinced Ed to make the move. So, it was nice to be together, especially while Mother was visiting, because I was working five days a week. Mother wanted to meet Margaret, so I called her. She invited us to come to her 17th floor condo, and she wanted to take us out to lunch. Mother was thrilled! I took my camera and got some great pictures of the two of them. Then, we went in Margaret's car to the Olive Garden.

I called Chicago to arrange my vacation for July 01-15, 1993. I made reservations to go to Cedar Rapids to visit friends and to Minnesota to visit Kim and her friend, Sheila. Then, I went to Virginia to visit Carol and Ray and my grandchildren. The flight from Dulles Airport to Palm Beach was uneventful (no bouncing around!). It was quite nice to know that I was returning to my new home in Lake Clarke Shores.

227

When I returned to the Gallery the nurses were all talking about Simone and her physical attacks on the Gallery housekeeper and on one of the night nurses. We were all aware of her verbal abuses, but now she apparently was crossing the line. That same day, one of the nurses told me that Simone had said that when I returned from my vacation she was going to fire me. I had been there since 8 o'clock in the penthouse with Wally, until he went to sleep for his morning nap. I then went downstairs to the kitchen to call my mother on the toll-free line. Simone was there, so I said, "Good morning, Simone." She didn't respond, so I said to her, "I have something I would like to talk to you about." She replied, "I don't want to hear it!" After a few strong, negative verbal exchanges, I had a flashback from Beverly Hills. This was the "Simone" I had known there! Knowing that Helen was no longer available to keep her under control, I suddenly realized that I couldn't continue at the Gallery. I knew there was staff on duty to care for Wally, so I picked up my purse and went home. I hadn't been there long when the phone rang. It was Bill Findlay, Wally's nephew. He said, "Gene, I'm sorry that you had a conflict with that *(expletive)*, *(expletive)*, *(expletive)* Simone Karoff!! If Helen were alive, this would never have happened. I'm coming to Palm Beach next week, and I'll see you then!" Bill kept his word, and I appreciated, and continue to appreciate, his support! I must say that there was no way for me to continue working in that environment, with Simone in command, even if the officers of the upper echelon of the various galleries had wanted me to remain. Enough was enough!

On May 06, 2013, I received the following words from Bill Findlay, which I feel led to place at this point in my life story: *Gene was the angel we were blessed to find when Wally most needed help in his challenging years. Gene soon became a member of the family. Her devotion to Wally and Helen will be forever, greatly appreciated. Best regards. Bill [William Findlay, William Findlay Fine Art, Established 1870]*

CHAPTER 63

1994
MARY MOON

CAROL came for a visit on February 15, 1994. She especially liked my patio and the walkway by the lake. We went to Key West on the 17th and celebrated my birthday on the 18th. On our return Carol wanted to meet Roz Borders. I called her, and we had lunch together the next day.

My many years of experience working for Wally Findlay were a big asset in finding other employment. I was told about an agency in Jupiter, Florida, called A Moment's Notice. I soon had a five day-and-night live-in assignment with a nice 94 year-old lady, Mary Moon. She lived on the 6th floor of a high-rise on Jupiter Island. From her balcony I was able to look east and see the Atlantic Ocean and look west and, almost under the building, was the Intracoastal Waterway. I did her shopping and took her for rides and to doctors' appointments. She preferred to eat at home, so I prepared her meals, administered her meds and took her vitals. She would often invite a friend from across the street, and I would fix meals for the two of them.

CHAPTER 64

1995
PERRY COMO

MARY told me that she had been a heavy smoker, but that she smoked her last cigarette ten years previously upon winning a new car based on her lucky number drawn by Perry Como. She said she didn't want her car to have an odor of tobacco smoke. Perry lived in The Colony on Jupiter Island, located about one-half mile from Mary's condo. At that time, he was very active in the community. It was while working for Mary that I returned to walking on a daily basis. Each morning I would walk at a fast pace to the Martin County line, which was three miles round trip. I really enjoyed my time with Mary, as well as getting some beautiful shots of the Intracoastal with its passing ships and of stormy weather and gorgeous rainbows. I took Mary to her regular medical appointments. The doctor found a large tumor in her right breast. She passed away two weeks later.

My son, Steve

Previously, I told about my two cruises to the Bahamas that were not very enjoyable, to say the least. I was seasick on both return trips. Now, my son, Steve, came up with an offer for a 3rd cruise that I just couldn't refuse. He paid my way as well as that of my sister Helen and her husband Ed on the Viking Princess. We met some of Steve's friends on that cruise. We all had a great time! I didn't even get seasick!

CHAPTER 65

1996
WALLY'S DEATH - FEBRUARY 16, 1996

FOLLOWING Mary Moon's death, I had employment through a temporary placement agency. They sent me to a couple living at The Breakers West for a five-day-and-night assignment. I was happy that it was only for a week, starting on Friday, February 09 through February 13, 1996. I shall never forget that last morning. I was awakened around 2:30 a.m. with chest pains!! I waited until the couple awakened and told them what I was feeling. They wanted me to call a doctor, but I refused, got into my car and left for home. On the way my cell phone rang. I pulled over and answered and heard the voice of one of Wally's nurses say, "Gene, this is Carla Kiser. Wally passed away this morning, February the 16th, 1996, around 2:30. The last word he said was, 'Gene.' I knew you would want to know this." It instantly struck me that my chest pains occurred at the time of Wally's transition! Only a week before I had stopped by the Gallery, not realizing, of course, that it would be the last time I would see him. He was glad to see me and even wanted to go for a ride with me.

A few months after Wally's passing, I received a call from Smoky, who worked in the Gallery frame shop. "Gene, Simone called me and asked if I would call you and ask you to pick her up. She's at the Brazilian Court. She would like you to go with her to the Flagler Museum Restaurant for dinner, but I don't think I would go, if I were you." Without much thought about it, I said, "Do you have her number?" I called her, and we had a very nice dinner, with not one word spoken about my departure from the Gallery.

Although Mother and I did not have an ideal mother-daughter relationship from my childhood through early adult years, I must tell you that we were very close in our later years. Even our names changed: She called me "Miss Smith" and I called her "Miss Jones." At the age of 98, she was still living alone in Montgomery. For the last eleven years, after moving to Florida, on a quarterly basis I drove my car 1,280 miles round trip to visit her on my two days off and taking an extra day from work. So, now, between jobs, I decided to go for a week. It was good to know that Helen and Ed would be at home, taking care of my house and feeding my cat.

Shortly after I arrived in Montgomery, I received a phone call from a lady I did not know. Helen had given her my mother's number. It was Harriett Ohland, and she wanted me to work for her as her companion. She lived at The Jupiter Inlet Colony. She had never seen me and, yet, she wanted me to come to work as soon as I returned to Florida. I must say I had a lot of questions in my mind. *Where did she get my home phone number in Florida? She hasn't even seen me, and she has offered me a great-sounding job!* It was to be another permanent live-in for five days and nights. *What would my duties be?* She said she had a housekeeper. Also, her husband, Louie, was confined to a wheel chair and had 24-hour nurses' care. I would be her chauffeur wherever she needed or wanted to go. So, I accepted her offer over the phone, including the wages involved, and agreed to be there one week later.

I knew about The Colony, because it was close to where Mary Moon had lived. Mary had wanted to show me Perry Como's home. The dwellings were located on the ocean, on the Intracoastal or on inlet streets. And, it had its own police, although there was no gate at the ivy-covered police station, located at the entrance.

Harriett's home was located on Colony Road, one street from the ocean front. As I went to the door, I had the intuition that I was going to like my new job. Louie's nurse came to the door with Harriett right behind her. The latter was a rather dignified-looking lady of short stature with "Bo" right beside her. Bo was a big, black Labrador retriever! Harriett took me to the sitting room, where I was introduced to Louie and his nurse. There was one more member of the family, and that was Leo, the cat. He was treated very well, but did not have the many privileges enjoyed by Bo.

After a few minutes of conversation, Harriett said, "Gene, I'd like for us to go for a ride, so that I can show you some places to which you will be driving me. There will be some grocery shopping, as you and I will either eat out or have our meals delivered here. The nurse will fix Louie's meals when we are out. For now, I want us to drive by Jacobson's Department Store and The Old Port Cove Yacht Club. You will be sleeping in the front bedroom. As soon as you unpack, we will go. Soon, we were headed for the garage and the car, with Bo right beside us. Harriett opened the hall door to the garage, and there was the largest, most beautiful, white Mercedes Benz 500 I had ever seen! I soon learned that I would be driving with Bo sitting up front with me and Harriett in the back seat. This brought back memories of my driving Wally's Rolls Royce with Helen and Wally in the back seat.

The first week with Harriett, we went to Jacobson's Department Store and antique shopping, and three nights we dined out. Harriett had a strict dress code; i.e., no slacks. That was just fine with me, for I loved wearing my high heels, and they looked better to me with a dress. During that first week Harriett and I had ample time to talk and get to know more about each other.

One thing I could not wait to find out was how the Episcopal Church in Tequesta had my phone number. Harriett's cousin, Laurel, was married to an Episcopal bishop, Alex Stewart. Their home was in Maine, so it was the bishop who called the church in Tequesta and asked if they would find a companion for Harriett. (Tequesta is located right across the drawbridge which connects Tequesta and Jupiter Island.) But I still don't know where that church got my phone number! To this day, I do not have the answer.

While waiting for our dinner at McCarthy's, at our first meal out, I was curious as to why she and Louie had moved to Florida. So, I said to her, "You said you moved here from New York. What city?" Harriett replied, "Louie and I moved to The Colony in 1995 from Lynbrook after Louie sold his business called Louis Ohland, Inc.—Prime Meats. Our meats were sold and delivered to the most prestigious clubs and restaurants in New York City and Long Island." Harriett wanted a companion 24/7, and she wanted me to find a two-day replacement for my days off. The next week I went to A Moment's Notice. There was a lady sitting in the office, waiting to be interviewed. I struck up a conversation with her. Within a few short minutes, she appeared to be what I was looking for. Without having her own interview, she went with me. Harriett liked her instantly. Problem solved!

Soon, I began to feel as if my home was in Tequesta and not in Lake Clarke Shores. I really did enjoy my home on my days off, and I was grateful to have Helen and Ed there when I was working. My sister was an immaculate house-keeper. But there was no garage for my car! Ed had just begun working for a real estate broker, so I said to him, "I would surely like a condo with a garage. Would you try to find one for me in Tequesta or right here in Lake Clarke Shores? You and Helen can continue to live here and pay the mortgage payments. Ed replied, "OK, I'll get to work on finding a place right away. We love it here in Lake Clarke Shores. Finding you another place will help my sales." What I wanted in my price range took Ed some time to find.

At work, not only was I Bo's chauffeur, but I had to take him for his daily walk, also. That meant walking him on a leash. My dogs of years ago, Nicky and Toby, never needed a leash. They walked on their own. Well, I thought I was doing quite well walking Bo; however, I did notice that sometimes he would pull me rather hard. On one of my daily walks, I met Perry Como and one of his friends. They said, "Hello." And then, his friend added, "Your dog is taking you for a walk." I didn't really appreciate that remark, but I quickly realized that I needed to learn more about how to walk a big dog like Bo.

On another day, I was walking and went to Jupiter Island where Mary Moon used to live. On my return, I walked around The Colony. I always had my tape recorder with me, so that I could listen to music through my earphones. It was on my way back that I spotted Perry Como, this time he was alone. I quickly took off my earphones and caught up with him. "Good morning, Mr. Como. My name is Gene Winn. My mother lives in Alabama, and she has a friend who is terminally ill. Mother tells me that her friend talks about you often and says, 'Nobody sings like Perry Como.' Would you please give me your autograph for her?" He said right away, "I would be very happy to do it." I said, "Thank you, Mr. Como. I know this will mean so much to her." As I walked away, my next thought was, "Well, why didn't I get an autograph for myself?"

My relationship with Harriett would get a little strained at times. It was not that we didn't like each other, but we sometimes had different opinions about things. At times, we would get into an argument. I soon learned that she liked to get into a disagreement. Overall, it was a good job. Harriett loved to go antique shopping. She had a good eye for a bargain. On my dresser today is a beautiful dish, which she had noticed and said to me, "I have a dish just like that one, and I paid $75.00 for it." Of course, I picked it up and paid $10.00 for it.

Our most serious disagreement was in the Tequesta Publix Supermarket. I do not recall what started our argument, but before we could get out of the store, she had told me that I was fired. To that I immediately replied, "You didn't fire me. I quit!" She then walked away but returned quickly, asking me, "What am I going to do if you quit?" Shortly after that, we were friends again.

I was in the sitting room talking with Harriett and Louie, and Bo, of course. Bo had his own private chair and would just sit there, as though he were taking part in our conversation. When the doorbell rang, I went quickly to the door and saw a nice-looking young lady who said, "Hi! You must be Gene Winn. I am Beth Sweigart. I am Louie and Harriett's niece." I said, "Oh, hello. It is so nice to meet you. Harriett said you would be here sometime today. They are in the sitting room. Come on in!"

Sisters-in-law Harriett and Jean Ohland

I became more acquainted with Beth at dinner. Harriett said we would be going to the Old Port Yacht Club, which would be my first of many times to go there. Jean Ohland and her husband were the next relatives to visit. Charlie was Louie's brother. Jean and Charlie were from Lynbrook, New York, as was Beth. My intuition failed me at my first meeting with Jean. I certainly did not recognize her as a life-long friend. After we were introduced, I went to my room. Shortly thereafter, she knocked on my door. I opened the door, and she said, "I don't like you!" I must say that I must have looked surprised. She continued, "I don't like your legs!" I was shocked at that remark, but after thinking it over I thought it might be meant as a compliment. Soon, we started referring to each other by new names. She called me Dixie Belle, in short, DB; my new name for her, excuse my language, was Damn Yankee, in short, DY. Now, in 2013, we are still good friends and continue to use the same names. She is my elder, only by six months. Her husband, Charlie, passed away in 2004. She lives alone in her big house, goes to the gym regularly and takes care of her cat, Sugar, and her dog, Heidi.

I was beginning to think that my brother-in-law, Ed, was not going to find a suitable condo for me. Then, he called me from his work to say, "I have made an appointment for us to look at a condo on your next day off." It was located a few blocks from Wellesley. So far, I had been disappointed with the previous ones he had shown me. So, I was pleasantly surprised to see exactly what I had been hoping for. It was located on Lake Mango Road. It had three bedrooms, 2½ baths and a single-car garage. The floor of the living room, hallway and stairs to the second floor were all marble. It was very close to the water of Lake Mango. I loved it instantly! Over the course of several weeks, my name was on the mortgage, and I moved in.

Four generations: Eunice, Gene, Carol, Suzy

Carol invited Helen and Ed and Mother and me to spend Christmas with them in Virginia. I drove Helen and Ed to Montgomery, so that Mother could join us and we could all fly to Dulles Airport. I don't mean to imply that Mother needed to be escorted. She was quite capable at the age of 95 to live alone and to travel alone. When she was 92, while visiting Carol and Ray, she suddenly had to go to the ER, due to severe stomach pains. The outcome was gall bladder surgery. After several days of recuperation in the hospital, her doctor told her she would not be able to go back to her home in Montgomery for at least one month. She was back in Alabama after one week of being dismissed from the hospital!

My grandson, Tom, who was working in the Capitol, had obtained a pass for a guided tour of the White House, signed by Senator Tom Daschle on December 27, 1996. It was a cold day with snow on the ground, but Mother wasn't about to let it make her miss the tour. Because of her age, the guide said Mother and I should go to the second floor on the elevator, which went into the kitchen. So, we got to see a little more of the tour than the rest! It was good to have most of the family together for the holidays, except for Kim and Steve, who had other commitments.

My 1996 Christmas vacation was very enjoyable. I had the happy anticipation of my return to Florida, my new town home and going back to The Colony to work. Harriett told me she had two friends who lived in Boca Raton, south of Palm Beach. She said she would like for us to go to lunch at the Palm Beach Club. I had always wanted to go there, when I was working for Wally. The closest I ever got to it was on our daily rides around Palm Beach. Wally had some kind of disagreement with the club management, so he would never go back there. This was the first of several visits to the club while I worked for Harriett. I liked her friends, Roma and Elizabeth, very much. And I certainly enjoyed the food as well as the beautiful view of the ocean.

CHAPTER 66

1997
HARRIETT OHLAND

THE Old Port Yacht Club continued to be my favorite place for dining out. On their buffet table you could choose from almost any kind of seafood you might want. Yours truly was a sort of "center of attraction" one night. I had ordered Oysters Rockefeller. When I was about half way through eating my delicious serving of food, I suddenly felt something strange in my mouth. I soon discovered that I was on the verge of swallowing a large pearl! I immediately got the attention of other diners wanting to see it. Of course, the brief baking of the oysters and the spinach dulled the luster of the pearl. It has since had a home in a small covered dish on the Queen Anne desk in my bedroom.

I must say that my life has been closely connected to the world of fine art. Let's see, there were Carol and Steve's father, my father, *Wally Findlay Art Galleries* and, now, Harriett Ohland. Her paintings had been on exhibition in New York galleries and now in Tequesta Art Gallery. I especially liked her painting of the rowboat and the duck, which was on the wall in my bedroom. I also liked her chicken painting in her kitchen.

One aspect of my job was that it afforded the time to go on my daily walk. On one specific morning I wished I had stayed at Harriett's and just washed her big Mercedes, which I had done on numerous occasions. On that never-to-be-forgotten day, I had walked out of The Colony and was about where Mary Moon had lived on Jupiter Island, when the toe of my right shoe caught on a rough spot in the pavement, causing me to fall flat on my face. I didn't lose consciousness, but I realized it could be serious. I finally was able to stand up and started walking back to Harriett's. I soon met a lady, walking toward me who didn't stop but said as she passed, "You should go to the Emergency Room!" As I went back into the house, Louie's nurse saw my face and without saying a word to me, she called 911. This did not please Harriett, as she did not want an ambulance coming to her home. I tried to cancel the 911 call, but once they have been called, they come anyway. They soon arrived. I was taken to Jupiter Hospital. The x-ray showed that I had a concussion. For several weeks, I had a black-and-blue face!

My effort to find out where the Episcopal Church had gotten my home telephone number for Harriett was still a mystery to me. Then, I received another call that really surprised me. Perry Como's daughter, Terry, called me to say she needed someone to stay with her mother, who was ill, and would like for me to go for an interview with Perry and Roselle at their home in The Colony.

Of course, I agreed to go at the time she specified. The interview took place at Roselle's bedside with Perry close by. I am not a nurse, and it was apparent that she needed a trained nurse. She passed away a few months later.

I do know that when one *really* knows, not just believes the word of God; e.g., "Be not afraid, it is I," well, I still have a ways to go, for I am afraid of thunderstorms. It was at work one day that the weather turned extremely stormy. This is a regular weather pattern in Florida. To be sure, had I been at home and not at Harriett's, I would have been totally traumatized! When I returned home from work, I discovered that my garage door would not open, so I went to the front door, unlocked it, and entered a very hot house. I went directly to the air conditioning control and discovered it was not working. After checking both floors, I went into the master bedroom, then into the closet in the bathroom, which was very bright for a normally dark closet. I looked up and saw a large hole in the roof! I'm still praying that, by the grace of God, in the midst of thunderstorms, I will attain the complete assurance of "Be not afraid, it is I."

It must have been obvious to anyone, even the insurance company, that lightning had struck my house! When the adjuster arrived, he immediately said, "Lightning struck your house." You wouldn't think that I would need to get my attorney involved before I would receive a settlement. It only took two years for them to pay for the damages!

My grandson, Ben

My grandson, Ben, came down for a visit from Fredericksburg, Virginia, where he was attending Mary Washington University. He later earned his bachelor's degree there with a double major in American Studies and Historic Preservation. He was a long-time student of military history. I knew that with his love of history since he was a little boy, I had found the perfect restaurant for us to have our first luncheon together. It was the 391st Bomb Group Restaurant, and had a World War II theme. Diners could view the planes landing and departing from the Palm Beach International Airport. My thrill there was to listen to my favorite entertainment, and that was the Big Band music, which was playing constantly.

We went on a tour to Jupiter, which included the Burt Reynolds Theater and then to Jupiter Island and up to Hobe Sound and, finally, back to Harriett's in The Jupiter Inlet Colony. Then, being an animal lover, Ben got to meet Bo and Leo. Harriett, knowing his interest in history, thought he might like the two swords hanging in her living room. Ben was extremely grateful for her generosity in giving him those Civil War relics.

CHAPTER 67

1998
ROSALIND BORDERS

JESSIE Nagle and I had close contact with each other since I had moved away from Cedar Rapids in 1980, by phone and by letter and later by email. At times, we would visit each other in person. This year, 1998, Jessie suggested that we go to Las Vegas. On July 16, I flew to Cedar Rapids. The next day we took a flight to Las Vegas. We had a great time at The Luxor Las Vegas, shaped in the form of an Egyptian pyramid. The name and the description of the hotel intrigued us both. After three days of the slots (pennies and nickels only!), sightseeing and eating great food, Jessie flew back to Cedar Rapids. I flew to Minneapolis to visit Kim before returning to Florida.

My grandson, Tom

I visited the U. S. capitol on many occasions over a period of ten years, while my grandson Tom served as a congressional aide. On several trips to visit Carol, I would go to Tom's office in the capitol. He would take me to lunch in the Senate dining room. On one special occasion, Steve was with us. We rode on the Senate subway, and Tom introduced us to several Senate employees. I have many great photographs, taken inside and outside of the Capitol. One time, on a visit to see Tom, after lunch we went back to his office. Some of the office workers were having lunch in a separate room. Tom gave me one of the books which were stacked and ready to be mailed. They were all intent on seeing me examine the book. To my surprise, I discovered photos on separate pages of Mother, Daddy, Tom's paternal grandmother, his maternal grandfather and ... yours truly! Not only was I astonished but also very proud that my grandson was responsible for the layout of this book, titled Social Security Issues.

I was also introduced to employees in Senator Robert C. Byrd's office. Tom had drawn a portrait of him, which was hanging on the wall of his outer office. He also did a portrait of Senator Thomas A. Daschle. I have a copy of the note of appreciation sent to Tom by the latter. Oh yes, I must mention the tribute to John Glenn at a Senate dinner on June 16, 1998, in which Tom presented his drawing of the Friendship 7 Space Craft.

Suzy and the gator

My plan was to keep the Lake Clarke Shores condo as long as Helen and Ed were there, but they began to talk about returning to California. So, I had him list the property with his real estate firm. It was sold shortly afterward. I thought I should have Mother, Carol and Suzy to come for a visit before they made their move. Mother got her very first view of an alligator, as I did when I first moved in. After all the years that I had lived in Florida, I had never seen one. There were several in Lake Mango. Shortly after I moved in, I was standing at my bedroom window, looking at the beautiful sky over the lake. Suddenly, I looked down, and there was a real, live gator! Without another thought, I quickly grabbed my camera, ran downstairs and out on the grass and got my first picture of an alligator.

My pet gator

Mother, then at the age of 97, was continuously saying to Helen and me that one of us should move to Montgomery to be with her. Helen and Ed were going back to California. I decided moving to Montgomery had to be me! I deeply hated to leave my new home in Florida. I loved my fish pond by the front door and the lake with alligators (I know what you're thinking, but I really took a liking to them! Just don't go up and try to pet one of them.). I called Roz Borders to give her the listing. Like the Lake Clarke Shores property, it wasn't long before I had a buyer.

My good friend, Roz Borders

I was going to miss my friend, Roz. She was two years younger than my older daughter, Carol. Age has nothing to do with our friendship. We had been talking about having a garage sale, so we decided to have two, one weekend at my place, and the next weekend at her home. She lived across I-95 from me and a short distance from the Intracoastal. Roz's son, Blair, a tall, nice-looking young man, was with us with a watchful eye, sort of like a security guard.

Now I had to find someone to move my furniture. Did I dare ask my son-in-law, Ray, to move me again? He is a one-of-a-kind son-in-law, so when I asked him, he simply said, "Sure!" On December 04, 1998, I drove my white Honda behind Ray in a big, yellow Penske rental truck, headed for Alabama.

Mother lived on the 2nd floor of the Ahepa Senior Apartments. On my previous visits to see Mother, I had gotten to know Sandy, the apartment manager. There was a 1st floor unit available, which she leased to me. She also found help for Ray in unloading the truck and in taking some of the furniture to a storage shed nearby. My apartment was pretty crowded but cozy!

My cousin, Becky Shirley, had been taking Mother to her medical appointments and grocery shopping. She was a nurse, and we had been very fortunate to have her available to take Mother wherever she needed to go. Her husband, Bill, was my second cousin. Their son, Daniel, helped to get me started on my new computer, which he installed in a hall closet. I spent much of my free time trying to understand my computer class lessons and brushing up on my typing skills.

It had been a long time since I lost my Kitty in Beverly Hills. I didn't think I would ever find another "special" cat. Shortly after I moved to Montgomery to be with Mother, she and I went to the Montgomery Animal Shelter. As we stood by a certain cage with several kittens in it, we both spotted a little orange tabby kitty, and we both thought that with her big, green eyes she was saying, "Please take me with you." Soon, I had another cat, this one named Suzy. As I am writing these lines she is fifteen years old.

My mother, making a point on her 98th birthday

CHAPTER 68

1999
CARING FOR MY MOTHER

MOTHER and I would go out to eat several times a week. Now she could visit her friends, which she enjoyed doing very much. I was happy to take her in my car. On Tuesday, March 10, 1999, Mother turned 98. This was going to be the second birthday party that I had for her in the Ahepa Party Room. Her friends and many of the local residents attended the parties. We played games, a favorite of the guests being Bingo. I kept LP music playing with our favorites, the Big Band Music. Of all things, and the shock of a lifetime, my mother danced with a man! And I have a photo of it!! Did she forget what she told me as a child, **"You're going to dance your way to hell!"** It was in September of that same year that I had my first professional tap dance lessons at the Academy of Dance. Becky Shirley went with me to take pictures. See my tap shoes in the picture!

Suzy's grandmother with her tap shoes

Mother was becoming more and more dependent on the wheel chair that I had bought for her. It was light weight and easy for me to lift in and out of the trunk of the car; however, she was becoming more and more unsteady on her feet and had some pretty bad falls. I realized that I needed to find a good nursing home for her. The Crowne Nursing Home was highly recommended. So, I called them and soon had a date set for an interview on October 26. Mother and I met with Tracey Pattillo, a pretty, young lady with the ability to make us feel right at home. She took us on an interesting tour of the facility. We left the interview with a moving date set for November 01, feeling that the recommendations we had received were absolutely correct. Now, I had a big job ahead of me! The family chose what they wanted from the household furnishings, and I had to sell the rest.

Becky and Bill told me about an attractive, single-wide mobile home that a friend of theirs wanted to sell. It was located in Sunshine Village on the east side of Montgomery. They took me to see it. I liked the park and loved the mobile home. Very soon, I signed mortgage papers and made plans to move.

My mother, Eunice Arnold Shirley

I stayed very busy, looking after Mother, taking her out to lunch, my computer lessons and my morning walk. I walked four or five times a week, either to *Oak Park* one way or to Oakwood Cemetery the other way. At the latter, I would go uphill to the Hank Williams Memorial Site, which brought back memories of my playing in his band in 1953. Stella's mother, Mrs. Morrison, was buried a short distance from Hank. Mother and I went several times to Deatsville, north of Montgomery, to visit Kim's aunts, Ann and Betty, and cousin, Debbie.

Kim's cousin, Debbie, with my mother

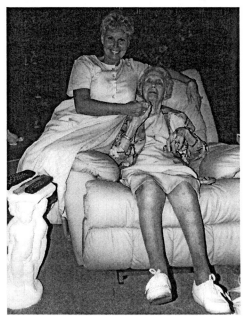

243

CHAPTER 69

2000
GHOST IN THE U. S. CAPITOL

I SOON began to realize that I needed to earn some money. Living on social security was not taking care of my expenses. I could see my savings dwindling away! So, I put in an application for a part-time job at Dillard's Department Store. This was a new line of work for me, but I enjoyed the experience. Mother and I went to her church, Highland Avenue Baptist, every Sunday; however, when my work at Dillard's required me to be there on the weekend, it interfered with our church attendance. I knew how much going to Sunday School and worship service meant to Mother, so I started looking at the classified section of the newspaper and found a position I thought sounded interesting, which was that of a sales person at Greenwood Cemetery. After a five-day training session, I was accepted for a sales position. Frank Hester, my manager, was very patient in teaching me the pre-paid funeral plan. I did sell several plans. One of the first was to my cousin, Bill Shirley, and his wife, Becky. Frank accompanied me to their home to present the plan and make the sale. A sad note as I write these lines in September 2013 is that Bill passed away last May. On the positive side, Becky has had to pay very little in addition to what the plan gave her.

A good friend, who worked with me at *The Ranch Restaurant* back in the 50s and for several years had lived in the Ahepa Senior Housing, Louise Groom, was admitted at the Crowne Nursing Home and became Mother's roommate; i.e., for one week, when Louise passed away. She had made it clear that she wanted to be cremated but, of course, Mother did not approve of crema-tion. As we were on the way to the funeral home for her memorial service, Mother suddenly asked, "Has Louise been fumigated yet?" (Of course, she meant "cremated.")

Nell Wilson, my childhood friend, and I renewed our friendship. As a result, I was reunited with several of my classmates and other acquaintances of long ago. I was invited to attend a monthly social gathering of the Sellers Drug Store Gang. You may remember my writing about Sellers Drug Store, which was located about a block from my home, when I was eleven years old. My very first time at the meeting, I was happy to see Mike Richardson, who I had not seen since 1946. It was great to meet his wife, Sarah. Several of my grade school classmates attended, such as Gloria Hall, Sarah Vann, Ray Wilson and Marjorie Guy.

Suzy, my granddaughter, played the viola and the violin; however, from an early age she seemed to be attuned to the business world. At age eight or nine, she delivered her homemade poster to the neighborhood, on which she stated that she would shovel their walks clear of their Minnesota snow, stating a price for her services. Not long after her college graduation, she began having success in the world of business. Now, she was going to get married! She and her husband to be, Joe, planned a big wedding on Saturday, May 13, 2000 at St. Mary's Catholic Church in Alexandria, Virginia. Suzy wanted Mother to be there, and Becky Shirley agreed to accompany us as Mother's nurse. This left me free to help Carol with the wedding arrangements.

A few days before the ceremony, Carol and I went to Tom's office in the capitol. We needed his expertise with some of the final wedding plans. His office was now located in the basement. We were there late that evening and, being in the basement, it was rather spooky, especially after Tom told me a Capitol ghost story, which was a new one for me. He said, "It happened not far from my office. A telephone service man, who was employed by the Capitol, was installing telephone lines in a small office, when he heard a man's voice say, "What are you doing?" He replied, without looking up, "I'm installing a phone in this office." The voice then asked, "What's a phone?" The repairman then turned around and, not seeing anyone in the office, left and didn't finish the job. Well, I decided I would take a little stroll down the deserted basement hall. I didn't get very far, when I felt the need to make a quick retreat to Tom's office!

It was rather crowded to have Thanksgiving Dinner in my new mobile home. All of the family was there as follows, except Kim: Carol and Ray, Suzy and Joe, Steve, Mother and I. We enjoyed a delicious dinner with all the trimmings at 4:30 p.m. Thursday, 23 November 2000.

CHAPTER 70

2001
MY MOTHER PASSES AT 100 YEARS OF AGE

Celebrating my mother's 100th birthday!!

MOTHER'S picture and a write-up were published in the Montgomery Advertiser on her centennial birthday celebration on March 11, 2001. Her many friends and some of the Crowne Nursing Home patients were present for her 100th birthday party. Carol, Suzy and Becky helped me with the preparations. I played my violin, which was the last time she heard me play. Also, Carol sang "This little light of mine, I'm going to make it shine," a Sunday School song Mother taught her when she was a little girl.

Mother was becoming increasingly sad, because Helen was in California, and she thought she would never see her again. She would often say to me, "I don't know why Helen went back to California. I will never see her again!" At the same time, Helen was having problems with Ed. He was not working and was becoming more and more confused. It was clear to me that I had to help them move to Alabama. Becky and I flew out to Apple Valley to help them pack and load their furniture on a rental truck.

You will remember my Nigerian friend, Bright Aregs. Well, I wrote him before I left Montgomery to let him know that Becky and I would be arriving to help Helen and Ed with their move to Alabama. He drove to Apple Valley for a short visit with us. Through conversation, it was apparent that he was doing well with his studies and work.

In the meantime, Helen had their car serviced for the trip cross country. While the car was being worked on, she decided to go back to the service bay.

While there, some heavy metal object fell on her foot, breaking one of her toes. The shop refused to pay for her medical attention, saying that she had no business being in the service area. I secured an attorney for her, and about a year later, she received a check for $5,000.00. Becky drove the truck, and Ed rode with her, and I drove Helen's car for her.

Mother's health was on the decline, but it had not affected her mental ability to understand the needs of the family. Not long after her birthday, we had a serious talk about finances. Although I liked my job at Greenwood, I was in need of the kind of job in which I had much experience, which would adequately supplement my social security. I did not want to deplete the rest of my savings, as I had been doing since moving to Alabama.

Well, Mother loved Alabama, and I am sure she would have preferred to stay there; however, she quickly and willingly agreed that all of us should make the move to Florida. The big question then was: How do I accomplish this? Only by the grace of God! The first thing I had to do was to find a nursing home for Mother. A good friend of mine recommended the Sutton Place Nursing Home in Lake Worth. Mother was discharged from Crowne Nursing Home on June 20, 2001. Her admittance date in Lake Worth was June 22.

I called the mobile home sales location in North Palm Beach, and sight unseen, but by faxing floor plans and documents back and forth, I soon had a mortgage note signed. The home had three bedrooms, a large living room, dining room, kitchen, three bathrooms and a two-car carport. It was located only a few blocks from the nursing home. I took the salesman's word that the mobile home park where the unit was located was one of the best for over-55 seniors. My son, Steve, had been looking for a mobile home in Montgomery. So, he moved into my single-wide there. Now what? I say again, thank God for Bill and Becky!

We soon had a large U-Haul truck rented and packed with our furniture and other belongings. Bill drove the truck, accompanied by Ed. Becky drove my car with Mother. I drove Helen's car with her. We did not attempt to make the 640-mile trip in one day. We spent a night in the Gateway Motel in Lake City.

I was not very pleased with the mobile home park in Lake Worth; however, the new home was everything I had hoped for. And it was close to Mother's location at the nursing home. She seemed to feel all right about everything with Helen and me close by.

Ed was becoming more and more confused. At times, he would leave the house and wander off. I could see that Helen was not going to be able to cope with this situation. I went with her and Ed to the Veterans Administration. The doctor said that Helen needed to find a nursing home for him.

Mother's health was really going downhill. The main problem for her was that she had difficulty swallowing. On August 10, 2001, Mother and I were driven to the doctor's office by a nurse's aide in the Sutton Place van. I will never forget looking at her in the seat behind me and seeing the pleasant look on her face as she looked out of the window at the passing scenery. At the doctor's office I was informed that she needed tube feeding only.

The next Monday evening, when I went to say good night to her, she was sitting up in her bed. I sat down beside her. We talked about the fact that she would be seeing Daddy and Papa and her sisters and brothers when her earthly journey came to an end. I said to her, "That will be a wonderful reunion!" After a few minutes, I said "Good night!" I was awakened by a phone call at 4 a.m., telling me that Mother had passed. Her body was sent to Leak's Memory Chapel in Montgomery, Alabama. The memorial service was held there on Friday, August 19, with the burial in Greenwood Serenity Gardens.

Helen did not go to Montgomery to the funeral. She felt that she needed to stay at home to see Ed at the nursing home. When the business matters were taken care of, I started my long journey back to Florida. I kept thinking of Mother, and how her strictness and religious views had really aided me in the search for answers to my spiritual questions, as well as the tenacity to deal with the tribulations of my childhood and young adulthood. As the years progressed, we had a wonderful mother/daughter relationship!

Now, I needed to begin looking for a job. So, I went to the Reimer Employment Agency in Palm Beach. At my very first interview, the agent said to me, "I have an ideal job for you. This client needs someone to be her personal assistant, but looks like her friend and not just an employee. I believe she will be happy with you! She lives in Tamarac, which is close to Ft. Lauderdale." This would not be very far for me, since I could take the Florida Turnpike and go south about 30 miles. Her home was located very close to the turnpike.

My interview was set for the next day. Gertrude liked me, and I now had a job. It was a five-day overnight job. What I liked most about the job was that she loved Bingo. We would go to the Seminole Casino in Hollywood almost every day to play. Also, my salary was very good; however, after seven or eight months, I decided to get employment closer to Lake Worth, where I lived. Also, the short-time jobs paid well.

I obtained my Florida license #2077, by completing a 50-hour training course at the Health Careers Institute on Congress Avenue in West Palm Beach. This was required for the home care and nursing home employment positions to which I might be sent.

CHAPTER 71

2002
LAKE MANGO

SPEAKING of home, Helen and I had become very dissatisfied with the mobile home park in which we lived. Our clothes started to ruin from being bleached by the water in the washing machine. The management notified the community not to drink the park water due to the threat of cancer contamination. The last straw was when a family moved into the single wide next to us with six children and, I later learned, they kept a boa constrictor on their screen porch. I tried to find a senior mobile home park, so that I might have my home moved, but there seemed to be none available close by.

Roz and I frequently met for lunch, since I had moved back to Florida. At lunch one day at the Olive Garden, I said to her, "Roz, I just have to find a solution to the problem I have at the mobile home park. Helen and I just don't feel that we can stay there any longer." She immediately replied, "I have a very nice home, not far from here. In fact, it's on Lake Mango, where your town home was located. With Helen sharing with half of the expenses, you could manage that, couldn't you? Why don't we go take a look?" I replied, "That suits me. Let's go!" So, the next thing I knew, I had signed a rental contract, plus paying a deposit on a lovely home on Lake Mango with "my" alligator.

Helen and I were very pleased with our new home. The floor plan was perfect for our furniture, and the large patio was just the right size for my plants. To my surprise and delight, there was a banana plant in the back yard which had a stalk of bananas developing on it. Suzy the cat was now five years old and stayed on the patio most of the time, where she could watch the alligators which would sun themselves on the lake bank just outside of our fence.

CHAPTER 72

2003
DR. RADU MAVRODINEANU

ROZ would often stop by on her way home from work. One afternoon, I was completing paper work for one of my patients. When the doorbell rang, I opened the door and said, "Hi, Roz! Come in, you look like you need a glass of lemonade. I just finished making a pitcher full. We can go out on the patio." She replied, "I can't stay long, but that sounds very good. I need to tell you about a job for which I think you will be perfect. I manage the property belonging to Radu and Monica. They are an elderly couple, and their home is on the Intracoastal, just a few blocks north of my home."

After a moment, she continued, "Radu has Parkinson's and Alzheimer's diseases. Monica cannot care for him, and she seems very depressed. She sleeps a good part of each day. I have been told by an officer at their bank that there is a concern over a maid who works for them. There is a rumor that she is involved with Radu and trying to gain control over their finances. Anyhow, she has to go! I'm wondering if you would consider seeing that they are properly cared for. This would mean that you would have a five-day shift, and you would have to fill the remaining shifts with employees you feel are trustworthy. They have a cousin, who is also their godchild, and is now in charge of their finances. Her name is Ioana Razi, a doctor who lives in Washington, D. C. Even though her husband is very ill, she is coming to West Palm Beach next week. I have told her about you, and she would like for me to set up an appointment with you. Well, what do you think?" I replied, "My goodness! That sounds like quite a challenge! But I would like to try it." Roz said, "Good! I know you can do it! I'll call Dr. Razi and make the arrangements. Oh, and I'll give you a little background on Radu. His professional title is Dr. Radu Mavrodineanu, a renowned analytical spectroscopist and scientist of international reputation. He has written several books in his field."

I was very impressed with Dr. Razi. Not only was she busy with her practice of pediatrics, but her husband was gravely ill. I met her at the Hampton Inn, about a mile from the Palm Beach International Airport. We both knew that this was going to be a demanding job; however, she seemed to have the confidence to believe that I could handle it. After visiting Monica and Radu, she returned to D. C. Her husband passed away ten days following the interview I had with her.

Now, I really had a huge job ahead of me! I was soon able to fill the overnight shifts. I worked five days and soon had the other two day-time shifts filled. Radu, for the first couple of months, was able to carry on a normal conversation.

He loved playing his piano and was pretty good at it. He and Monica really liked cats, so much so that they had ceramic cats sitting around in every room in the house. Monica, at first, only wanted to be left alone. She would sleep most of the day, just as Roz had said she would. Shortly after I started working for them, I asked Monica if she knew how to play dominoes. She didn't, but she said she would like to learn. Well, she did learn and, then, she wanted to play whenever she was awake. In fact, she would ask anyone who came to her home if they would like to play dominoes. This was a good thing, for now she did not seem to be depressed.

Monica's cousin, Anca, and her husband, Alex Burghele, visited several times while I was there. I added them to my life-long friends. We still communicate with each other, even though I live in Georgia, and they live in Germany. Almost one year after I started working for Radu and Monica, he passed away. The couple, who had moved into their home, so they could be there overnight, became aware that Radu had lost consciousness. Being unable to rouse him, they called 911. He was taken to the hospital, where he died a few days later, on December 17, 2003.

Dr. Razi made the decision to move Monica to Virginia, and arranged for her to live at Sunrise Nursing Home in Arlington, not far from her own home in Georgetown. I accompanied Monica to Ronald Reagan National Airport, where Dr. Razi, Carol and my granddaughter, Suzy, were waiting to receive us. I was a little uneasy about Monica's reaction to leaving her home and realizing that she was going to be living in a nursing home. I need not have worried! She enjoyed the flight, and was very happy to see Dr. Razi. Her very first words to her were, "Thanks for making my move to Virginia possible."

We said our good-byes and left in Carol's car. Just as we got on the George Washington Memorial Parkway, I discovered that I had Monica's cup in my travel bag. My next thought was, "I have to get this cup to Monica. She probably will not want to drink anything without it." I didn't think this was so strange, taking into account that, when I am at home, I must have by my plate the silver spoon that I found in the aftermath of Camille in 1969. I said, "We have to get this cup to Monica. Suzy, call Dr. Razi, here's her cell number. Explain to her Monica's need to have her cup." Carol then said to Suzy, "Tell Dr. Razi that I will drive close to her car so that you can hand her the cup!" We all gave sighs of relief when this feat was accomplished! After a week's visit with Carol, I returned to Florida and went back to work, taking short-term cases, both at private and nursing homes.

Helen was busy at the Presbyterian Church, where she and Ed were members, and going to visit Ed at the nursing home. The last time he was able to leave the nursing home, he made a short visit to our home on Lake Mango. Then, we went to Helen and Ed's favorite place for lunch, Wendy's! And for dessert? A "Frosty," of course. Helen liked Frosties so much, she would buy several to take home and put in the freezer. Ed passed away on December 13, 2003. His memorial service was held on December 17 at Lakeside Presbyterian Church on Flagler Drive in West Palm Beach. Helen had his body cremated.

CHAPTER 73

2004
MOVE TO VIRGINIA

I TURNED 76 on February 18, 2004. I thought that Carol and Ray must have been thinking that I was too old to be living alone in Florida. I thought I was doing quite well with a job and going twice weekly to the aerobatics class at the YMCA. I am very sure that my son-in-law, Ray, is the absolute best! After all, how many sons-in-law would move their mothers-in-law all over the country? And now, he was not only going to move me from Florida to Virginia, but he and Carol had purchased a very nice town home in a new development in the town of Tappahannock for me to live in. For years, I wondered why they had me living a hundred miles from Leesburg, where they lived. I finally learned about the high property taxes in Loudoun County, as opposed to the much lower taxes in Essex County.

On May 03, Ray arrived at Lake Mango to move Suzy and me. I hired two movers to help Ray load my furniture in the big 40 ft. Penske rental truck. Helen's furniture was moved to a storage location in West Palm Beach. She could hardly wait to leave for her daughter Peggy's home in California. She took Ed's ashes on the flight with her for burial in a military cemetery.

Ray is allergic to cat hair. I did not realize this could cause such a reaction from being close to a cat. So, I was a little worried about his coughing. On our trip to Virginia I tried to keep Suzy by my side next to the door, as far away from Ray as possible.

Of course, I'll never forget the first sight of my new home. Carol had purchased two white rocking chairs for the front porch and several hanging baskets of flowers. Carol, Suzy, Tom and Ben were there to welcome me. I soon began to feel right at home in Tappahannock, which is located on the shores of the Rappahannock River. After moving in, I had friends on each side of my house, Bob and Shirley on one side, Liz and Andy on the other, across the street Leo and Dottie and two doors from them, Betty.

The Riverside Wellness and Fitness Center was located very close to me. So, it didn't take long for me to join the club and sign up for water aerobics. It had a great place to walk, with a pathway circling the exercise machines. My routine was to walk, either before or after my class. One morning, as I was walking, I noticed a lady on one particular machine. When I came back around the path, she had gotten off and was walking with a cane. We were both headed toward the locker room, went in, and introduced ourselves, and we became instant friends! I invited Beverley to go home with me for lunch. I had not known about the Red Hats. Beverley was the queen mother of the Red Hat Club in Warsaw, located at the other end of the Rappahannock Bridge. She invited me to join, which I did, and I soon had many new friends, including Betsy Ware and Sandy Wade.

CHAPTER 74

2005
RAPPAHANNOCK COMMUNITY COLLEGE

I HAD worked most of my life, so I thought, why stop now? I could use the extra income. Very soon, I found myself in a totally new work environment. After accepting the job, I thought, "Are you crazy? You know how you are about noise. You're going to work around all these noisy kids?" To my surprise, I really loved my new job, which was at the Essex County Intermediate School. My duties included working in the library, in the main office and in the classrooms. It was there, on my very first day, that I made another life-long friend, Elsie Washington. We were both born on February 18, but she is a lot younger than I. And George Towns, known to his many friends as "Baby George," was a sixth grade English teacher. Everyone in Tappahannock seemed to know and love him. I certainly had no idea of what his influence and help would mean in my coming years in Tappahannock.

One day, after I had been working at the school a couple of months, in talking with Baby George, I told him about my violin playing and mentioned that I had not played for twenty-five years. So, he said, "Gene, would you play for the music class?" "Remember, I just said, I hadn't played for years. Oh yes, I played for my mother's funeral in 2001. I'll have to think about it." Well, I did play for the class. It must have been all right, for then he asked me to play in two Baptist churches.

My sister, Helen, didn't stay in California. She and her daughter, Peggy, had a serious disagreement, so she just came back to the Palm Beach International Airport ... with no place to go. She called a friend from her church, who picked her up and took her to her home for the weekend. Her husband talked Helen into going back to California, so she took the next flight. After an even shorter period of time she was back at the same Florida airport. She called her good friends, William and Patsy Edwards, who lived in Palm Bay. She had known them since her husband, Ed, was at his first pastorate in Calera, Alabama, following their graduation from Toccoa Falls Bible College. They picked her up and took her home with them. After several weeks, they took her to West Palm Beach and helped her find an apartment.

I realized that at her age of eight-three and being without a vehicle, she was too old to be living in Florida alone. She only had a couple of friends from her church. So, what did I do? Well, of course, I asked my son-in-law, Ray, if he would please go to West Palm Beach and bring my sister and her furniture to

Tappahannock. My furniture had filled the town house, so we found a storage rental very close for Helen's furniture and excess personal effects.

My friend and neighbor, Betty Wilson, across the street from us in Tappahannock, attended the Warsaw United Methodist Church across the Rappahannock River. She invited Helen to attend services with her. She later became a member. Knowing that she had been a church pianist, she was given a key to the church, so that she could get in and practice on their piano.

An opportunity came for me to take a Nurse Aide training course at the Rappahannock Community College, just over the bridge in Warsaw. I realized that this training would be very helpful in my work with elderly people. I signed up for the classes, which began in October 2005. On December 07, I received my Award of Completion for the Nurse Aide Training Program, which consisted of 165 contact hours.

My Nurse Aide uniform

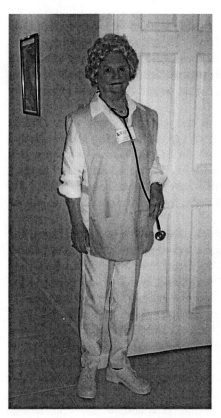

The Registered Nurse instructor, Lelia Poteet, was a pretty lady and, at the same time, a stern, no-nonsense teacher. I'm sure that the nine young students in the class must have thought, "What is this old lady doing in here with us?" Ms. Poteet didn't seem to feel that way. In fact, she was very patient with me.

One morning, during a break, I was talking with her, telling her a little about my life and varied work experience. Well, from that time on, she would say, "Gene, you should write a book!" I had heard this from a few people before, and it was just something I would never consider. I didn't like to write, and I never could spell well at all, which would make any writing of mine more difficult. Ms. Poteet didn't stop saying that I should write a book. In fact, she even announced to the class, "Ms. Winn is going to write a book!" At the conclusion, would you believe it? She wrote on my final grade sheet, "I'm looking forward to your book!!" She even arranged for me to play my violin at the celebration party following the graduation.

My Nurse Aide Instructor and the inspiration for writing this book, Lelia Poteet

I'm sure that Lelia did not realize that the comments she was making about my writing were going to change the direction of my life. I was not unhappy in Tappahannock, I was enjoying the friendship of numerous friends, and most of my family lived in Virginia. However, God had a totally different plan for my life.

The very next week after graduation, I started writing from my first memory. I meditated, and I wrote, and I meditated some more, and I wrote some more, as if I were obsessed. And, really, there was no thought that I was to write the story of my whole life. But that is what transpired! In the current year of 2013, at the age of eighty-five, in the month of November, I am putting the finishing touches on my book, *DANCING MY WAY THROUGH HELL!* May I say this? From my life experiences in Cedar Rapids, Beverly Hills, Palm Beach, Tappahannock and right up to facing Lelia Poteet at Rappahannock Community College with her steady and strong encouragement for me to write my autobiography, and through prayerful meditation, and without a shadow of doubt, I *know* that God guided me every step of the way. Thanks, Lelia!

CHAPTER 75

2006
NORTHERN NECK SYMPHONY ORCHESTRA

Playing in a concert of popular classical music

As a result of Baby George asking me to play at school and in churches, I received an invitation to play with the Northern Neck Symphony Orchestra. Rehearsals began on January 09, 2006, every Monday night until March 04, the night of the performance, to be held in Kilmarnock, Virginia. The written invitation brought back early memories that I loved so much. Of course, I wanted to play! My last orchestra experience was at age 28, fifty years previous to this occasion. The invitation came as a result of Anthony Washington (Elsie's husband), introducing me to Margaret, who worked at Rappahannock Community College with him. The program to be presented was not new to me, for I had played some of the music by Mozart, Ravel and Tchaikovsky in Mrs. Seibels' orchestra in Montgomery. After the last performance with Mrs. Seibels, my playing was strictly by ear. Of course, I could not play classical pieces without reading the music. After all those years, it was not going to be easy!

I knew that to become a member of an orchestra, one would have to audition and be accepted; however, I was told that, if I wanted to play, to just show up! On that Monday night of January 09, I did appear, in spite of my fears that upon arrival I would need to go into a private room for an audition. No one did that! I managed to at least keep up with the rest of the musicians. I appreciated the presence of some of my family members, Carol, Ray, Tom and Suzy.

The wonderful experience I had of playing in the Northern Neck Orchestra is like a recording, playing over and over in my head. I owned four violins, the fourth having been my mother's, but I didn't really like to play them, not even the Stainer. It was an expensive instrument, but I just didn't like its tone. However, with my love for the violin rekindled, I began practicing with my old "Dino" tapes. I was making progress with my writing, although much time was spent on research, along with meditating, hoping to spark my brain to recall memories of long ago. On the other hand, my early spiritual questions and the search for my "Secret Garden" were clearly remembered.

On May 06, I boarded a flight from Washington/Dulles Airport for Cedar Rapids to visit my friend, Jessie Nagle. After a few days with Jessie, I rented a car to go to Des Moines to visit Steve and on to Minneapolis to visit Kim. I came back to Tappahannock on May 14.

I placed a three-line ad in the Rappahannock Record for a job, resulting in my next employment. Mr. Robert Bennett was in the early stages of Alzheimer's. When he took his afternoon nap, I would work on my book. When I had completed twenty-three pages, I was unsure of some names and dates relating to my school days at Toccoa Falls. So, I called the Alumni Office. I had been writing about my two best friends from Montgomery, Muriel and Stella. I remembered while speaking to the lady in the office, "I should ask how I could contact Stella." You will remember that she came to the school after I had left. She later married Richard Richey, the same "Richard" with whom I had been in the tenth grade English class on the third floor of Earl Hall. When he finished Bible College in 1949, they went to the mission fields of Costa Rica and Spain.

I had no contact with Stella since the mid-40s. I was told that she had passed away, but the lady gladly gave me Richard's phone number in Gainesville, Georgia. I called him on June 01 to express condolences and to ask about the circumstances of her death. We then talked about Toccoa Falls and the people we both knew from our school days. The first call lasted about an hour, and we still had more to talk about.

I had a telephone plan which included free long-distance calls, so I set the time I would call the next evening. We talked almost every night for two months. At the end of July, Richard suddenly said, "May I ask you something?" I replied, "Of course, anything!" Then, he said, "Do you think two people can fall in love over the telephone?" After a moment's hesitation, I said, "Well, I think they would have to see each other." Then I said, "Would you like to come to Virginia to visit me?" He thought that was a good idea, and I reserved a room for him at the nearby Day's Inn.

Helen and I had just washed the dishes from lunch when the doorbell rang. I opened the door, and there was Richard, holding a bouquet of red roses in one hand and a bouquet of wild flowers in the other, the former for me, the latter for Helen. And what was my first impression of him? Well, I would have recognized him anywhere. He was a good-looking man, who certainly didn't look to be 77. Helen was equally impressed, feeling that he had come to visit both of us. She and Richard talked about old friends they knew from school in the early 40s.

Richard had not had his lunch, so I said, "Why don't we go by the motel so that you can check in and, then, we will go to Lowery's for an early dinner? He said, "That's fine with me. I am hungry!" After dinner, we told Richard "good night" early that evening, and I said to him, "Helen and I get up at 8 o'clock in the morning, so feel free to come at 9 or later. Richard said, "I'll see you then." He was at the door at 9 o'clock the next morning, and he was carrying a violin. "This was Stella's better violin. Why don't you play it, and see how you like it? I've noticed that you have several violins standing in the corner. Maybe you'll like this one the best of all of them." I guess I had told him in one of our telephone chats that I didn't like the tone of my best violin. After I played Stella's violin a short time, I really did like its tone. When I told him this, he said, "Now, it's your violin. I brought it just for you." I said, "Are you sure? Thank you very much!!"

Richard noticed my two statues of Venus de Milo in my living room. I told him why I really treasured them. My childhood friend, Muriel, had given me one, when I visited her in her home in Port St. Lucie, Florida, several years ago. The other one I purchased myself. I explained to him that Venus was the first thing I had seen in a meditation. I then told him that I hoped that my grandson, Tom, would give me another one for Christmas. I had seen one in a gift shop in Fredericksburg, where he lived.

I said to Richard, "Would you like to go to Leesburg to visit Carol and Ray but, first, we could stop in Fredericksburg and have lunch with Tom? After we go to Leesburg, we could go around D.C. to Annapolis to visit my granddaughter, Suzy, her husband, Joe, and their two-year old son, Jack. He replied happily, "Of course, I was hoping for the opportunity to get to know your family."

The next day was August 07. We left Tappahannock to have lunch with Tom in Fredericksburg. We arrived a little early, so I said, "Richard, do you see that gift shop on the corner? Since we're a few minutes early, I would like to see if my Venus is still there." There were so many interesting things to see in the three rooms of the shop. Also, I was glad to see that the Venus was still there.

We went across the street to La Petite Restaurant to meet Tom. After lunch, we went to his historic home on nearby Fauquier Street. It had belonged to Charles, the brother of President George Washington. After a short visit, we left for Leesburg to spend the night with Carol and Ray.

My granddaughter Suzy's son and my great grandson, Jack

The next morning Carol went with us to Annapolis to visit Suzy and her family. When we got there, we took some neat pictures at the U. S. Naval Base. All of my Virginia-Maryland family really took a liking to Richard. I began to realize that I had fallen in love with this man. However, I had not been thinking about another marriage, and especially at my age of 78. I had a nice home and many friends, and I was still able to find jobs! These were my thoughts as we made the return trip to Leesburg and Tappahannock.

I was driving along, perhaps a little over the speed limit, and as we got closer to home, all of a sudden Richard said, "I want to ask you something. What would you think about our making this relationship a permanent one?" Believe it or not, I quickly said, "OK." Then, there was complete silence. I was thinking, "What did I just do?" I wondered if Richard was thinking that as well. I looked over at him, and he was fast asleep. With the strain ended, he just went to sleep.

When I pulled up in front of the house, Richard said, "How about popping the trunk for me?" I replied, "OK, but would you get my bag out, please?" What I saw next really surprised me. Richard began taking a large package out of the trunk. As he came around the Civic, he said, "I think this has your name on it." Of course, when he helped me open the box, I saw that it contained my Venus from the gift shop in Fredericksburg.

The next few days were busy ones, calling family and friends as well as looking for a church for the wedding. I said, "Why don't we ask Baby George if he can get Beulah Baptist for us?" A quick chat worked out the church as well as September 09, 2006 for the ceremony. In fact, Baby George became the coordinator and prepared a beautiful program for the occasion. Richard and I were happy to repeat the words which appeared on page two, as follows: "This date I will marry My Friend, My Soul Mate, my Companion and my Love." In addition to the Bride and Groom, the following participated in this order: the Reverend Murphy Brooks, Cora Armstrong, George Townes, Jr., my grandsons Ben and Tom, my daughter Carol, my sister Helen O'Neal, Mary Burrell (mother of fifteen children!), my granddaughter Suzy, my son-in-law Ray, Cora Armstrong, the Reverend Murphy Brooks, Nicholas Melillo, Pastor Brooks.

The wedding was beautiful, and it was followed by a nicely prepared reception in the Fellowship Hall of the church. We left immediately afterward for a short honeymoon in historic Williamsburg. I really enjoyed the ripe figs on the property!

I had a lot of packing to do, and Richard had to return to Georgia to arrange for another ceremony for us, so that his family and friends could be present. He flew from Atlanta to Richmond, and Helen and my neighbor, Betty Wilson, and I picked him up at the Richmond Airport. On October 09, we drove to Greensboro, North Carolina, where we spent the night with our friends, Jack and Dena Fail, traveling on to Gainesville, Georgia the next day.

Our Gainesville wedding was held at Lakewood Baptist Church on October 16, which, incidentally, was Richard's 78th birthday. The senior pastor, Dr. Tom Smiley, officiated. The church provided a nice reception. God blessed Richard and Stella with two adopted infants, a girl and a boy, in 1962 and 1964, respectively. Rebecca and Stephen both live in Georgia. They each have a daughter, Megan Diana (24) and Chelsea Elizabeth (23), respectively. The day after our Georgia ceremony, we flew to Costa Rica, where we spent a delightful two weeks, divided between Royal Pines Resort, owned by our good friends, Olman and Xiomara Madrigal, on the skirts of Volcano Poás and their time share at

Playa Hermosa (Beautiful Beach) on the western side of the country. Having served as a career missionary for many years there, you can see why Richard was invited to speak and I to play my violin in two churches and a senior citizens group.

We returned to Gainesville on October 31, leaving two days later for Virginia to bring my furniture and personal effects to Georgia. We spent the night with friends in Statesville, North Carolina. During the night, Richard had an attack of diverticulitis. He had experienced two previous attacks. We rushed on to Tappahannock the next day, with yours truly at the wheel, and I had him admitted at Riverside Hospital. His colon was removed; he was in intensive care for a week and in a private room for another week. Of course, he had to fully recuperate in my home, where I served as his nurse. It was December 17 before we could make the move to Georgia. Guess who drove the big Penske truck? Right! My son-in-law, Ray the faithful! He firmly declared that he was not ever going to move me again, that this was the very last trip! We moved into the town home Richard had rented for us; until we could find something more suitable.

CHAPTER 76

2007-2008
IN SERVICE TO OTHERS

My daughter, Carol, and her husband, Ray

We are in both Anglo and Hispanic churches on a regular basis and are happy to participate when we are invited. From Richard's long years of mission service in Costa Rica, Guatemala and Spain, of course, he speaks fluent Spanish and does verbal and written translations. Two special occasions involved programs at the First Vietnamese Church here in Gainesville and at the Chinese Christian Church of Athens. In these cases, would you believe that I played my violin in Vietnamese and in Chinese? Every year we spend a week in February at our time share on Tybee Island. You will remember the experience I had on the sidewalk of the DeSoto Hotel in Savannah the summer of 1945. On our way to Tybee Island in February 2007, we made a swing through South Georgia and visited my cousin, Ginger, in Albany. We took her out to eat that evening, and we enjoyed staying in her home that night. The next morning, before, leaving, Ginger went with us to the local cemetery, where Papa, Aunt Detty and Uncle Dave are buried.

My cousin, Ginger, in Albany, Georgia

We made a trip in April 2007 to Ormond Beach, Palm Bay, Palm Beach and West Palm Beach. We had lunch in West Palm Beach with my wonderful friend of many years, Roz Borders, thus giving Richard the opportunity to meet her. Among other places, I took Richard to The Breakers, where I went so many times in the past with

261

Wally Findlay. In this picture I took of Richard, he gives the appearance of being the CEO of The Breakers. What do you think? In October 2007, we drove to Minnesota and Iowa to visit Kim and Steve, respectively. We had good visits, and they were glad to meet Richard and he to meet them.

My husband, Richard E. Richey, at The Breakers, Palm Beach

Carol and Ray visited us in July 2008. While they were here, we took them to the Oar House, located on the banks of the Chestatee River, near Dahlonega, Georgia. Carol took this picture of us, which we have considered to be one of our very best.

At the Oar House

On October 04, 2008, we attended the wedding of my grandson, Tom, at Berkeley Plantation on the James River in Virginia.

My grandson, Tom, and his wife, Megan

My sister, Helen, came on October 08 and visited us for a month. We took her to Toccoa Falls, where she and Ed studied so long ago. She showed a lot of pleasure as she saw all the signs with her name on them in the Alpine village of Helen, Georgia. I especially like the picture Richard took of us feigning a sisterly fight in front of our little Magnolia tree, which is now about thirty feet high.

Fighting sisters in 2008, Helen at 85, Gene at 80

Among the first people I met in Gainesville were Richard's long-time friends, W. A. and Louise Van Valkenburgh, although he is affectionately known as "Cap." Due to Richard's strong promotion of Costa Rica as a tourist attraction, they have gone there annually for many years. Of course, it thrilled them to know that we went there on our honeymoon back in 2006. They have kindly invited us to their home on Lake Lanier each year for Thanksgiving Dinner. It was Louise who invited me to my first meeting here of the Red Hats Club. At that meeting I met two ladies who have become close friends, also, Hazel Prosser and Pat Inman.

Our Gainesville friends, Cap and Louise Van Valkenburgh

Presenting our "Music and Message" to the Senior Gadabouts, First UMC, Gainesville

95 year-old Red Hat friend, Hazel Prosser, visited us and had lunch in our home.

CHAPTER 77

2009-2010
LOCAL – REGIONAL – NATIONAL - GLOBAL

Toccoa Falls Homecoming, October 2009

AT the time of our annual trek to Tybee Island, Carol and her husband, Ray, spent four days with us (tour of Historic Old Savannah with lunch at the famous Pirates House, lunch with our friends, the Beardshaws, at the Old Cotton Exchange on River Street, a visit to Burnside and Rio Vista Islands with the Beardshaws, shopping for Carol and me while Ray and Richard visited the Savannah Wildlife Refuge. We drove to Tappahannock, Virginia for ministry at Beulah Baptist Church in nearby Minor, Virginia, the church in which we were married on September 09, 2006. I played my violin, and Richard spoke in Sunday School and in the morning worship service. On October 10, 2009, we went back to Toccoa Falls, where we went to school in the 40s, for the Homecoming Celebration. I was invited to participate in the Alumni Concert and played "Give me that old-time religion." In early December, we made a mission trip to the East Coast of Florida, staying in a time share on Jensen Beach for a week. While there, Richard was able to meet my friends, Bob and Donna Konrad, one day for lunch. I still have a tape I recorded ten years ago of Bob saying that I would not be staying in Florida, that I would be moving to the mountains, and I would be writing a book. True, yet hard to believe!

Playing at the church Richard started in 1985

I want to share with you a picture Richard took of me in the Albernas home in Gainesville on May 27, 2010. Pedro is from Cuba and is a registered nurse. Minerva is from Cancún and is a graduate of the University of Mexico in computer science. She has maintained both of our computers in top running condition ever since Richard and I were married, and she did the same thing for his computer for years before our marriage. We enjoy our mutual home visits.

In the home of Pedro, Minerva, Susy and Osmani

The last Sunday of January 2010 marked the 25th Anniversary of the founding of First Hispanic Baptist Church of Gainesville, Richard being the first pastor, 1985-92. A special service was held on Saturday evening at Lakewood Baptist Church, continuing on Sunday in the Hispanic Church's own facilities. Richard gave details on the early days of that ministry. Our programs are well liked, especially by senior citizens. The following picture was taken at Lakewood Baptist Church on August 24, 2010. The senior pastor, Dr. Tom Smiley, who performed our Georgia wedding ceremony back in 2006 is visible, looking over the neck of my violin.

Playing the old hymns for the Golden Nuggets

An outstanding experience for me on August 31 and September 01 was to record a compact disc titled "Songs of Faith" in the studios of Mark Dowdy, called Rivercrest Music. Duplicates have been made for us *by* Lakewood Baptist Church and First Hispanic Baptist Church of Gainesville. Over eight hundred CDs have been freely given away.

Happy in churches and nursing homes

On October 20, we made a mission trip to Costa Rica (meeting in a dear lady's home with a group of senior citizens; she had her 102nd birthday while we were there and passed away the following February). We also had meetings in three churches where Richard was well known. I played my violin, and he preached at each one. We had a nice stay at a time share on the Pacific side of the country, owned by our good friends, Olman and Xiomara Madrigal, the same ones who provided so well for us there on our honeymoon four years previously.

Roatán harbor, Honduras – December 2010

We had a wonderful cruise on the Norwegian Pearl, departing from Miami on December 05, returning on December 12. We went ashore on the Island of Roatán, Belize, the Mayan Coast of Mexico and Key West. We had special opportunities to share the story of our lives with passengers, crew, officers and even the captain of the Pearl and with others as we went ashore from place to place. I had the privilege of giving my CD "Songs of Faith," which I made in September of this year, to a number of people, including Captain Lars Bengtsson.

CHAPTER 78

2011-2012
MUSIC AND MESSAGE

Playing my violin at The Bell Minor Home

A NUMBER of opportunities have been given to us in churches, senior citizen groups and nursing homes. The Bell Minor Home was the first, with a regular monthly commitment, beginning on June 15, 2011. The picture above is typical. The next regular commitment developed at a rehabilitation center known as The Oaks at Limestone. The following picture gives an idea of our meetings there.

Playing the old hymns for residents at The Oaks

While at Tybee Island in February this year (2011), we were in ministry at the First Hispanic Baptist Church of Savannah. I played two old hymns on my violin, and Richard shared words of testimony with the congregation. The minister said publicly that he wanted us to return when we could have more time for our "Music and Message." I can only try to give a summary of this program. It refers to my violin playing of the old hymns which mean so much to both of us; e.g., *No one ever cared for me like Jesus, Just a closer walk with Thee, What a Friend we have in Jesus, I'd rather have Jesus, The old rugged cross* and others. As the reader of this story of my life, I trust that these old hymns mean something to you, also. Our bimonthly newsletter reaches 21 states and 14 foreign countries.

Olman and Xiomara Madrigal, our best friends from Costa Rica, at the Oar House in Dahlonega, Georgia

Just as we visited Olman and Xiomara in their country in 2006 and again in 2010, so they came to the States and visited us. We enjoy showing them around our country, just as they are proud of their beautiful little country in Central America.

Celebrating Doug and Pat's 50th Anniversary on the Norwegian Pearl, December 2011

We made another cruise on the Norwegian Pearl in December 2011 with our good friends from Costa Rica, Olman and Xiomara, and from Gainesville, Doug and Patricia Inman. A special time was enjoyed by all as we celebrated the Inmans' 50th wedding anniversary in the Summer Palace, the main dining room on the Pearl.

"Songs of Faith" shared on Grand Cayman Island

We shared on ship and on shore the story of our lives together and placed my CD "Songs of Faith" in open hearts and hands on board and ashore in Jamaica, Grand Cayman and Cozumel. In December 2012, we had the same activities on the Norwegian Sun, this time in Cartagena (Colombia, S.A.), Aruba, Curaçao, St. Maarten and St. Thomas (U. S. Virgin Islands).

Abby Villagracia receiving my CD on the Norwegian Sun, December 2012

My violin student, Andrea Palacios

On June 20, 2011, I gave ten year-old Andrea some extra help with her violin in our master bathroom, (excellent acoustics!). She received lessons at school, also. We were invited to a concert given by the music department of McEver Elementary School on March 22, 2012. Andrea scored among the "Top Five" violinists! Richard snapped this picture at the close of the concert that day.

Richard's step grandson, Jimmy

Richard's son, Stephen, has a stepson named Jimmy García, who is making great advances with his piano playing. He takes lessons at Lancaster Music Company in Gainesville and has a piano at home for practice. We invited him to accompany us, along with his mother, Ivonne, to share on our "Music and Message" program, playing two or three piano numbers at two of the nursing homes we visit, on

July 16 and 24 this year. Several residents are not visible, but you can see the interest in those who are in this picture. Keep up the good work, Jimmy!

My grandson, Ben, and his wife, Elizabeth

We were happy to have my grandson, Ben, and his wife, Elizabeth, in our home for the night of January 22, 2013. They treated us to dinner at our local O'Charley's Restaurant in Gainesville. Richard snapped this picture of them.

Richard with Ruthann and Don Sedrel and Jessie Nagle

Richard is seen here with good friends in Cedar Rapids, Iowa. You will remember my long association with the late Jessie Nagle. Don is the son of "Stretch," mentioned by me so many times in relation to the *Armar Ballroom.* He and his wife, Ruthann, are bikers and own two Harley Davidsons. Richard was reminded of his two Indians in Costa Rica in the early 50s, a Warrior first and then a Chief. I am not a supporter of "cycles," as Richard calls them.

Toni Armellini and her husband, Jack O'Brien

It is wonderful to have renewed contact with Toni Armellie, a good friend from my K-Mart employment days in Thousand Oaks, California. Today, she is a happy Mrs. Jack O'Brien. I have just received this picture of their wedding reception, even as I write these words. Congratulations, Toni and Jack!

271

Our good friends in Simi Valley, Ed and Shelby

You will remember my good friend during my two employment periods in the Simi Valley K-Mart, Shelby Treece. She and her husband, Ed, just sent us a picture taken of them on November 23, 2012. We look forward to being in their home later this year.

My good friend and neighbor, Pat Inman

How many *really* good friends does one have in a lifetime? Probably, very few! Pat and I have been close friends since our first meeting at a Red Hats Club Christmas party in 2010. We have so many common interests, such as cats, visiting in each other's home, talking by telephone every other day, going on a cruise together, she loves my violin and I love her artistry with water colors and … tap dancing! Right after we first met, she took me to a Home Depot to buy a 36 square-foot tap board. Yes, I said "tap board." I'm 85, and I'm still tapping! And she supports the writing of this book 100%, since the day we met!

I really want to share with you a couple of pictures of my dear mother, one in which she was trying on a dress of mine in Florida and another taken in Montgomery, both of them in her mid-90s. Also, I want to share one more picture of my cat Suzy, in which she is posing in front of a portrait of Mother. To us, it appears that she is coming out of the frame to keep an eye on us. I hope our publisher will be able to accommodate these three pictures, in order, as I have mentioned them here.

(left) Mother, trying on my dress in Florida
(right) Mother, in the home of Maggie, her life-time friend, in Montgomery
(center) Suzy, with Mother apparently coming out of her portrait

CHAPTER 79

2013
NOTABLE INDIVIDUALS

I WISH to give an update on my Nigerian friend, Bright; however, I must now call him "Doctor Bright A. Aregs." I am once again in contact with him, and he has kindly provided me with his current profile, as follows: Dr. Aregs is the President and the Principal Consultant of Eagle Advanced Technologies Corporation. EATCORP is a high technology professional company which provides satellite communications network infrastructure for the high tech security systems of cities and highways. He is a Space Scientist, having been in the American Space Industry for thirty-two years. He has worked on various NASA programs in numerous capacities.

Dr. and Mrs. Bright A. Aregs

I have been able to peruse Dr. Aregs' profile at length and have identified that he has earned two bachelor degrees, two master degrees, two doctoral degrees as well as several post graduate diplomas. His specialties have been in areas, such as electrical engineering, industrial technology, telecommunications, project management, business administration, space craft and space mission design and analysis, liquid rocket propulsion. He has also earned multiple certifications in the fields of industrial technology, electrical and electronic engineering, aeronautics and astronautics. I am especially proud of my good friend, Bright, for his position as Anchor of DX2099 Analytical Chamber, a television talk show on Africa Independent Television in Africa and in the United States. I have seen the program, and it is educational, informative and provocative. Bright lives with his wife, Rukayat, and their twin sons in Porter Ranch, California.

The late Gloria Cassity Stargel, good friend and renowned author

Gloria Cassity Stargel was a well-known writer and a good personal friend. She appeared on radio and television programs in the United States and Canada. Her award-winning articles appeared in Guideposts, Journal of Christian Nursing, Home Life, Christian Reader and Decision, published by the Billy Graham Evangelistic Association. We were in her  home on many occasions, especially in 2012. We visited her several times in the hospital in her last days, at which time she held me by the hand and urged me to move ahead with the writing of this book. Gloria passed away on March 02, 2013 and was followed by her husband, Joseph Stargel, one-time mayor of Gainesville, on June 19, 2013.

CHAPTER 80

HAPPY CONCLUSION!

Life Achievement Award received from Toccoa Falls College

As I approach the end of my life story, I want to share a surprise we received toward the end of last year. On Saturday evening, October 13, we attended the Alumni Awards Banquet in Gate Cottage, located at the entrance to beautiful Toccoa Falls, to which I referred several times in the early pages of this book.

Richard and I were presented a Life Achievement Award, which dealt with struggles and victories throughout our lives; mine, as covered in the details of my story and Richard's, in his lifetime of foreign and home mission ministry. We love and appreciate the contributions Toccoa Falls High School and Bible College made to our lives and to thousands of others since its founding in 1907 by Dr. Richard Forrest, for whom my Richard was named by his parents, who lived in the "old" Gate Cottage in the late 20s.

I almost forgot one of my fondest memories of the past. When I would be the chauffeur for Harriett Ohland and Bo in her luxurious Mercedes Benz 500, she would be in the back, and Bo would be sitting in the front seat to my right. I snapped this picture of him, showing to one and all that he was in charge!

"I almost forgot you, Bo, I'm so sorry!"

A very happy experience for me this year came through a telephone conversation with my second cousin, Susan, who lives in Columbia, South Carolina. She told me that her parents, Dorothy Ann and Bob Hamilton, had moved from Arizona to South Carolina. She gave me their telephone number, and we have talked often with the realization that we have a lot in common. We saw each other several times briefly over the years, the first time when she was eighteen months old, and I was five years old.

Happy Couple! Beulah Baptist Church – Minor, Virginia – 09 September 2006

In a session with spiritual intuitive Bob Konrad in 1997, I was told that I would not remain in Florida but would move to the mountains and write a book. At that time, I thought that was an outlandish idea, and I forgot it completely. However, in 2005, Lelia Poteet, my Nurse Aide Instructor in Virginia, told me, and more or less insisted, that I should write a book on the story of my life. She even wrote on my final grade sheet, "I am looking forward to your book!"

Bob and Donna Konrad with us – Ormond Beach, Florida

In 2009, I came across the old tape of that session from 1997. Hearing the tape brought back the memory of that reading. My reaction to it then was, "This time you are 100% wrong. I don't like to write, I can't spell, it will never happen!" Well, my home today is in the foothills of the Blue Ridge Mountains of North Georgia. I have now written my book. This picture was taken with Bob and Donna Konrad on October 25, 2013. We enjoyed a delicious meal together with great fellowship!

This book was foretold, before I was aware of the possibility. I believe there is a message I am supposed to share with others. I have come to realize that my musical talent and my forgiving spirit are mine by the grace of God. During the first thirty-six years of my life, through traumatic events which occurred, I continued the search for answers to my spiritual questions. I seriously wanted to understand the words of the Greek philosopher, Socrates, *"Know thyself."* These two words led me to the discovery of the reason for the very existence of humankind, and the realization that what we do and what we think about another, we do and think about ourselves. In other words, whether it is positive or negative, it will come back for or against us. Also, we need to understand that God loves His entire creation, saint and sinner alike.

In the Gospel of Matthew, Jesus advises us to love our enemies and pray for those who persecute us. In my search for a way out of the hell in which I was dancing, I discovered that the key to my freedom was through forgiving. It was through the grace of God that my heart and eyes were opened. I realized the power of forgiveness and how it brought me the freedom to love others. Because I was able to forgive as the Master suggested, **I journeyed my way out of the hell in which I was living.** Through forgiving, I discovered who I truly was, a child of God. Because I was able to forgive, I have danced through life with joy, peace and happiness. When I forgave, **that old dance** of physical, sexual and mental attacks, as well as anger and resentment, disappeared!

In my lifetime, I have never written poetry; however, three years ago I was meditating in a recliner in our living room, while Richard went to our little post office in Murrayville. When he returned fifteen minutes later, I handed him a slip of paper on which I had written verbatim the following words:

THE REAL "ME"

Look at me, what do you see?
I know what you're going to say,
That I'm old and grey; well, that's OK.
What you don't know is that in all these years
I've had time to grow.
And with life's ups and downs,
I've discovered the *real* me,
And that is that *my soul lives eternally.*

One of our favorite pictures was taken on a cruise we made on the Norwegian Pearl in December 2010. We simply handed our camera to a fellow passenger, asking her to take a picture of us. Only one, but it turned out to be a winner! I want to close the book so that you can see me standing happily beside my true soul mate and, yes, he is the "Richard" from one of the early pages in this book.

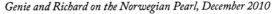

Genie and Richard on the Norwegian Pearl, December 2010

CPSIA information can be obtained at www.ICGtesting.com
Printed in the USA
LVOW08s0128180314

377845LV00001B/1/P

9 781460 236802